MW01254860

MAN AND THE INCARNATION

GUSTAF WINGREN

MAN AND THE INCARNATION

A Study in the Biblical Theology of Irenaeus

Translated by
ROSS MACKENZIE

A translation of *Människan och Inkarnationen enligt Irenaeus* by Gustaf Wingren, published by C. W. K. Gleerup, Lund, 1947.

The Scripture quotations are from the Revised Standard Version of the Bible, copyrighted 1946 and 1952 by the Division of Christian Education, National Council of the Churches of Christ in the U.S.A., and used by permission.

Wipf and Stock Publishers
199 W 8th Ave, Suite 3
Eugene, OR 97401

Man and the Incarnation
A Study in the Biblical Theology of Irenaeus
By Wingren, Gustaf

ISBN: 1-59244-856-9
Publication date 9/10/2004
Previously published by Muhlenberg Press, 1959

FOREWORD

THE two most recent complete editions of the principal writings of Irenaeus bear the dates 1853 and 1857 respectively. During the century which has passed since their publication the work of textual criticism has, of course, continued, and the discussion on questions raised by textual criticism has at times been lively. The urgent need at the present time, and it has been fairly generally discussed for a lengthy period, is that of a new edition. This discussion has probably helped to discourage theologians from carrying out research into Irenaeus, and their attitude has been to choose to wait until the promised new text appeared. Since the original appearance of this volume in Swedish, there has appeared a new edition of the text of Book III of the *Adversus haereses—Irénée de Lyon contre les Hérésies, Livre* III, introduced and edited with notes by F. Sagnard, O.P., *Sources Chrétiennes*, Paris 1952. This will, in its completed form, be a most valuable source book for scholars of Irenaeus, although I myself have not had the opportunity of consulting it for the present work in English. Nevertheless, since undertaking the present theological study of Irenaeus, I have had the advantage, in addition to the printed editions, of being able to consult an expert in the text of Irenaeus, who is an authority in the manuscript material, Docent Sven Lundström, and I should like to take this opportunity of expressing my thanks to him for his readiness to discuss problems of etymology, and for his expert references to philological literature.

I also take this opportunity of expressing my thanks to the Rev. Ross Mackenzie, B.D., who has translated this work for the English edition.

G. W.

INTRODUCTION

It is not usual to connect the words *Man* and *the Incarnation* in the History of Dogma. Such double concepts as Law and Gospel, faith and works, or sin and grace, are frequently to be found, and become fixed in our understanding. And we could, of course, turn to Irenaeus and by using an accepted method of investigation such as this derive from his writings a good deal that would be of interest; but in doing so we should, I feel, find that much of what is essential in his work would be slightly to the side of our main line of investigation, and we should be compelled to digress slightly in order to be able to deal with it. If we ask, on the other hand, What idea of *man* does Irenaeus have? What does Irenaeus say man is? or, What is the relationship between man and the Incarnation, i.e., the becoming-man in Christ? we should then have to come down to the problem with which Irenaeus himself was concerned, and his theology would lie open to us in all its monumental simplicity. For Irenaeus the central problem of theology is *man and the becoming-man*, or *man and the Incarnation*. This is not the only problem with which he is concerned, but it is his main one. I propose to adopt this analytical framework in the present inquiry, and I believe that if we do so we shall be able to work our way through Irenaeus without deviating from the main line of investigation, and be able to find in his writings every important theological concept, and make each the object of a systematic analysis.[1]

[1] The primary source *Adversus haereses*, henceforth cited as *A.h.*, is quoted from W. W. Harvey's edition of 1857. But since Harvey has his own system of chapter and paragraph numbering which is different from the traditional one, I always give in brackets the position of the passage in question in A. Stieren's edition of 1853 which follows the traditional division. The *Proof of the Apostolic Preaching, Epideixis*, henceforth cited as *Epid.*, is quoted from J. Armitage Robinson's translation, London 1920; and other translations have also been consulted (cf. the Bibliography). Since there are only fragments from the Greek original of *A.h.* preserved, and our interpretation of Irenaeus must in consequence depend for the most part

If it is a purely historical understanding of Irenaeus's thought which we are looking for, there is this straightforward analytical method available, although from the point of view of systematic theology there is the possible objection that this whole method of interpretation is made to depend on an out-of-date hypothesis—man and the Incarnation—which cannot be easily accommodated to our modern theology. Neither the Middle Ages nor the Reformation thought directly in the categories of the early Church, and all modern Christian theology is to a

on the Latin translation of the writing referred to, there has been keen debate about the date and trustworthiness of this Latin version. No unanimity has been achieved with regard to the date. There are some who uphold the position that the translation was made very early, e.g., F. R. Montgomery Hitchcock, *Irenaeus of Lugdunum*, Cambridge 1914, p. 44 (*c.* A.D. 200); A. d'Alès, "La date de la version latine de Saint Irénée," in *Recherches de science religieuse*, 1916, pp. 133–7; C. H. Turner in his preface to the *Novum Testamentum Sancti Irenaei*, Oxford 1923, p. xxiv; and Hans Lietzmann, *Geschichte der alten Kirche*, VOL. II, Berlin and Leipzig 1936, p. 208, Eng. trans. *The Founding of the Church Universal*, henceforth cited as *Church Universal*, London 1938, pp. 205 ff. There are others who hold that the translation is late and should be placed in the region of A.D. 421 when it is explicitly mentioned for the first time, e.g. Hermann Jordan, "Das Alter und die Herkunft der lateinischen Übersetzung des Hauptwerkes des Irenaeus," in *Theologischen Studien Th. Zahn dargebracht*, Leipzig 1908, pp. 135–92; A. Souter, "The Date and Place of the Latin Translator of Irenaeus," in *Novum Testamentum Sancti Irenaei*, p. lxviii—Souter argues that the Church was almost universally Greek-speaking in Irenaeus's time, and that therefore a translation was unnecessary then; and F. C. Burkitt, "Dr. Sanday's New Testament of Irenaeus, with a note on Valentinian terms in Irenaeus and Tertullian," in *Journal of Theological Studies*, henceforth cited as *J.T.S.*, 1924, p. 67—Burkitt agrees with the date suggested by Souter. On the whole of this problem cf. Sven Lundström, *Studien zur lateinischen Irenäusübersetzung*, henceforth cited as *Studien*, Lund 1943, pp. 90–109. On the other hand, with regard to trustworthiness the unanimity is very great. The Latin text is slavishly faithful to its original and reliable in so far as it understands the original. See in this connexion H. J. Vogels, "Der Evangelientext des hl. Irenaeus," in *Revue Bénédictine*, henceforth cited as *Rev. Bén.*, 1924, p. 21 f.—the Latin text is more *reliable* than the original Greek citations which are preserved to us; John Chapman, "Did the Translator of St Irenaeus use a Latin New Testament?" in *Rev. Bén.*, 1924, pp. 34–6; and Benedikt Kraft, *Die Evangelienzitate des heiligen Irenäus*, Freiburg-im-Breisgau 1924, which criticises Stieren's and Harvey's Greek texts, e.g. p. 7 f. In his paper mentioned above Lundström has attempted to trace the misunderstanding of the Latin translator in rendering certain passages from the Greek original. It may be added here in conclusion that the classical account of the history and present status of the Latin manuscripts of *A.h.* is Friedrich Loofs's "Die Handschriften der lateinischen Übersetzung des Irenaeus und ihre Kapitelteilung," in *Kirchengeschichtliche Studien H. Reuter gewidmet*, Leipzig 1888, pp. 1–93; cf. also Erich Köstermann's article "Neue Beiträge zur Geschichte der lateinischen Handschriften des Irenäus," in *Zeitschrift für die neutestamentliche Wissenschaft*, henceforth cited as *Z.NT.W.*, 1937, pp. 1–34, where, unfortunately, new notations are introduced.

certain extent different from the dogmatics of the early period, although certain European confessions have relatively uninterrupted connexions with the Church Fathers, e.g. Greek Orthodox and Anglican theology, neither of which required a complete reformulation during the massive theological conflicts in Europe at the beginning of the new period in which medieval Scholasticism and the Lutheran Reformation were immediately opposed. From our modern point of view the thought of the early Church seems at times to be wholly *sui generis*. One might suppose that this would be an excellent reason for devoting a great deal of effort towards the understanding of the faith of the Fathers *from within*. The early Church opens up to us a world of thought which is largely untouched by the whole of our modern controversies, viz. the thought-world of the early Church. In a theologian like Irenaeus there are parts of the Biblical message which are interpreted in greater clarity and power than in any later period of Christian thought. It is my own hope that in the formula which I have suggested—man and the Incarnation—we possess the key to understanding Irenaeus and his age.

There is, however, a point which I have not yet mentioned, and which, from the point of view of systematic theology, is of the greatest importance. As theologians, we require to have a positive doctrine of *man*—a theological anthropology. Both in the New Testament and in Luther we do, of course, find a certain interpretation of man, but in both cases the interpretation is axiomatic. Neither the New Testament nor Luther speaks directly about man in such a way as to provide us with a considered anthropology, and so it is from other evidence in each instance that we have to draw the interpretation of man. It could not be said that a thoroughgoing anthropology was characteristic either of the Bible or of the Lutheran Reformation. Irenaeus, on the other hand, lived wholly within the period of the heretical Gnostic doctrine of man, and he was forced to draw up a precise anthropology on the basis of Scripture, and to use the Old and New Testaments as his primary source for his doctrine of man. We cannot, of course, evolve a Christian anthropology for our own period simply by adapting the Biblical interpretation of an earlier period; we must, rather, return to the sources themselves, viz. the Biblical record. If, however, we regard the theologians of the Church as being, in their various periods, our guides to the Bible, or interpreters of the Biblical theology, then we must assign to Irenaeus a place of very great importance.[2] Indeed, as far as a theological interpretation of man is concerned, it would be difficult to find anyone to surpass Irenaeus either then or in the later periods.

Particularly related to this is the fact that the classical documents of Christianity, viz. those of the early Church and the Reformation, all speak about God's work of salvation in Christ, i.e. they direct our attention to what God is doing, and not to what man is. When theological thinking begins to refer to *man* as such, it very often does so almost in a spirit of protest against theocentricity, stressing the co-operative parts played by both God and man in the act of redemption. If, however, man is set in opposition to God from the beginning, and this conception about man and God as being in opposition has once become hardened, it becomes quite impossible afterwards to withdraw from this position.

Positive statements which are made about man then become limitations on the sovereignty of God, and positive statements about the omnipotence of God are seen to be limitations on man's freedom. Irenaeus speaks at great length about man, but —and this is unique—not in opposition to the theocentricity of early Christianity, which, in fact, he himself represents, but in opposition to the Gnostics' false idolisation of man or contempt for man. The Gnostic belief was that some men were "pneumatic," and could, therefore, be saved, while others were "sarkic," and were incapable of receiving the message of salvation.[3] The Gnostics' idolisation of man stems from the

[2] With reference to Irenaeus and the New Testament, see Albert Dufourcq, *Saint Irénée*, 3rd edn., Paris 1904, p. 184; cf. W. von Loewenich, *Das Johannes-Verständnis im zweiten Jahrhundert*, henceforth cited as *Johannes-Verständnis*, Giessen 1932, pp. 4, 138–41; and J. N. Sanders, *The Fourth Gospel in the Early Church*, henceforth cited as *Fourth Gospel*, Cambridge 1943, pp. 66, 84, 87. The abundance of Biblical references in Irenaeus is made clear from figures of Biblical citations and allusions in S. Herrera, *S. Irénée de Lyon exégète*, Paris 1920, p. 6, although we ought, perhaps, to take his figures with certain reservations—there are many other errors in other passages in Herrera's book.

[3] This is Irenaeus's own description of the position taken by his Gnostic opponents. See *A.h.*, I. i. 4 (Stier. I. vii. 5). On the general reliability of Irenaeus's state-

same root as their contempt. Irenaeus destroyed the basic assumption of both interpretations by asserting that God alone saves through Christ, that this salvation is offered to all, and that all men stand on exactly the same level before God. The Incarnation has, therefore, this unique position of being the *locus* of God's entering into the world of men, in such a manner that not only is there a change in the condition of certain spiritual groups, but that *man* is actually sought by God.

Besides all this, Irenaeus had a conception of the relation between Christ and man which was different from the usual understanding of that relationship. I have devoted all that follows in this Introduction to an attempt to describe precisely how Irenaeus deals with this relation, and it is not possible here to put the upshot of my observations into one or two sentences. This, at least, however, must be said in the meantime—the connexion between man and Christ which Irenaeus makes excludes any conception of God and man as being in opposition to one another. It is in this light that we must see the juxtaposition which Irenaeus typically makes of man and the Incarnation.

The only aim of the present enquiry is to set out in detail the subject-matter which we find in Irenaeus, and to centre it on the general concept of man and the Incarnation as clearly as is possible.

(1) The first part, "From Life to Death," will deal with man and his progress from his creation by God to his defeat and bondage to the Devil. The Son of God is with God from eternity, and when man is created, he is created in the Son to become the image of God. Man's bondage to the Devil, however, has completely disrupted his appointed end.

(2) The second part of the book is headed "Christ," and describes the Incarnation. The Son of God, who existed before man, and in whom man was created, Himself becomes man.

ments on Gnostic sources, cf. Carl Schmidt, "Irenäus und seine Quelle in *Adv. haer.*, I. 29," in *Philotesia P. Kleinert dargebracht*, Berlin 1907, pp. 335 ff. I am of the opinion that what he says here is generally true. On the question of the three classes of men—pneumatic, psychic, and choic (hylic)—see Ernst Klebba, *Die Anthropologie des hl. Irenaeus*, Münster 1894, p. 138 f. The same subject is also dealt with by Hans Jonas, *Gnosis und spätantiker Geist*, henceforth cited as *Gnosis*, Göttingen 1934, Vol. I, pp. 212–14, even although he clarifies the issue very little.

This means that not only *God*, but also *man*, is manifested in the Incarnation. In Christ we encounter man as he was ordained to become in Creation, and *this* man has to endure the same struggle against evil as we have, only in His case the end is not defeat by temptation, but victory. The culmination, therefore, of the Incarnation, is not death but life—the life of the Resurrection.

(3) The third part will return to describe man in bondage to sin, but now man moves towards the destiny which was ordained for him in Creation—"From Death to Life." Since Christ *is* the image of God and man *was made in* the image of God, so man, as man, in the midst of his bondage carries his destiny—which is to become like Christ—within himself, and when he becomes like Christ he becomes completely man. Transformation into the likeness of Christ is realised within the Church, the Body of Christ, and is completed only in the resurrection from the dead in the Kingdom of the Son when God becomes all in all. Thus, in the Church the original Creation breaks through afresh and extends towards the resurrection, when the Devil and death will be destroyed and annihilated. Not until the Consummation will Creation be fully realised, for not until then will God's primal decision concerning man, *Let us make man in our own image* (Gen. 1.26),[4] be accomplished, and this fulfilment of God's purpose is wholly dependent on the fact of Christ's becoming man, His conflict, and His victory.

The concept of the image of God, of likeness to God, is of fundamental significance in Irenaeus, both for defining the purpose of man's creation, and for determining the meaning of the Incarnation. In four different places in this book I have inserted sections with the heading, "*Imago* and *Similitudo*," and in these, Creation, the Incarnation, the Church, and the eschatological Consummation, are related. The heading of another section which appears also four times is "*Recapitulatio*." The meaning of this central concept cannot be fully dealt with in one context alone. Recapitulation is through Christ, but it is also achieved through men: it is the plane of Creation breaking

[4] It is from this Biblical passage that the terms *imago* and *similitudo*, *εἰκών* and *ὁμοίωσις*, are drawn. Gen. 1.26 f. keeps recurring in Irenaeus in widely different contexts.

through in the Incarnation and in the victory over evil through the temptations and Passion of Jesus by which our captivity is destroyed, and a way opened from death. Within the Church and the resurrection man is drawn into this recapitulation in such a way that he realises his origin and achieves the purpose of his creation. The best confirmation that a particular interpretation of Irenaeus is a correct one will be whether or not we have given the terms *recapitulatio* or *anakephalaiosis* a definite and objective meaning. Although we may analyse this difficult and yet tremendously rewarding concept repeatedly, we shall nevertheless find that it has only one basic meaning throughout.[5]

The result—and of course at this point in the book it is purely an assertion, but it is one which I hope will emerge as fairly well established by the end of our present inquiry—is of so much the greater importance, as the whole of our main source, the *Adversus haereses*, is without doubt a compilation of many different sources. Quite often Irenaeus explicitly says that he has taken various theological arguments from some of the earlier writers,[6] but in spite of this there is a remarkable unity throughout his writings. The explanation is, perhaps, that in the early years of the primitive Church it was the great

[5] A completely different problem is the question of translation. We probably do not have a single word with which to render the meaning of *recapitulatio* or ἀνακεφαλαίωσις. It has been argued whether *recapitulatio* means the restoration of Creation or the perfection of Creation, while again there are others who assert that it means *renewal*, or the emergence of Christ as "Head"—κεφαλή, *caput*—of the Church. The attitude of Irenaeus himself may well be such that these different senses are all implied in the word. We do not therefore have to speak about a shift between several meanings. It is commonly said that the Swedish word "lagom" is difficult to translate into another language, and at times must be paraphrased "not too much and not too little." On the grounds of such a difficulty of translation it might be asserted that "lagom" has two different meanings, one "not too much," and the other "not too little," but this is wrong, for in the word "lagom" there is a single unitary idea. There is a comparable illustration in this principal concept of Irenaeus, and if we are wanting to hold the meaning of the concept *in a single word*, then we must stick to the Greek or Latin and use ἀνακεφαλαίωσις or *recapitulatio*. But it is in fact possible to describe what Irenaeus means by this word. As we get near the centre of his theology, we find, for example, that the restoration of Creation and Christ's establishment as Lord, as "Head of the body," are in fact related elements in a unitary concept, and that other aspects of *recapitulatio* also become comprehensible.

[6] Cf. Harnack, "Der Presbyter-Prediger des Irenäus," in *Philotesia P. Kleinert dargebracht*, pp. 5 ff.; W. Bousset, *Jüdisch-Christlicher Schulbetrieb in Alexandria und Rom*, henceforth cited as *Schulbetrieb*, Göttingen 1915, pp. 272–82.

pioneering thinkers who were responsible for compilations, i.e. who drew together to form a unity the diverse theological thinking of their predecessors. There are some scholars who have all too often approached a writer like Irenaeus from the angle of a nineteenth-century cult of personality and search for originality, and have been quick to point out what, on this basis, they assume to be his inferiority. But we do not imagine that if Irenaeus had evolved an idea of his own he would have rejected it as being of no value. It was the Gnostics who were the innovators, flinging out ideas which had no basis in the Apostolic witness. In all his writings Irenaeus sought only to stamp out these objectionable innovations, and forge into a unity what the Church throughout the world had taught since the days of the Apostles. This, indeed, is Irenaeus's singular merit, that he co-ordinated the thought of his predecessors, and his strength as a systematic theologian lay exclusively in the fact that everything that belonged to the primitive period—the Scriptures, the Old and New Testaments, and the different parts of the New Testament in their turn, and finally the various authorities of the early Church—all this is collated and fused into a harmonious whole.[7] In this work of unifying theological concepts Irenaeus has no equal.[8]

Our impression of this homogeneity has on the whole been confirmed by Friedrich Loofs's great posthumous work on Irenaeus,[9] in which this expert patristic scholar sets out with all his scholarship and critical discernment to separate the different sources in the *Adversus haereses* from one another, but completely and entirely fails to do so. For several years after the publication of Loofs's extensive book there was little or no discussion on the points which he raised, for his theory of the divisions between

[7] An excellent comparison of the teachers of the early Church who exercised an influence on Irenaeus is provided by Montgomery Hitchcock, *Irenaeus of Lugdunum*, pp. 19–34, in which there is included almost everything that can be known about this subject apart from guesswork. The question of the relationship between different Biblical writers (e.g. Paul and John) and Irenaeus is not here discussed.

[8] Cf. W. Bousset, *Kyrios Christos*, Göttingen 1913, p. 413, and Hjalmar Lindroth, ("Irenaeus' kristendomstolkning och kyrkosyn" ("Irenaeus's understanding of Christianity and his view of the Church")), in *Svensk teologisk Kvartalskrift*, henceforth cited as *S.T.K.*, 1939, pp. 22–5.

[9] *Theophilus von Antiochien adversus Marcionem und die anderen theologischen Quellen bei Irenaeus*, henceforth cited as *Theophilus von Antiochien*, Leipzig 1930.

the various sources had been based on detailed analysis, and had in consequence to be verified by no less detailed an analysis.[10] It was F. R. Montgomery Hitchcock who set himself to this particular task, and he did so with the most methodical care. Loofs had held that the most important source in the *Adversus haereses* was the recently lost writing *Contra Marcionem* by Theophilus of Antioch, but that in addition there were, besides his wholly arbitrary idea of "*Irenaeus selbst*," three or four further sources, of which the most important theologically was the so-called IQA.[11] Hitchcock examined the two proposed sources IQTU (Theophilus) and IQA separately,[12] and with regard to the former demonstrates that phrases from this assumed source of *Adversus haereses* are more closely paralleled in the parts of *Adversus haereses* which Loofs says belong to "*Irenaeus selbst*" than they are in any extant fragment of Theophilus we possess;[13] indeed Hitchcock goes the length of repeating Karl Müller's earlier argument that Theophilus of Antioch was a writer who must have been *unknown* to the author of *Adversus haereses*.[14] Similarly, as regards IQA, Hitchcock finds

[10] We find comparatively open recognition of Loofs in Folke Boström's *Studier till den grekiska theologins frälsninglära* (Studies in the doctrine of salvation in Greek theology), Lund 1932, p. 15, and also in Wolfgang Schmidt, "Till förståelsen av Irenaei teologi" ("Towards an understanding of the theology of Irenaeus") in *Teologisk tidskrift*, henceforth cited as *Teol. tidskr.*, 1934, p. 190. Albert Ehrhard in his *Die Kirche der Märtyrer*, Munich 1932, p. 217 f., takes a deprecatory attitude from the outset.

[11] In Loofs, *Irenaeus selbst* is an arbitrary factor, because exactly the same argument can be adduced to prove that these parts of *A.h.* are also an unrelated source —on as good grounds it may be argued that they were an apology influenced by Justin which had got lost. According to Loofs *Irenaeus selbst* is theologically related to Justin, as indeed it is. Cf. Loofs, *Theophilus von Antiochien*, pp. 339ff.

[12] IQTU is examined in two articles, "Loofs's theory of Theophilus of Antioch as a source of Irenaeus," in *J.T.S.*, 1937, pp. 130 ff. and 225 ff.; and similarly IQA is discussed in a detailed essay, "Loofs' Asiatic source IQA and the Ps-Justin *De resurrectione*," in *Z.NT.W.*, 1937, pp. 35–60.

[13] *J.T.S.*, 1937, e.g. p. 135 f. Cf. pp. 255 ff.

[14] This is an exaggeration. Cf. E. Klebba, *Anthropologie des hl. Irenaeus*, pp. 42, 66; Hugo Koch, "Zur Lehre vom Urstand und von der Erlösung bei Irenäus," in *Theologischen Studien und Kritiken*, henceforth cited as *Theol. Stud. u. Krit.*, 1925, p. 204 f., note; and Emmeran Scharl, "Der Rekapitulationsbegriff des hl. Irenäus," in *Orientalia christiana periodica*, henceforth cited as *Orientalia*, 1940, p. 397. But it is amazing that Hans von Campenhausen can quote a passage in Irenaeus as a definite statement by Theophilus, as though Loofs's hypothesis were proved. See his *Die Idee des Martyriums in der alten Kirche*, Göttingen 1936, p. 112, n. 9, and p. 164, n. 3.

that its alleged characteristics are not limited to the textual similarities which have been mentioned, but are quite common, and therefore of no use for the purposes of defining the divisions between the sources in *Adversus haereses*.

Loofs built on a detailed analysis of *Adversus haereses*. In what follows I have taken the opportunity of quoting Loofs on more than one occasion and discussing his meaning in relation to specific texts. Here by way of introduction I shall look only at the main outlines of his theory, and the general difficulties which are sufficient to make his hypotheses unacceptable, in so far, that is, as these hypotheses aim at separating the sources. All Loofs's attempts to get at special sources in Irenaeus begin in his observations of peculiarities of thought or vocabulary in a stated passage in the *Adversus haereses*, which determine that that particular fragment is to be separated from other parts of the same section.[15] In this way he penetrates to at least five different primary sources, and when he later attempts to relate these to writings outside Irenaeus it becomes evident that there is not *one* such document extant—all of the assumed sources have regrettably disappeared.[16] It is puzzling that Loofs was able to see the consequences of his primary contention, and yet, although he was quite clearly confused in his assertions, continued to develop his thesis.[17] Loofs, in fact, treated any discrepancies or differences that occur in the *Adversus haereses* as indications that there are various sources traceable within it, and having established what he took as the sources, he then proceeded on the assumption that each one of these sources is homogeneous, and therefore contains only one dominant line of thought, but not more than one.

But can all this be ascertained about a document that is unknown to us? In point of fact this unknown piece of writing may in turn have the same characteristics as *Adversus haereses* and a great many other documents of the early Church which

[15] Loofs, *Theophilus von Antiochien*, pp. 16 ff. (on IQT and IQTU), 103 ff. (IQP), 211 ff. (IQA), 313 ff. (IQS and IQE; cf. p. 325). See in conclusion p. 342, where Loofs's outlines what he believed belonged to *Irenaeus selbst*.

[16] For this reason Loofs concedes that no source can be defined with final certainty. *Op. cit.*, pp. 375–84, 397.

[17] *Op cit.*, pp. 341, 429: "Eine Aufrollung dieser Fragen an dieser Stelle würfe uns wieder an den Anfang zurück und verbietet sich daher."

we have preserved) and contain ideas which Loofs finds to be anything but consistent with one another.[18]

It is completely impossible to solve a problem which provides nothing but unknown quantities, and only one known factor—the number of such quantities. This is a case in point. We do know that *Adversus haereses* is constructed on sources that are moulded together to form a unity,[1] but none of these sources is extant. Loofs, taking up the task of separating the unknown sources from one another, was faced by the equation $x + y + z = 100$. The fact that this problem is insoluble does not make him any less a scholar, but the proper study of patristics is with problems which *can* be solved—and of these there is an accumulated mass available which has not yet been touched.

When we come to deal with Irenaeus's literary relationship to writers before his own time, we discover that up to the present period there has been far too little work done on the basic problem of the inner relationship between the New Testament and Irenaeus. These are the "sources" upon which Irenaeus has worked so carefully. He was the first within the Church to make extensive and copious citations from Paul and John, and his

[18] When Loofs makes his reconstruction of IQT on p. 394 he puts in ". . . wenn er klar gedacht hat." There is no basis for this, and it has to be decided whether the thought of Theophilus in a lost work was clear or not. We do know that in his extant work, *ad Autolycum*, according to texts available to us, Theophilus holds together in his thought ideas which Loofs holds to be irreconcilable (see p. 396). The possibility that in his lost work Theophilus thinks "unclearly" (in Loofs's sense) is therefore as great as the possibility that he thinks "clearly." But then it becomes meaningless to attempt to guess what the situation was. Loofs tends to treat almost all the extant documents of the early Church as being composed from various lines of thought. The question why the sources of *A.h.* are so uniform, theologically considered, has an obvious answer—they have the uniformity of being lost! Loofs has therefore to reconstruct them, and he sets about his work so methodically that he posits a new source in which he comes upon a new line of thought—and this is why his sources become uniform. It is as if he is arguing that the documents from the early Church which we do in fact possess contain ideas which are incompatible with one another, while the ones that are lost are clear and consistent!

[19] On the unity, see the moderate and well-balanced criticism in Bonwetsch, *Die Theologie des Irenäus*, Gütersloh 1925, p. 29 (against Loofs's earlier work). It should also be borne in mind that Irenaeus wrote *A.h.* in stages and at long intervals: see Otto Bardenhewer, *Geschichte der altkirchlichen Literatur*, Freiburg-im-Breisgau 1902, p. 502. In conclusion it may be added that V. Cremers in his controversy with Loofs assumes an interpolation in an originally unitary text of Irenaeus, "Het millenarianisme van Irenaeus," in *Bijdragen der Nederlandsche Jezuieten*, henceforth cited as *Bijdragen*, 1938, p. 63, but even this is purely hypothetical.

task was to wrest these New Testament writings from the Gnostics, and use them as his weapons against them. Before Irenaeus undertook his work, which was both controversial and exegetical in character, there had been no development in any significant theology of Scripture in the Church with which he might identify himself. There may, perhaps, be some interest in investigating Irenaeus's relationship to the earlier writers of the primitive Church who appear between the New Testament and himself, but this is a problem of little account in comparison with the major question of what appraisal we are to make of Irenaeus's own interpretation of the New Testament. To what extent does he make use of early Christian concepts, or break away from early Christianity? If we turn to a recent period in the history of Dogma, say, to the eighteenth century, we find that enormous contributions have been made in understanding the Biblical theology of the period between Irenaeus and the New Testament—contributions such as those which Luther made—and it was these which interpreted the Bible to the eighteenth century, or, perhaps, obscured it. But there is about as great a distance in time between Paul and Irenaeus as there is between the *Theologia deutsch* and Luther. The immediate problem is that which concerns the relationship between Irenaeus and the New Testament.[20]

On the other hand, there are two other conditions which demand fulfilment. One is that we must get a historically accurate, organic view of the New Testament as a whole, and not of Johannine or Pauline theology by itself, and so on. When the great histories of dogma were being conceived in Germany at the end of the nineteenth century, it was possible to regard early Christianity from an organic, i.e. from the liberal point of view, but for many years now this approach has proved deficient, and it has left behind a vacuum in the form of

[20] Cf. the general criticism in Paul Beuzart, *Essai sur la théologied 'Irénée*, Le Puy-en-Velay 1908, p. 169. With ref. to Paul, see Bousset, *Kyrios Christos*, p. 442. On the position of the fourth Evangelist in this connexion, see Loewenich, *Johannes-Verständnis*, p. 4, and Sanders, *Fourth Gospel*, p. 66. The whole discussion about the *regula veritatis* and related concepts in Irenaeus form part of this problem, as does the hotly debated question of the relation between tradition and Scripture in Irenaeus's thought—this is the point present-day inter-confessional controversy has reached in its interchange of ideas.

an atomistic system of exegetics, with a paralysing effect on the history of dogma itself as well. The establishment of a theology of the New Testament on a new basis would make possible the revival of the history of dogma as a subject of study. The other condition which has to be fulfilled is that, if we can, we should attempt to get a fundamental understanding of the theology of Irenaeus as a whole. One of the main questions which emerges from studies in Irenaeus at the present time is whether or not his thought is in fact consistent.

Our study of man and the Incarnation in Irenaeus has the sole aim of providing an answer to this latter question of how we are to come to a fundamental understanding of Irenaeus. We shall be interested primarily in the extant writings of Irenaeus, and not in any other literary evidence, and if we refer to other authors it will only be in order to throw light on Irenaeus. It will be quite obvious that the important question which I have just mentioned of the relationship between Irenaeus and the New Testament cannot be answered in a simple positive or negative formula.[21] On the one hand it is evident that there are several Fathers in the early Church, and not least Irenaeus, who ought to be able to make direct contributions to a correct understanding of the thought-world of the New Testament. On the other hand there seem to be traces in these Fathers of a certain distortion of the New Testament, and a blunting of its message in comparison with the early Christian

[21] Among those who reject outright the theory of an affinity between Paul and Irenaeus are Johannes Werner, *Der Paulinismus des Irenaeus*, Leipzig 1889, in his summary on pp. 211 ff., and Eva Aleith, "Paulusverständnis in der alten Kirche," in *Z. NT. W.*, 1937, pp. 70–81, in spite of certain modifying reservations. In his *Die Lehre des hl. Irenäus von der Erlösung und Heiligung*, henceforth cited as *Lehre des hl. Irenäus*, Mainz 1905, Franz Stoll disputes the argument in Werner's above-mentioned book, and on the same point at issue has a one-sided defence of the theory—see pp. 17 f., 26, 81 f. On the question of the internal relationship between the Johannine writings and Irenaeus agreement is more general but is also more moderate—see Aleith, *op. cit.*, pp. 74, 80, but the theological relationship between the other parts of the New Testament and Irenaeus is hardly mentioned and tends to be passed over in unjustified silence. A distinctive feature of the New Testament such as the long speeches in Acts offers quite obvious points of correspondence with the theology of Irenaeus. There are, however, cardinal problems in the study of Irenaeus which are pushed aside; namely the question whether Irenaeus was justified in referring to the Apocalypse for his eschatology, and the problem of the relationship between the belief in demons of the Synoptic Gospels and Irenaeus's basic view of man as the captive of Satan, the Serpent.

kerygma.[22] As I have mentioned, however, the comparison between these two is not the object of our present discussion, and instead I propose to begin immediately with the interpretation of Irenaeus.

[22] E.g. Oscar Cullmann's theory in his *Königsherrschaft Christi und Kirche im Neuen Testament*, henceforth cited as *Königsherrschaft Christi*, Zürich 1941, p. 6, n. 4, and p. 47, which would be worth detailed discussion; cf. the same author's *Die ersten christlichen Glaubensbekenntnisse*, Zollikon-Zürich 1943, p. 56, Eng. trans., *The Earliest Christian Confessions*, London 1949, p. 61 f. Cullmann holds that Christ's dominion, which in the New Testament is a dominion in the present time, is projected by Irenaeus into the eschatological future. Points of view similar to Irenaeus have been adduced from several sources. There is, e.g., a very lengthy treatment in Carl Schmidt, *Gespräche Jesu mit seinen Jüngern*, Leipzig 1919, pp. 492–8. For Cullmann's general interpretation of Irenaeus see also his study *Christus und die Zeit*, Zollikon-Zürich 1946, pp. 48 ff., Eng. trans. *Christ and Time*, London 1951, pp. 56 ff.

PART I

FROM LIFE TO DEATH

CHAPTER I

CREATION

God the Creator

OUR best starting-point for a full understanding of the concept of God in Irenaeus is the sovereignty of God—the absolute power of the Creator. The Gnostics' pessimism in regard to the world forced them into assuming a God who had nothing to do with the world, and they kept large parts of reality separate from God's sphere of influence. Against this, Irenaeus maintained that if God is held to be powerless in any respect, then that before which He is powerless is in point of fact *God*. We make certain deductions about the universe, deducing one proposition from another, but there is some point at which we have to stop, an already existing reality which cannot conceivably have originated from anything else, and it is this which we designate as "God." But if we conceive of some substance, or matter, that is independent of God, then this independent substance is sovereign, and God is not, and it makes no difference however actively God may work and "create" with this substance as the basic stuff of His Creation, He is still not *Creator*, and what we ought consistently to call God is really matter, because the point at which we have stopped is that which does not require to depend upon any prior cause. But it is precisely this which characterises God, and which cannot be expressed about anything else except God, namely, that He cannot be deduced from anything.[1]

[1] See the whole discussion in *A.h.* from II. i. 1 to II. xxii. 5 (Stier. II. i. 1–xvii. 11). The passage II. x. 2 (Stier. II. x. 4) deals with matter: "Attribuere enim substantiam eorum quae facta sunt virtuti et voluntati ejus qui est omnium Deus, et credibile et acceptabile et constans et in hoc bene diceretur: quoniam quae impossibilia sunt apud homines, possibilia sunt apud Deum; quoniam homines quidem de nihilo non possunt aliquid facere, sed de materia subjacenti: Deus

By this it is implied that all things and all forms of life have originated from God. Whatever exists in heaven or on earth has had its origin in something else, but the matter from which everything has originated must in its turn have originated somewhere; but God has created the whole world from *nothing* out of His own unlimited power. The matter from which everything in Creation was to be formed must itself have been made from nothing, because it is only from God that Creation can originate, and because there is nothing greater than God and nothing equal to Him. It is only God who has a scheme for Creation and the will to create, and there is none to assist Him in His Creation other than His own "hands," in other words God Himself. The hands of God are His Spirit and His Son, who are thus uncreated; they belong to the Creator, and are active in all Creation.[2] It is as impossible for us to state how the Son and the Spirit originated as it is to penetrate into the mystery of God's existence at all. God and his "hands" are inseparable.[3]

It may be stated at this point that the Son—and also, as we shall see, the Spirit—is revealed to us in Jesus Christ. Now since the Son appears to us in Christ, it would be plausible to argue that belief in Him could only come with the Incarnation. But Irenaeus strenuously opposes such an interpretation, and in the

autem quam homines hoc primo melior, eo quod materiam fabricationis suae cum ante non esset ipse adinvenit." Cf. II. xlvi. 1–4 (Stier. II. xxx. 1–5) and the important argument for the resurrection of the body in v. iv (Stier. v. iv. 2). The proposition that God is the source of all things occurs also in the *Epideixis*, e.g. in *Epid.* 4. There are two monographs on the concept of God, one by Johannes Kunze, *Die Gotteslehre des Irenaeus*, Leipzig 1891, which has a commendable emphasis on God's creative power, but which decidedly overestimates the philosophical aspect in Irenaeus. The other book is the longer *God in Patristic Thought*, London 1936, a textbook of liturgical study by G. L. Prestige, which also deals with Irenaeus. See, e.g., the discussion in this work on p. 46 f. of God as *agennetos* and *agenetos* in Irenaeus, and cf. on the whole discussion Bonwetsch, *Theologie des Irenäus*, pp. 53–5.

[2] "Nec enim indigebat horum Deus ad faciendum quae ipse apud se praefinierat fieri, quasi ipse suas non haberet manus. Adest enim ei semper Verbum et Sapientia, Filius et Spiritus, per quos, et in quibus omnia libere et sponte fecit," *A.h.* IV. xxxiv. 1 (Stier. IV. xx. 1). See also IV. xiv (Stier. IV. vii. 4), and cf. Joseph Barbel, "Christos Angelos," in *Theophaneia*, VOL. III, Bonn 1941, p. 64.

[3] In Loofs, *Theophilus von Antiochen*, pp. 16 ff. this "pre-temporal Trinity" is treated as a concept unknown to Irenaeus himself, but see Montgomery Hitchcock in *J.T.S.*, 1937, pp. 131–4.

Epideixis his opposition to this interpretation becomes almost tediously monotonous. Irenaeus frequently connects this with the statement in the Johannine Prologue about the Word which was in the beginning with God, and which became flesh in the birth of Jesus. "Because, for God, the Son was (as) the beginning before the creation of the world; but for us (He was) then, when He appeared; and before that He was not for us, who knew Him not."[4] The fact that we had not seen the Son or known about Him does not, therefore, mean that the Son did not exist. Irenaeus avoids the idea of a world which existed before the Son as studiously as he does speaking about matter which exists independently of God, for to maintain either of these propositions is to diminish the sovereignty of God, and to make as incredible the idea that God can work miracles upon the earth as that Christ will one day rule over the whole world.[5] For a complete understanding of the theology of Irenaeus we must keep firmly in our minds from the very first the belief that God and His Son *are* before everything that has been created, and before any matter or any world they *are*.[6]

In the section that follows I propose to examine in particular the creation of *man*. Man is created in the likeness of God—God says to His Son and the Spirit, His own hands, "Let us make man in our image, after our likeness" (faciamus hominem ad imaginem et similitudinem nostram). In the present section, where we are dealing with God as Creator in general, my purpose is to lay stress on the following proposition, namely, that the Son of God, who was made man in Jesus, exists *before* man, and, indeed, when man is created he is created through the Son and *for* the Son, so as to reach his destiny in the Son, his Saviour. Man's coming into being is something which occurs after the Son, and since the Saviour existed before man came

[4] *Epid.* 43, *St Irenaeus, The Apostolic Preaching*, ed. J. Armitage Robinson, pp. 108 ff. Cf. *Epid.* 52, and several other references from 40 to 52. Another important New Testament reference to this is Col. 1.15 f.

[5] The thought of the Son as being the first-born before the whole of Creation, and the One in whom everything has been created, is inseparably linked with the idea that everything is to be judged by the Son. See *Epid.* 48.

[6] Cf. E. Scharl in *Orientalia*, 1940, p. 387, and Adolf Harnack, *Lehrbuch der Dogmengeschichte*, 4th edn., Tübingen 1909, VOL. I, p. 584, Eng. trans. of 2nd German edn., *History of Dogma*, London 1899, VOL. II, p. 263.

into being, it was proper that something to be saved should come into being, lest the Saviour should exist by Himself alone.[7] This point requires to be emphasised quite strongly, since the concept in primitive Christianity and in the early Church of the world as having been created in the Son has disappeared in modern theology. Oscar Cullmann holds, not without some justification, that the celebrated controversy between Karl Barth and Emil Brunner rests on the false alternative of *the work of Creation* (without Christ altogether) or *the work of salvation* (in Christ).[8] Irenaeus holds, on the contrary, that everything is created in the Son, or the *Verbum*, the same *Verbum* which becomes flesh in Christ. In this fundamental premise he continues an early Christian line of thought.[9]

In point of fact the concept of pre-existence is often established on very inadequate Biblical foundations, creating only a variation of the un-Biblical separation of Spirit and matter. Matter as such is then held to be disclosed in reality and value —matter has an ideal pattern and is only a shadow of this eternal idea. The concept of pre-existence in early Christianity proceeds from God's sovereignty, that is, from God the Creator, who controls what is in existence, and who cannot be confounded by anything that originates from outside Himself, for nothing outside God has any existence. God does not, as it were, discover that there is something in existence farther forward in history, but rather, if anything new comes into existence, then it has come from the Creator, and therefore existed previously in Him. It follows that the question whether in its pre-existence it existed in a spiritual or a material way is irrelevant, and does

[7] "Cum enim praeexisteret salvans, oportebat et quod salvaretur fieri, uti non vacuum sit salvans," *A.h.* III. xxii. 1 (Stier. III. xxii. 3). This passage has been the cause of a lively discussion which I propose to deal with in a different connexion. Cf. III. xix. 1 (Stier. III xviii. 1), IV. xi. 5 (Stier. IV. vi. 7), and the important passage on Christ as *in universa conditione infixus* in V. xviii. 2 (Stier. V. xviii. 3).

[8] Cullmann, *Earliest Christian Confessions*, p. 51.

[9] Loofs, *Theophilus von Antiochien*, pp. 347 f., 393, holds that the idea of the pre-existent Logos-Son, belongs to "Irenaeus selbst" and is not characteristic (p. 444) of early Christianity. Ernst Barnikol makes a determined attempt to eliminate the concept of pre-existence from the New Testament in his *Apostolische und neutestamentliche Dogmengeschichte als Vor-Dogmengeschichte*, 4th edn. Halle 1938, pp. 57 ff. The relevant passages in Irenaeus are carefully scrutinised and stated by Bonwetsch, *Theologie des Irenäus*, pp. 62–6.

not even need to be asked.[10] There is a clear understanding of this concept of pre-existence, which is linked together with the idea of Creation, in Eph. II.10, in which the writer speaks of "good works, which God prepared beforehand, that we should walk in them." For Irenaeus the whole of the history of salvation is a series of "works" done by God with the Son and the Spirit as his "hands," and God has done them all in order that in them man might partake of Life. The power of God is, therefore, impeded neither by the Devil, God's adversary, nor sin, nor death, and the victory over these enemies of God, which is won through Christ, and which extends to their utter destruction in the Consummation, has been ordained by God from the very beginning, and exists in God as Creator. The existence of the Devil and his conflict with God in men does not involve for Irenaeus the same intolerable encroachment upon God's sovereignty as the existence of matter before God's creation of the whole universe. The Devil, too, has been created by God and has no life in himself, but has his existence by the power of God, and only for so long as the Creator and Father wills: his time is fixed by the decree of God.[11]

Hence, if it is a characteristic of God to create, it is characteristic of man that he is created, i.e. that he is made, not that he is, but that he becomes, or increases.[12] And these two facts, God's creation and man's continual becoming, are identical—the same reality seen from two different aspects. At times the

[10] Cf. Harnack, *History of Dogma*, VOL. I, pp. 797-806; R. Liechtenhan, *Die göttliche Vorherbestimmung bei Paulus und in der posidonianischen Philosophie*, henceforth cited as *Göttliche Vorherbestimmung*, Göttingen 1922, pp. 17–24, 122–4; and Cullmann, *Christ and Time*, e.g. pp. 70, 91. See *Epid.* 67 (beginning).

[11] "Nihil enim in totum diabolus invenitur fecisse, videlicet cum et ipse creatura sit Dei, quemadmodum et reliqui angeli. Omnia enim fecit Deus," *A.h.* IV. lxvi. 2 (Stier. IV. xli. 1). There is a general reference to the power of God in comparison with the power of the creature: *Οὔτε οὖν φύσις τινὸς τῶν γεγονότων, οὔτε μὴν ἀσθένεια σαρκὸς ὑπερισχύει τῆς βουλῆς τοῦ Θεοῦ. Οὐ γὰρ ὁ Θεὸς τοῖς γεγονόσιν, ἀλλὰ τὰ γεγονότα ὑποτέτακται τῷ θεῷ, καὶ τὰ πάντα ἐξυπηρετεῖ τῷ βουλήματι αὐτοῦ*, *A.h.* V. v. 3 (Stier. V. v. 2). On the idea of the risen Christ as still awaiting the hour appointed by the Father, cf. *Epid.* 85.

[12] "Facere enim proprium est benignitatis Dei: fieri autem proprium est hominis naturae," *A.h.* IV. lxiv. 2 (Stier. IV. xxxix. 2). Cf. Louis Escoula, "Le verbe sauveur et illuminateur chez Saint Irénée," in *Nouvelle revue théologique*, henceforth cited as *N.R.T.*, 1939, pp. 393 ff.; see further *A.h.* IV. xxv. 1–2 (Stier. IV. xiv. 1–2) and esp. IV. xxi. 2 (Stier. IV. xi. 2).

description in Irenaeus of man's increase has been represented as an instance of an almost modern theory of evolution, but Karl Prümm has justifiably insisted that this aspect of Irenaeus's thought has also first to be seen against its Gnostic background. The Gnostics proceeded from beneath, in differences, for instance, between certain aspects of the Old Testament and contradictory passages in the New Testament, and classified "God" in the categories of an Old Testament God and a New Testament God. It is against this disintegration in the idea of God that Irenaeus contends.[13] God is one, but man becomes, and for him there are many stages of development.[14] In both Testaments we encounter the same God, and it is only to be expected that, in spite of this fact, they contain differences, for God is the creating One, i.e. man is continually in process of becoming.[15]

Because of this relationship it is impossible for man to obtrude on God's existence. Any knowledge which man possesses of God is dependent on the active revelation of God, and where God has not revealed the mystery of His own person, man knows nothing. Irenaeus is decidedly averse to speculation, and frequently observes that Scripture does not tell us everything, but only what we need to know, in order that we may be able to have faith and obedience. There are blanks in our knowledge at several points, e.g. no one knows what God did before the creation of the world, and so no one can say how the Son proceeded from the Father; the period before the Last Day is and remains unknown, and the reason why certain created beings (man and the Devil) fell into sin is likewise hidden.[16] Where there are blanks of this kind in our knowledge it is because they have to be, and it is futile for us to attempt to amplify our limited knowledge of God by our own thinking. Man may properly study what lies "before his eyes," and what is clearly written in Scripture: both these ways lead to incontrovertible knowledge, although, of course, it is limited know-

[13] K. Prümm, "Göttliche Planung und menschliche Entwicklung nach Irenäus *Adversus haereses*, in *Scholastik*, 1938, p. 208; cf. p. 350.

[14] *A.h.* IV. xix. 2 (Stier. IV. ix. 3) and IV. xxxiv. 6–7 (Stier. IV. xx. 6–7).

[15] *A.h.* IV. xliv. 2 (Stier. IV. xxviii. 2).

[16] *A.h.* II. xli. 4 (Stier. II. xxviii. 3) and II. xlii. 3–xliii. 2 (Stier. II. xxviii. 6–7).

ledge.[17] However persistently we may try, we cannot reach any knowledge of what God is like in His majesty, in his *magnitudo*, despite the fact that God is so close to us, and that He never ceases to know everything that is in every man.[18] When van den Eynde speaks about the simple "theology of faith" in the early Church as an expression of the common life of faith within the local congregations, and holds that the theology of Irenaeus, but not the theology of Alexandria, belongs to this less intellectualised theology of the early Church, we should note that the unwillingness of Irenaeus to employ *la théologie savante* is founded on principle,[19] for Irenaeus could not have admitted either Gnostic or Alexandrian speculation without destroying the basis of his theology.

As we have just seen, our inquiry has to be directed not only at the unequivocal affirmations of Scripture, but at everything "before our eyes," and the Gnostics proved deficient in both of these respects, for they had no interest either in a balanced exegesis of Scripture, or in the visible, external world. It is at this point that another aspect of Irenaeus's belief in the Creator presents itself. The Gnostics held (and here I am referring to sensual *gnosis*) that it was a necessity to experience everything, even what was evil; yet they were never known to take part in anything that required resilience or adaptability, but, being the sensualists they were, either devoted themselves to every kind of excess, or kept ascetically remote from the world. Irenaeus held that we ought by rights to be finding the Gnostics occupied on occasion with medicine, botany, painting, sculp-

[17] *Ὁ ὑγιὴς νοῦς, καὶ ἀκίνδυνος, καὶ εὐλαβὴς, καὶ φιλαληθὴς, ὅσα ἐν τῇ τῶν ἀνθρώπων ἐξουσίᾳ δέδωκεν ὁ Θεὸς, καὶ ὑποτέταχε τῇ ἡμετέρᾳ γνώσει, ταῦτα προθύμως ἐκμελετήσει, καὶ ἐν αὐτοῖς προκόψει, διὰ τῆς καθημερινῆς ἀσκήσεως ῥᾳδίαν τὴν μάθησιν ἑαυτῷ ποιούμενος. Ἔστι δὲ ταῦτα, τά τε ὑπ' ὄψιν πίπτοντα τὴν ἡμετέραν, και ὅσα φανερῶς καὶ ἀναμφιβόλως αὐτολεξεὶ ἐν ταῖς θείαις γραφαῖς λέλεκται, A.h.* II. xl. 1 (Stier. II. xxvii. 1); cf. II. xli. 4 (Stier. II. xxviii. 3).

[18] *A.h.* IV. xxxiii (Stier. IV. xix. 2–3). This fundamental "hiddenness" is not given a clear enough emphasis in Friedrich Böhringer's analysis of the doctrine of the Devil in Irenaeus, *Die Kirche Christi und ihre Zeugen*, henceforth cited as *Kirche Christi*, 2nd edn. Stuttgart 1873, VOL. II, pp. 476–8. Cf. in this connexion Herrera, *S. Irénée de Lyon exégète*, pp. 139–46.

[19] For the distinction between these two types of theology, see Damien van den Eynde, *Les Normes de l'enseignement chrétien dans la litérature patristique des trois premiers siècles*, henceforth cited as *Normes de l'enseignement*, Gembloux and Paris 1933, pp. 132–41. Cf. Lietzmann, *Church Universal*, p. 214 f.

ture, or different types of handwork, agriculture, seafaring, and also gymnastics, hunting, the art of warfare, and politics—but in every one of these pursuits we look for the Gnostics in vain.[20] And yet it is the corruptible things, too, which have been made by God, and the whole earth is the Lord's, despite the fact that it is transitory and destined to pass away[21]—God the Creator is at work even in the least of His creatures which reproduce, and by so doing continue His Creation.[22]

In this present connexion particular attention should be given to the statements in Irenaeus about the Roman Empire, and what God is doing for the benefit of mankind and the preservation of His world by using a pagan power such as this as His instrument. These statements of Irenaeus are given in great detail and lucidity, although they are infrequently mentioned in theological literature. His interpretation of Mt. XXII. 7 is quite characteristic. The verse, "The king was angry: and he sent his troops and destroyed those murderers and burned their city," is an allusion to the destruction of Jerusalem by the Roman army. The Roman armies are called God's armies—the king (God) sent *his* armies. And the Lord may speak thus "since all men belong to God." Some lines farther on this theme is expanded: "Every man, as a man, is His creation, even though he may be ignorant of his God."[23] Irenaeus puts the theme in question into its proper context by quoting in full three passages from Scripture, and his selection of passages is highly significant. The first is from Psalm XXIV: "The earth is the Lord's, and the fulness thereof" (Ps. XXIV.1). The second is Paul's statement about the powers that be as the servants of God (Rom. XIII. 1–6), and the third is Mt. V.45, the passage

[20] *A.h.* II. xlix. 1 (Stier. II. xxxii. 2). Cf. Andreas Bigelmair, *Die Beteiligung der Christen am öffentlichen Leben in vorconstantinischer Zeit*, Munich 1902, pp. 296–8, 327. Note too the original illustration of the unpractised wrestler who is booed by the audience. *A.h.* V. xiii. 2 (Stier. ibid.).

[21] *A.h.* IV. vi–vii (Stier. IV. iv. 2–3).

[22] *A.h.* II. xlvii. 2 (Stier. II. xxx. 8). Creation is not finished but still continues. There is a more exhaustive treatment of the belief in Creation in my essay "Skapelsen, lagen, och inkarnationen enlight Irenaeus" ("Creation, the Law, and the Incarnation according to Irenaeus"), in *S.T.K.*, 1940, pp. 133 ff.

[23] ". . . et propter hoc ait: Mittens exercitus suos: quoniam omnis homo, secundum quod est homo, plasma ipsius est, licet ignoret Deum suum", *A.h.* IV. lviii. 8 (Stier. IV. xxxvi. 6).

about the sun and the rain on the just and the unjust.[24]

Also of interest is the defence which Irenaeus attempts to make of the passages Ex. III.21 f. and XII.35 f., the description of how, before the Exodus, the Israelites took jewels of gold and silver from the Egyptians. As Christians, he maintains, we act in a similar kind of way towards non-Christians around us, and make free use of what they produce for us by their efforts in giving the world peace, and creating the possibility of unimpeded intercourse and secure sea-communications.[25] It belongs to God's nature to give us such worldly gifts as these, although they come to us from the Creator through other men, and although these others have no knowledge of God.[26] The belief in Creation, which underlies passages such as this, sees man as being on the earth for God to make use of in the same way as he makes use of the fig-tree to give us figs—it is not necessary that it should first be converted or received into the congregation!

Of very great importance, however, is the extended analysis in Irenaeus of Lk. IV.6, the declaration of the Devil at the temptation of Jesus that he, the Devil, can give away all the kingdoms of the world, since he has power over them (*A.h.* V.24).[27] The whole of the exegesis of this passage forms part of a larger systematic context dealing with the Devil as Falsehood and the Lord as Truth (from V.21 onwards). When the Devil claims that he possesses the kingdoms of the world he is lying,

[24] *A.h.* III. xxxix, God as the One who directs all men and gives His counsel to the leaders of the heathen (Stier. III. xxv. 1). The destruction of Jerusalem took place according to the will of God, and the fall of Jerusalem and the beginning of the Church are two stages in the same process, the supersession of the old Covenant by the new.

[25] *A.h.* IV. xlvi (Stier. IV. xxx). This does not prevent Irenaeus from applying the principles of the Apocalypse to the State, but in negative statements of this sort he is not concerned with what the heathen State produces from the *good of the earth*. Jahveh gave His own people jewels of silver through the Egyptians who were evil, and from whose power His people were on the point of being liberated. The Church now is Israel. Linked up with this is a double view of the surrounding heathen State.

[26] "... non quasi mundus alienus sit a Deo, sed quoniam hujusmodi dationes ab aliis accipientes habemus, similiter velut illi ab Aegyptiis qui non sciebant Deum," *A.h.* IV. xlvi. 3 (Stier. IV. xxx. 3). The attack on the narrative in Exodus came from the Gnostics who were looking for signs of the discreditable nature of the Old Testament demiurge.

[27] The figures in Harvey and Stieren coincide in this chap.

because "the hearts of kings are in the hand of God." It is not Satan who administers the kingdoms of this world, but God.[28] When Christ contradicts the Devil at every temptation with a word from the Old Testament, the word of the Law, He speaks the truth and declares *which* God His Father is, viz. the God of Creation and the Law.[29] The Devil is continually active, and never gives up his desire to embroil the whole of mankind in warfare and strife, but all that he is able to do by this is to *disturb* God's government of the world; it is an impossibility for him to get the whole of the created order into his control, for *God rules*.[30] When men sinned and began to destroy one another, God put a "fear of man" into mankind, because men no longer knew how to fear God. In subjection to the mastery of their fellowmen, and bound by their laws, men were to learn to be righteous at least in some measure. So men are forced into curbing one another and treating with respect the repressive control which confronts them. The laws of authority are "a garment of righteousness." Severity checks sin,[31] and new rulers continually gain power as new generations of men are born. In both of these the continuing work of Creation is discerned: "The One by whose command men are born commands also rulers to be appointed who are fit to govern those over whom they rule at the time."[32]

But the demand for obedience to authority is only one aspect of the fundamental view of kings as the servants of God. The other side is that all rulers, independently of whether or not they are Christian, are to be judged in the Last Judgement by the God who appointed them. The Judgement will be upon all without exception. And if the rulers have done anything contrary to the law, as tyrants do, it will inevitably bring upon

[28] *A.h.* v. xxiv. 1. He cites passages from Prov. and Rom. XIII.

[29] *A.h.* v. xxi. 2–v. xxiii. 2. This important combination of ideas is unfortunately neglected by Jean Rivière in *Le dogme de la rédemption, Études critiques et documents*, henceforth cited as *Dogme de la rédemption*, Louvain 1931, in which he attempts to establish what Irenaeus means by saying that the Devil is defeated *juste*, pp. 137–41. See III. xxxii. 2 (Stier. III. xxiii. 1).

[30] *A.h.* v. xxiv. 3.

[31] *A.h.* v. xxiv. 2. It is continually stressed that God and the Devil are the two protagonists, and mankind lies between these two.

[32] *A.h.* v. xxiv. 3.

them destruction and ruin.[33] The sun rises on the evil and the good now, but it will not always be so, and the God who is so long-suffering now to His Creation will some day cause His Judgement to come upon mankind.[34]

There is a further point in the teaching of Irenaeus where his belief in Creation emerges in a precise definition in a comparable way, and that is his interpretation of Holy Communion. In more recent theology, and especially in Anglican quarters, the Holy Communion is regarded as "an extension of the Incarnation," and in this definition there is something which was part of the theology of the early Church. But it is, in fact, an Anglican theologian who has pointed out that Irenaeus tended rather to connect Holy Communion with the belief in *Creation*: God has created the world through His Word, His Son, and in the Eucharist there is "an extension of His creative energy."[35] Christ took the bread from Creation and said of it: "This is my body." The wine too had been produced by the earth, and of it He said: "This is my blood."[36] When the Gnostics took these gifts of Creation, they treated them as having been created by the Demiurge, a lower Creator-God, and not by the God and Father of Jesus Christ. It was a matter of astonishment to Irenaeus that the Gnostics could celebrate Holy Communion at all, using bread and wine as food and nourishment, and he could not see how they were able to relate the elements to Christ. A precondition for such a connexion as this is that in Christ we see the Son of the Creator of the world. Christ is the Word made flesh, He is the *Verbum* through which the vine bears its fruit, the springs flow, and the earth has strength to produce the stalk, the ear of corn, and the grain of

[33] "Et propter hoc etiam ipsi magistratus indumentum justitiae leges habentes, quaecumque juste et legitime fecerint, de his non interrogabuntur, neque poenas dabunt. Quaecumque autem ad eversionem justi, inique et impie et contra legem, et more tyrannico exercuerint, in his et peribunt; justo judicio Dei ad omnes aequaliter perveniente, et in nullo deficiente," *A.h.* v. xxiv. 2; cf. v. xxiv. 3 and also *Epid.* 8.

[34] *A.h.* III. xl. 3 (Stier. III. xxv. 4).

[35] Montgomery Hitchcock in his above-named work, *Irenaeus of Lugdunum*, p. 278, and the same author's forthright article "The Doctrine of the Holy Communion in Irenaeus," in the *Church Quarterly Review*, henceforth cited as *C.Q.R.*, 1939–40, p. 213, in which he represents Irenaeus as a good Anglican receptionist, pp. 220 f., 225. See the criticism even in J. Werner, *Der Paulinismus des Irenaeus*, p. 111 f.

[36] *A.h.* IV. xxix. 5 (Stier. IV. xvii. 5).

wheat for bread.[37] The Creator has power to give life to the grain which is cast into the earth and is changed, and it is the same Creator who has power to nourish and feed us with Christ in the Eucharist, so that when we die and are buried in the earth we may await the resurrection from the dead. The bread and wine of the Holy Communion both testify that the Creator of the world is in Christ, and that our earthly bodies share in the life which the Creator wills to bestow upon mankind through the incarnate Son.[38] Farther on in our study we shall have cause to return frequently to this profound relationship between Creation, the Incarnation, the Church, and the resurrection of the body.[39]

God is life; the Devil is death. Irenaeus regards all life as being in the hand of God, and death as a lost connexion with God, a lost contact with the source of life, and captivity to the enemy of God. He therefore held together in his understanding natural life and the Spirit, Creation and the Sacraments, and man's body and his communion with God. By the very fact of our being in the presence of *life* in all its countless forms we are confronted by a wholly divine activity in which God is directly at work in His Creation.[40] Whatever affects life adversely is wrong and contrary to the will of the Creator, but at the same time too it is *death*, something which destroys life like poison in the body. It is from God that man has proceeded, and so the only life he has is the one which he has received from God. But at this point let us leave the idea of Creation in general and turn our attention to the man whom God has put into His created world.

Imago and Similitudo

In Gen. 1.26 both *image* (צֶלֶם) and *likeness* (דְּמוּת) are mentioned together. These two substantives are rendered in

[37] Cf. *A.h.* IV. xxxi. 3 (Stier. IV. xviii. 4), and see also the unusual passage in *Epid.* 57 with its exuberant imagery.

[38] See *A.h.* V. ii (Stier. V. ii. 2–3) and cf. H.-D. Simonin, "A propos d'un texte eucharistique de S. Irénée," in *Revue des sciences philosophique et théologique*, henceforth cited as *Rev. des sciences*, 1934, pp. 286 f., and *A.h.* III. xi. 9 (Stier. III. xi. 5) and IV. li. 1 (Stier. IV. xxxii. 2).

[39] See Anders Nygren, *Den kristna Kärlekstanken genom tiderna*, Stockholm 1936, VOL. II, pp. 190–205, Eng. trans. *Agape and Eros*, London 1953, VOL. II, pp. 276–88.

[40] Cf. *A.h.* V. iii. 3 (Stier. ibid.).

Greek as εἰκών and ὁμοίωσις respectively, and in Latin as *imago* and *similitudo*. This combination of words occurs in a very large number of places in Irenaeus, mostly as a hendiadys. There are, however, passages where Irenaeus uses only one of the words, and there are other places where he makes a distinction in meaning between the two. The majority of the interpreters of Irenaeus's anthropology have concentrated on these latter passages, with some loss in the total understanding of their meaning. We shall have to examine the whole of this discussion when we come to deal with man and his faith in Christ, man in the Church, for by then we shall have drawn together all the necessary material for discussion. There are other problems too which we are unable to study at this particular point—the question of free will and of immortality, for example—and so we limit ourselves here solely to the relationship between the Son on the one hand (or, rather, the Son and the Spirit), and man on the other, as this relationship existed when man was created. This relation between the Son and man, having been established by God from the beginning of Creation, is an expression of the same truth as the statement that man is created in the *imago* and *similitudo* of God.

Prümm states that there is hardly any verse in the Old Testament which is more frequently quoted "in der alten Christenheit" than Gen. 1.26. The statement is true enough of Irenaeus, but otherwise it is somewhat of an exaggeration.[41] It cannot be said that this quotation abounds in theological literature before *Adversus haereses*.[42] In Irenaeus, on the other hand, repeated allusions are made to the verse in question, sometimes in reference to the Creation of man, at other times with allusion to Christ Himself, or again to Christ's dealings with men in the present, or even in connexion with some futurist or eschatological expectation, which man awaits in faith.[43] In regard to the

[41] Karl Prümm, *Christentum als Neuheitserlebnis*, Freiburg-im-Breisgau 1939, p. 64.

[42] Gen. 1.26 is not often quoted in the Apostolic Fathers; for other literature of the early Church see the commentary on *Die apostolischen Vater*, ed. K. Bihlmeyer, VOL. III, Hans Windisch, *Der Barnabasbrief*, Tübingen 1920, p. 328 (Barn. v. 5), and Montgomery Hitchcock in *Z.NT.W.*, 1937, p. 56. Later on we shall have the opportunity of mentioning a passage in Tertullian and two in the Apostolic Fathers.

[43] Cf. F. Vernet's article "Irénée" in *Dictionnaire de théologie catholique*, VOL. VII, PT. II, Paris 1923, p. 2452 f. and the excellent discussion by Wilhelm Hunger,

points of contact in Irenaeus with contemporary thought it is of very great interest to note that the Gnostics—at least the Valentinian *gnosis*—also built on Gen. I. 26 f.[44] The Valentinians, it is true, were Irenaeus's chief opponents, but for this very reason we may well assume that they had a real influence on him, as indeed several scholars maintain.[45] It was a characteristic of this Gnosticism that, in accordance with the division into *higher* and *lower* which was applied to the whole of the Gnostic world-view, it made a sharp distinction between *imago* and *similitudo*. The exaggerated influence of Valentinian Gnosticism on Irenaeus is, however, closely bound up with the tendency which has been found recently of putting into the centre of discussion the relatively few passages in which Irenaeus appears to distinguish between *imago* and *similitudo*, in a manner which is reminiscent of the scholastic scheme of nature and supernature. But even among those who for reasons such as these over-emphasise the Gnostic influence there is nonetheless general agreement that the Valentinian interpretation of Gen. I. 26 f. exercised at the most a subsidiary influence, and was important only in that it impelled Irenaeus to take up the interpretation of the passage in earnest, but was not his basic reason for doing so. His interest in the passage was Biblical and Pauline.[46]

At the same time, however, there is an obvious difference between the theology of Irenaeus and the Pauline theology in their general interpretation. In Rom. V.12–21 Paul compares

"Der Gedanke der Weltplaneinheit und Adameinheit in der Theologie des hl. Irenäus," in *Scholastik*, 1942, pp. 167–76.

[44] *A.h.* I. i. 10 (Stier. I. v. 5); cf. I. xi. 2 (Stier. I xviii. 2).

[45] Prümm in *Scholastik*, 1938, p. 213 and Emil Brunner, *Der Mensch im Widerspruch*, 3rd edn. Zürich 1941, p. 523, Eng. trans. *Man in Revolt*, London 1939, p. 503 f. (a description of A. Struker's book which I do not have available, *Die Gottebenbildlichkeit des Menschen in der urchristlichen Literatur der esrten zwei Jahrhunderte*, 1913). Cf. Klebba, *Anthropologie des hl. Irenaeus*, p. 23 f.

[46] So also, for example, Bousset, *Kyrios Christos*, p. 437; see however p. 443 with its interpretation of Paul that was characteristic of that period. More recently E. Käsemann, *Leib und Leib Christi*, Tübingen 1933—see pp. 81 ff, 147 ff., 163 ff.—admittedly has maintained that in his use of the term *eikon* and related words Paul came under the Gnostic influence. On the question of speculation in general within Gnosticism on primitive man see W. Bousset, *Hauptprobleme der Gnosis*, Göttingen 1907, pp. 160–203; and C. H. Kraeling, *Anthropos and Son of Man*, New York 1927, pp. 17 ff; and also Jonas, *Gnosis*, pp. 344–51. With regard to Paul cf. Ernst Lohmeyer, *Die Briefe an die Philipper, an die Kolosser und an Philemon*, henceforth cited as *Briefe*, Göttingen 1930, pp. 55, 140 (On Col. I. 15 and III. 10).

Adam and Christ. Through Adam sin and death have come into the world, but through Christ has come righteousness and life. Paul focuses his attention on the *defeat*, the "fall," of Adam.[47] By so doing he is not denying that Adam was created by God, but it is not this which, as an Apostle, he has to proclaim. The Gospel is about what Christ has done. And so in Paul's theology Adam and Christ are set over against one another. Irenaeus found himself involved in controversy with Gnostics who denied what was self-evident to Paul, namely that Adam was created in the image of God, as it is written in Gen. 1.26 f., and created by the God who sent Christ into the world.[48] The Gnostics likewise rejected the Law and the Old Testament which God the most high had given, and so Irenaeus was forced not only to try to demonstrate how both the Old and the New Testaments were derived from God, and how both the Law and the Gospel were addressed to men by the same God, but also to make it clear to his own period that Adam was created by God to live, body and soul, in accordance with His will. For this very reason it is important to speak of Adam's sin as a *fall*. Irenaeus also lays strong emphasis on the fact that Adam's defeat and Christ's victory are the extreme opposites of one another.[49] If, however, we examine what Adam was created *for*, what appears is not the contrast between Adam and Christ, Irenaeus maintained, but, on the contrary, the connexion between them.[50] And it is this connexion which we must first of all now define.

There is a suitable starting-point for our discussion in Loofs's

[47] See Nygren, *Pauli brev till Romarna*, Stockholm 1944, pp. 214–19, Eng. trans. *Commentary on Romans*, Philadelphia 1949, pp. 218–24, 232 f. Against this background the individuality of Irenaeus stands out with the greatest clarity. He takes up for discussion a subject which in the N.T. is a subsidiary one. Cf. Franz Stoll, *Lehre des hl. Irenäus*, pp. 40, 51.

[48] See Heinrich Schlier, "Vom Menschenbild des Neuen Testaments" in the volume of essays entitled *Der alte und der neue Mensch*, Munich 1942, p. 25, and Edmund Schlink, "Gottes Ebenbild als Gesetz und Evangelium" *op cit.*, pp. 79 ff.; cf. p. 83 where Irenaeus is mentioned with others as one who laid a theological foundation in his doctrine of *imago* and *similitudo*. Brunner's massive work of Christian anthropology, *Man in Revolt*, London 1939, which first appeared (in German) in 1937, had probably both a positive and a negative influence on this compilation referred to—in both books the idea of *imago* occupies a prominent place. It is remarkable that this important Pauline concept is left completely unexamined in a volume which appeared three years before Brunner's, Walter Gutbrod's *Die Paulinische Anthropologie*, Stuttgart 1934.

[49] E.g. *A.h.* v. xxi. 1–2 (Stier. ibid.). [50] Ibid. See also *A.h.* III. 30 (Stier. III. xxi. 10).

analysis of a line of thought which appears in Irenaeus. Loofs isolates a special line of thought in *Adversus haereses*, according to which the historical Christ who lived on earth was the pattern which God had in His mind when he fashioned the first man. Christ was the man about to be, *homo futurus*, and the Creator, as it were, foresaw Christ. While the earth was being formed, Christ was in the mind of God, and matter took shape in the hands of God in accordance with this future pattern. In particular, Loofs links up this line of thought with a much-debated passage in Tertullian's *De resurrectione carnis*, where the Christological and anthropological concepts which I have just mentioned are quite prominent.[51] In Tertullian, however, these ideas have no systematic significance, and the idea of Christ as *homo futurus* is one which comes up only for a time and then disappears.[52] There is, however, one dominant idea in the main writing of Irenaeus, which Loofs was continually trying to split up into several parts, in which the line of thought of which I have just spoken would be fundamental.[53] It is characteristic of Loofs's interpretation of Irenaeus that this line of thought—the Christ yet to be—is set in sharp contrast to the idea of Christ as the pre-existent Son. The idea of pre-existence belongs to a quite different part of *Adversus haereses*, and it was solely on account of his general theological lack of depth, Loofs held, that Irenaeus as a compiler was able to attempt the task of joining together two such unrelated elements to form a unity which had to be forced.[54]

[51] Tertullian, *Opera*, ed. E. Kroymann, PT. III, *De resurrectione carnis*, Bonn 1906, p. 33. Loofs has a detailed exegesis of the text, "Das altkirchliche Zeugnis gegen die herrschende Auffassung der Kenosisstelle," in *Theol. Stud. u. Krit.*, 1927–8, pp. 44 ff.; note that Loofs punctuates the text differently from Kroymann, which is also of importance for the theological explanation of the passage in question. Tertullian is here expounding Gen. I. 26 f., among other passages. The same passage was referred to for illustration by Irenaeus in Klebba, *Anthropologie des hl. Irenaeus*, p. 25. Similar passages are found in Hippolytus and in two other places in the writings of Tertullian.

[52] Cf. Harnack, *History of Dogma*, VOL. II, p. 283, n. 2, where the passage referred to in Tertullian is similarly touched on.

[53] Loofs, *Theophilus von Antiochien*, pp. 135, 253 f.

[54] *Op. cit.*, pp. 288, 446 f. On "*Irenaeus selbst*" as the mechanically operating co-writer, see p. 355. Loofs's view of pre-existence in the N.T. appears on p. 444 f., n. 2. Cf. too his lengthy article mentioned above in *Theol. Stud. u. Krit.*, 1927–8, pp. 3 ff. on Phil. II. 5–11.

It is easier to see the significance of Loofs's reasoning if we take a parallel from the history of dogma. On the question of election it is sometimes suggested that God elects, but that He does so on the basis of His foreknowledge of what course man is going to take. But if this foreknowledge is allowed to become the principal thing, then obviously the decisive factor will be man's free will—whatever takes place does so independently of God and in isolation from Him, while God is added on later as the One who foresees, but in an essentially passive way. The view which underlies Loofs's dichotomy between the idea of pre-existence and the idea of the future is just the same. Christ is a reality in the future; the Son is not with God from eternity, but rather the future, historic Christ is foreseen by God. In the preceding section, however, it was made clear that a deistic concept of God such as this was altogether alien to Irenaeus. Irenaeus maintained not only that God has foreknowledge of everything, but also that His foreknowledge is an element in His creation of all things, and before we see them emerging in history these things are already real in God.[55] It is an artificial contrast that Loofs makes between what is pre-existent and what is of the future. The affinity between these two ideas is natural and primary. Mankind's prototype is the Son, the *Logos*, the *Verbum*, who, in His future aspect as Saviour, existed in God. It is perhaps a matter of some doubt whether Tertullian looks at the matter in the same way, for his references to the subject are scattered, but as far as Irenaeus is concerned this inner connexion is certain.[56]

"Man is created in the image of God, and the image of God is the Son, in whose image man was created. For this reason the Son also appeared in the fulness of time to show how the

[55] On this idea in general cf. Liechtenhan, *Göttliche Vorherbestimmung*, pp. 114–16, and with ref. to Irenaeus see Escoula in *Nouvelle revue théologique*, 1939, where, however, he accentuates the idea of predestination with all the emphasis on one side, pp. 387 ff., 395. If we are to represent Irenaeus correctly, the characteristic of sin as disobedience to God must not be obscured. The Irenaean view cannot be satisfactorily described if we do not bear in mind that according to Irenaeus there are certain matters of which we do not have any knowledge. Among these is the reason for the Fall. It can be demonstrated pragmatically that sin is a positive reality, an act of resistance which is defeated by God in Christ.

[56] Scharl makes this clear in *Orientalia*, 1940, pp. 390–2; cf. Hugo Koch in *Theol. Stud. u. Krit.*, 1925, p. 211.

copy resembles Him."[57] The Son was first, before Creation. Man, like every other thing, is created in the Son and the Spirit, i.e. he has been formed by God's own hands, but he is different from the rest of Creation in that in addition he was created in order to become like God—to become the very image of God. This is his destiny. Irenaeus does not say that he *is* this image, nor was this destiny wholly realised in Creation before sin entered into the world, because man was a *child*. This means, in part, that man has not arrived at his appointed destiny in Creation, because he is not the son of God in that sense, but it also means that, if he grew up to maturity without being confused by his adversary, he would reach the end which has been ordained for him by God. In our next section we shall look at the statements in Irenaeus about man as a *child* in Creation, and we shall postpone making references and offering a more detailed analysis till then, but this, at any rate, may be said in the meantime: a healthy, new-born child is unable to talk, for example, but it has every likelihood of being able to do so in the future, and provided only that the child grows, it will reach the stage of being able to talk. An injury to the child, however, may prevent it from ever beginning to talk. This is the situation of the first man. He is a child, created in the image of God, but he is not the image of God. That he lacks something, however, is not due to sin. No injury has yet happened to the child. He is uninjured, but he is just a child—he does not yet realise what he is to be. All the while, however, there is already in Creation one who *is* the image of God, the only-begotten Son.[58] There is nothing lacking in Him; He is more than man, and man, by being created "in the image of God," is created and established in Him, who was at a future point in history to become incarnate.

And yet at the same time there is an absolute distance between God and man. The Son is God, and therefore Creator; but man is created in the image of God, and is and remains

[57] *Epid.* 22. Cf. *Epid.* 11 and 55.

[58] See *A.h.* III. xxxi. 1 (Stier. III. xxi. 1) and III. xxxii. 1 (Stier. III. xxii. 3), and also IV. xi. 5 (Stier. IV. vi. 7), where Irenaeus lays stress on the fact that from the very beginning of Creation it is through the Son that God acts and reveals Himself. On the textual variants of the last-quoted passage see Loofs, *Theophilus von Antiochien*, p. 381, n. 1.

created.[59] This distinction between the Son and man is such that it may never be abolished, however man may become like the Son who is man's prototype. There is a passage in Irenaeus, in which he is emphasising this difference between Christ and man, where his very choice of words is significantly changed. Dealing with man, he states that having succumbed to his adversary man has become a captive of the Devil, and the question is, How shall anyone be able to overcome this adversary of mankind unless he is different from the man who has suffered defeat? But only the Son of God is stronger than man who has been created in the image of God, the Son in whose image man was created. The Son, therefore, was made man in the Incarnation in order to defeat man's adversary and to reveal the *similitudo*.[60] It is the Son's superiority to man which Irenaeus is emphasising here, and he demonstrates this distance by his statement that man was created in the likeness of the Son. The affinity between the Son and man and the distinction between them are part of the same reality, and both the distance between them and the bond which unites them are expressed by saying that man is created in the *imago* and *similitudo* of the Son; but it is a better definition simply to say that the Son *is* the *imago* and *similitudo* of God, and that man is *created in* God's *imago* and *similitudo*.

Man is created by God's hands, the Son and the Spirit, so as to become the very image of God.[61] The fulfilment of the purpose of Creation implies accordingly that man should grow in con-

[59] Cf. *A.h.* II. xlii. 2 (Stier. II. xxviii. 4) and—even more pronouncedly—V. iii. 1 (Stier. ibid.). See Bonwetsch, *Theologie des Irenäus*, pp. 104–7.

[60] "Quomodo autem eum qui adversus homines fortis erat, qui non solum vicit hominem, sed et detinebat eum sub sua potestate, devicit, et eum quidem qui vicerat vicit, eum vero qui victus fuerat hominem dimisit, nisi superior fuisset eo homine qui fuerat victus? Melior autem eo homine qui secundum similitudinem Dei factus est, et praecellentior quisnam sit alius nisi Filius Dei, ad cujus similitudinem factus est homo? Et propter hoc in fine ipse ostendit similitudinem, Filius Dei factus est homo, antiquam plasmationem in semetipsum suscipiens," *A.h.* IV. lii. 1 (Stier. IV. xxxiii. 4). Cf. *A.h.* IV. xxii. 1 (Stier. ibid.). In the quotation given here the simple *similitudo* is quite typically used as being synonymous with *imago et similitudo*.

[61] *A.h.* IV. Pref. iii (Stier. IV. Pref. iv) and IV. xxxiv. 1 (Stier. IV. xx. 1). Cf. V. xv. 2–xvi. 1 (Stier. V. xv. 2–xvi. 2) and V. xxviii. 3 (Stier. V. xxviii. 4) where he also speak of the *manus Dei*, but where it is God's acts through the Son or the Spirit in the Incarnation and the Church which are referred to.

formity with the Son, and since the Son is Christ, this coalescence with Christ in the Church, which is the Body of Christ, means that Creation is moving towards its consummation. We shall have more to say about this farther on, but it should be stressed at this point that, since the Spirit is given in the Incarnation and is inseparably bound with the Body of Christ, the Spirit too is active in Creation as well as the Son. Irenaeus will refer to the Son or the *Logos*, the *Verbum*, as "God's hand," but even more frequently he connects the Son with the Spirit and speaks of them together as "God's hands."[62] It is not only the Son, it is also the Spirit, who represents God's likeness. When man is formed after the image and likeness of God the Spirit too is active in that formation. This may be an appropriate point at which to mention some references to the Spirit as taking part in the formation of man, in spite of the fact that in so doing we are anticipating part of what is to follow.

There is a passage in the *Epideixis* which speaks of God as being triune in the following terms: "He is over all things as Father, He is with all things as the Word, since all things proceeded from the Father through the Word, but He is in us all as the Spirit who cries 'Abba, Father,' and forms man in the image of God."[63] Immediately before this Irenaeus had made the traditional identification of the Son with the Word and the Spirit with Wisdom—the Spirit forms the flesh, and "the flesh forgets its own property and assumes that of the Spirit by becoming conformable to the Word of God," i.e. to the Son.[64] In this last quotation the Spirit forms man in the likeness of the Son. There is a further related fact, which is that Christ's work of salvation consists in His bestowal of the Spirit: it is the Spirit which unites man with Christ.[65] Man's identity with the Son is

[62] Of the passages referred to in the previous note, v. xv. 2 ff., e.g., refers to God's *hand* (the Son) whereas the other passages speak of God's *hands* (the Son and the Spirit).

[63] *Epid.* 5. Cf. on the whole of this question Bonwetsch, *Theologie des Irenäus*, pp. 66 ff., and Scharl in *Orientalia*, 1940, p. 389; but see too p. 407: the subject of the verb *recapitulare* is always the Son, not the Spirit or the Father.

[64] ". . . caro a Spiritu possessa oblita quidem sui, qualitatem autem Spiritus assumens, conformis facta Verbo Dei," *A.h.* v. ix. 2 (Stier. v. ix. 3); cf. v. ix. 1 (Stier. ibid.).

[65] See Paul Gächter, "Unsere Einheit mit Christus nach dem hl. Irenäus," in *Zeitschrift für katholische Theologie*, henceforth cited as *Z.K.T.*, 1934, p. 526.

not finally achieved until the resurrection from the dead, and in Irenaeus as well as in early Christianity the resurrection is connected with the Spirit which forms the body, and in forming the body takes possession of it, making it a *soma pneumatikon*. In faith man already possesses the Spirit as an earnest, but the full dominion of the Spirit in the resurrection will perfect man in accordance with the Father's purpose in Creation, and conform him to God's *imago* and *similitudo*.[66] The Son and the Spirit are one in the Church and the resurrection, but not only there: they are already one at the beginning in the work of Creation.[67] From them, as the hands of God, man proceeds.

There are certain statements in Irenaeus about Christ's work of salvation which are put in such a way that we may at the same time deduce from them something about man as he was destined to be in Creation. Among these are all his statements of how Christ re-established man through the Spirit and restores him to his original status, and annuls the harm wrought by the Fall. The point is frequently made in *Adversus haereses* that what man lost in Adam, namely his conformity to the image and likeness of God, is restored again in Christ, and it was for this very reason that the Son, who was always with the Father, was made flesh.[68] The divine decree at man's creation comes to fulfilment through what is realised by Christ in His Incarnation: God's Word emerges as an effective reality.[69] There is hardly any passage in Irenaeus of greater importance than the one in which he describes in detail how it is only the man who receives

[66] *A.h.* v. viii. 1 (Stier. ibid.). Note how Irenaeus consistently avoids saying that man *is* the image of God. The resurrection is also the perfection of the *body*, which reaches its fulfilment only then.

[67] See lastly in this connexion *A.h.* IV. xiv. (Stier. IV. vii. 4); and cf. on this much debated passage Léon Froidevaux, "Une difficulté du texte de S. Irénée," in *Revue de l'orient chrétien*, 1931–2, pp. 441–3. In this passage the Spirit is called God's *figuratio*, by which is meant God's creative power. Loofs, *Theophilus von Antiochien*, p. 14, n. 2, provides the most reliable interpretation of the text.

[68] ". . . ut quod perideramus in Adam, id est, secundum imaginem et similitudinem esse Dei, hoc in Christo reciperemus," *A.h.* III. xix. 1 (Stier. III. xviii. 1). Cf. III. xxxii. 2 (Stier. III. xxiii. 1) and v. i. 1 (Stier. ibid.), and the last lines of v. xiv. 1 (Stier. ibid.).

[69] ". . . neque vere nos redemit sanguine suo, si non vere homo factus est, restaurans suo plasmati quod dictum est in principio, factum esse hominem secundum imaginem et similitudinem Dei," *A.h.* v. ii. 1 (Stier. ibid.).

the Spirit that is truly man.[70] If a man rejects the Spirit he remains in the power of his adversary, and by being so held he remains in a state that is contrary to his nature. The man, however, who receives God's Word returns to his original state: "Those who are created after God's *imago* and *similitudo* gain man's original state.[71] Accordingly, what is given in salvation is not a supernatural addition to what is purely human, as Roman Catholic theologians in particular frequently interpret Irenaeus to mean, but rather, the typical condition of mankind is his state of not being human—and what perverts man is his captivity to a power over himself—and Christ, by what He has done, frees man from his inhumanity and lets him become truly man.

The passage in Col. III.10 about the new man who "is being renewed in knowledge after the image of its creator" is an affirmation which Irenaeus finds of profound and particular significance. It implies that man, by faith in Christ, becomes a new man, becomes like Christ. And yet it was in the likeness of Christ, the Son, that man was created. The first creation, which was corrupted by sin, is begun again when man by faith is united with Christ who is the image of God.[72] In the "new man" Christ is active, and in Christ the Creator is active. God has not given up the work which He began when He said, "Let us make man in our own image," but in fact is active in creating man by His "hand," that is, by Christ; and when Christ, God's "hand" and "mouth," is accomplishing His work among men, the first creation is being brought to its fulfilment. These references in Irenaeus to the recreating power of Christ in the Incarnation are confirmed by similar statements about his view of Creation "in the beginning," which bear out what we have already discovered: from the very beginning the Son *is* the *imago* and *similitudo* of God, while man *is created* in the *imago* and *similitudo* of God.

[70] *A.h.* v. ix. 1 (Stier. v. ix. 2). Only from this can v. vi. 1 (Stier. ibid.) be understood. Those who make a distinction in Irenaeus between the natural and the supernatural always fail to interpret these passages satisfactorily.

[71] *A.h.* v. x. 1–2 (Stier. v. x. 1).

[72] "Et in eo quod dicit, *Secundum imaginem conditoris*, recapitulationem manifestavit ejusdem hominis, qui in initio secundum imaginem factus est Dei," *A.h.* v. xii. 4 (Stier. ibid.).

To reach an understanding of the concept of man in Irenaeus we shall have to avoid making distinctions between his various statements about Adam, the descendants of Adam, or man after Christ, etc.,[73] for Irenaeus would never have defined these different periods separately. In speaking of Adam he speaks of man, and in speaking of what Christ does for men he speaks of what Christ does for Adam; or again, in using the word *Adam* or the word *man* he is always in some way referring either to himself, or to those to whom he was preaching, to all men everywhere, that is, the dead as well as those yet to be born. There is a real difficulty, certainly, for us today in understanding such a view as this, only the difficulty is of a religious nature. As soon as we assume a view of man in himself as a creation of God, possessing nothing which has not come from God, and destined by the Creator for eternal life, we find that there are no insoluble difficulties connected with the concept of man which was held in the early Church. Certainly, we shall have to take time and trouble to understand it, but our whole understanding of man and everything connected with him is itself bound up with our belief in Creation. If we find that we are conceiving of man instinctively as being an isolated individual among other isolated individuals, we are proceeding on the assumption that the ground of his existence is something other than God. In this kind of individualistic view there is a difficulty in making any reference to Christ as Saviour.[74] The universal application of the work of Christ and its alteration of the status of the whole of humanity is a quite incomprehensible idea apart from the view of mankind as a unity, and the idea of man as having been created and destined for eternity. This understanding of man does not add any new difficulty to those which already exist in our comprehension of man, but is simply one of the assumptions which the Christian faith makes.

There is a helpful metaphor in Wilhelm Hunger where he says that Irenaeus regards mankind as a river—seen, however,

[73] Klebba, *Anthropologie des hl. Irenaeus*, approaches Irenaeus with this fundamental misunderstanding, which explains his frequent complaints that Irenaeus "mixes up" various things—see e.g. p. 22 f., 34. In referring to Irenaeus we should not even use the term "original state," since it tends to suggest a static scheme.

[74] Cf. Nygren in *Corpus Christi* (En bok om kyrkan), Stockholm 1942, p. 18 f., on Adam and Christ as the two by whom the destiny of mankind is determined.

not from the bank at a certain point in its course, and later seen again at another point from the bank, but seen at a glance from the source right down to the river-mouth, the same river all the way, and the same water with the same name.[75] The history of Adam is fulfilled only at the Consummation.[76] This aspect of the Irenaean anthropology will become a little clearer when we examine the statements in which he refers to a man as a *child.*

"*A Child*"

Both in the *Adversus haereses* and the *Epideixis* Irenaeus declares that man, as God created him, is a *child* (*νήπιος*, *infans*). His statements have frequently been noted, without any great importance being attached to them. These passages, however, are directly connected with a concept which is fundamental in Irenaeus, the concept of man "growing," of man as one who is constantly developing, or who ought to be so. By trying to discover what it means to speak of man as a child in Creation we shall succeed in avoiding a hard-and-fast attitude in the analysis of the term *recapitulatio*. It is clear from what we have already seen above that Irenaeus conceives of recapitulation, or Christ's work of salvation, as a restoration of Creation, a return to man's original state. Against this, however, a number of different statements have been adduced from Irenaeus in which he maintains that Christ completes Creation, making it into something better and richer than it had ever been from the beginning. There would appear, then, to be an inconsistency between this perfectionist view, and the kind of statement which is frequently repeated in Irenaeus, that what we lost in Adam we recover in Christ.[77] It is difficult to reconcile the pattern of *loss*

[75] *Scholastik*, 1942, p. 170.

[76] Hunger, *op. cit.*, pp. 171, 173, 176. The solidarity of all mankind in every age resides in men's common origin in God (Creation), and their common destiny (the Last Judgement), and therefore in both origin and destiny. Modern individualism is a direct consequence of the conception of man as a creature who exists for a certain length of time between birth and death, and no more. Individualism therefore concentrates on this period of time alone, this "life" which is held to have had a purely accidental origin and which comes to nothing at its end, but in doing so, individualism makes man into a creature existing wholly for himself.

[77] Cf. above, note 68.

and recovery with that of *imperfect beginning to perfection*, and it is only too clear that one cannot lose what one has never possessed. It was at this particular point, the double aspect in the concept of recapitulation, that H. H. Wendt put a wedge into the theology of Irenaeus, a wedge which was intended to prove to Irenaean scholars conclusively that the theology of Irenaeus consisted of at least two disconnected parts.[78] Perhaps the assumption must be that it was only in the nineteenth century that this dichotomy was revealed! Two distinguishable parts there are indeed in the Irenaean concept of recapitulation, but the unity which unites the two parts consists of the concept of *child* and the concept of *growth*.

If we take as an example a child's power of speech, it is not in the least illogical to argue that one may lose what one has never had. An accident may deprive a child of the power of speech before it has reached the age when it occasionally spoke a few words. If, however, the child which suffered from such a defect were cured by medical skill, the recovery of its health would be evidenced by the fact that it spoke, by doing something, that is, which it had never done before the accident occurred. The child recovers its power of speech which it never had. In this phrase "power of speech" there is a certain variation of meaning, but it is exactly this kind of variation which is characteristic of Irenaeus, and which is a quite different thing from maintaining that Irenaeus's thought proceeds on two different lines.[79] The same thing happens when Irenaeus deals with the concept of *growth*, and attempts to demonstrate that the full-grown man is exactly the same being as the undeveloped man, and yet is something completely different, because he has *grown* and become something different. In Irenaeus the thought vacillates between identity and change, and is con-

[78] H. H. Wendt, *Die christliche Lehre von der menschlichen Vollkommenheit*, henceforth cited as *Christliche Lehre*, Göttingen 1882, pp. 26 ff. This is the source of all subsequent division of the theology of Irenaeus and his writings. Harnack, *History of Dogma*, VOL. II. p. 272 f., follows Wendt, and many more follow in Harnack's footsteps.

[79] Irenaeus himself does not use the metaphor of power of speech, but it casts light on the Irenaean terminology as a whole. One might have chosen any of the abilities which a child possesses or does not possess. The full meaning of the language used by Irenaeus will not be seen until we have brought man's Fall into the discussion—the blow which strikes the child and injures it. We shall return to the point in the later chapter on Satan and man's defeat.

tinually fluctuating between the two.[80] The historian of dogma who, in dealing with this kind of problem, merely states that there is a general confusion, is justified in saying so provided that he himself clearly demonstrates how man's *growth* is to be interpreted, for what Irenaeus was attempting to undertake was nothing less than the interpretation of words such as *grow*, *growth*, and so on, terms which, for an interpretation of man, are central to the New Testament.[81]

Bonwetsch points out that Irenaeus never speaks of man as being "perfect" in his "original state,"[82] and while he is quite correct in what he says, I think it would be better to give up this rigid scheme with its three or four "states" which was so characteristic of later Scholasticism, both on the Roman Catholic and the Protestant side.[83] A theology of man's "original state" does not emerge before the controversy between Augustine and Pelagianism, and before that time we find hardly any account of the first paradisiacal world and its perfect man.[84] When Irenaeus refrains from saying that the man whom God created was perfect, he has no intention of repudiating any elaborate theory of perfection, and consequently no suggestion that there was any weakness, want, or mortality in Adam.[85]

[80] The dominion of sin is the interruption of man's growth, a contravention of nature, and death.

[81] E.g. Eph. II. 21, III. 16, IV. 15 f., Col. II. 19; these passages should be connected with the idea of "growing together with Christ" in Rom. VI and the other related passages; and also I Jn. III. 2, which proceeds from the concept of *son*, and II Cor. IV. 16–18, and also II Cor. III. 18. The growing likeness to Christ in death and resurrection of Phil. III. 10 f., and III. 21 is an integral part of the same complex of New Testament ideas upon which Irenaeus worked vigorously.

[82] Bonwetsch, *Theologie des Irenäus*, p. 74.

[83] Klebba, *Anthropologie des hl. Irenaeus*, pp. 27 ff. takes this approach. Sven Silén, *Den kristna människouppfattningen intill Schleiermacher*, Stockholm 1938, pp. 70–3, adopts the theories of division propounded by Wendt and Harnack in his view of Irenaeus.

[84] Cf. Antoine Slomkowski, *L'État primitif de l'homme dans la tradition de l'église avant Saint Augustin*, henceforth cited as *État primitif*, Paris 1928, in his summary on p. 143. This book does not go very deeply in its details, but is right in its main thesis. Cf. also O. Zöckler's more apologetic work, *Die Lehre vom Urstand des Menschen*, Gütersloh 1879, p. 41, an exposition which otherwise has as its dogmatic basis an unconcealed belief in evolution. See also Brunner, *Man in Revolt*, p. 84, n. 1; broadly speaking, Brunner's picture of Irenaeus is built on Klebba's book published in 1894.

[85] Neither in *A.h.* IV. lxii–lxiii (Stier. IV. xxxviii) nor in *Epid.* 12 does Irenaeus think of death as being a part of God's Creation. When he says that man lacks

The line is clear: death came through *sin*—every hurt in the life of man has its source in mankind's primal adversary, in evil, and disobedience. But on the other hand the yielding to temptation and defeat is so intimately associated with Adam that the only remaining contribution of the first man to the human race is his Fall, and his introduction of death into the world of men. Mortality thus is characteristic of original man, without itself having been created by God. Mortality is not of itself involved in the concept of *son*, but is a work of sin and the Serpent against the Commandment of God.[86]

This point is made clear in the *Epideixis*, in which it is maintained that the first two human beings were sinless and childlike, and were so because they had been created by God.[87] But having said this, Irenaeus goes on immediately to stress that there is a gulf which separates man from God, a gulf which has been made by the Creator Himself; and that in contrast to God man has a Lord over him, and a Will imposed upon his own. One expression for the dominion which the Creator has over His created child is the *Commandments* of God. At once, therefore, the ethical factor comes into the foreground at this point, in the sense of a regulated conduct of life from man's side, namely the Law.[88] From the very first Irenaeus connects life, that is, the physical factor, with the Commandments, the ethical, and continues to do so throughout his thinking. If man were to live in accordance with the Commandments he would continue in the state in which he once was, *that is, he would be immortal*, for obedience and life belong together.[89] Had he violated God's

perfection he is simply giving expression to the fact that man is *created*, and therefore he "grows," he "becomes," but he does not create like God. We must also take into account the fact that when Irenaeus speaks about Adam he is sometimes referring to fallen Adam, Adam who was conquered by the Devil, since there was nothing much that could be said about what Adam had done before the Fall: his first significant act was sin. See Reinhold Niebuhr, *The Nature and Destiny of Man*, London 1944, VOL. I, p. 296, and *A.h.* IV. xxiii. 2 (Stier. ibid.). But in so far as man's destiny is fixed by sin, passages like these say nothing about Creation—Creation, that is, which is intact, and which has its source in God.

[86] This is obscured in Hugo Koch's description of Irenaeus's view in *Theol. Stud. u. Krit.*, 1925, pp. 209 ff. (cf. p. 201, n. 1), which in other respects contains some of the best material ever written on Irenaeus.

[87] *Epid.* 14. On the term *child* cf. *Epid.* 46 and the beginning of 96.

[88] *Epid.* 15.

[89] Cf. Hermann Jordan, *Armenische Irenaeusfragmente*, Leipzig 1913, p. 129 f.: life and death are thought of as being in continual conflict. Jordan's compilation of

Commandment *he would become subject to death and be resolved into dust*, for sin and death belong together. Man is free, and can acquire any power at all, life as well as death. If "mortality" means that the possibility of death as well (through sin) remains open, then man is mortal from the time he leaves God's hand, since Irenaeus is always firm in maintaining that man is free and created free through the power of God.[90] Irenaeus, however, does not usually refer to this as mortality, but, on the contrary, man plunges into mortality when he yields to the temptation of disobedience. The man who chooses evil, says Irenaeus, or who gives up the struggle between good and evil, destroys himself in his inner man—"latenter semetipsum occidit hominem."[91]

We may now note here in parenthesis that just as the physical and the ethical are connected in relation to life or death for mankind in Creation, the same combination recurs in recapitulation. Christ defeats death by resisting temptation in the wilderness and on the Cross. The "physical" resurrection proceeds from the "ethical" death on the Cross. But Christ's ethical purity is consequent also on the fact that God dwells in Him. Christ's ethical works have their source in the physical Incarnation. And the man who receives the Spirit gains thereby an attitude to his neighbour which is induced by God, and which corresponds to the Commandment, *and* he gains everlasting life in the resurrection from the dead. The Church is to be understood as a creative ethical force in the non-Christian society simply because it is Christ's martyred Body which

fragments consists of a series of hypotheses with some useful observations interspersed among assumptions which he does not substantiate. On the continued discussion on his book cf. W. Ludtke, "Bemerkungen zu Irenäus," in *Z.NT.W.*, 1914, pp. 268 ff. and W. Durks, "Eine fälschlich dem Irenäus zugeschriebene Predigt des Bischofs Severian von Gabala," in *Z.NT.W.*, 1922, pp. 64 ff., which continues without very much evidence an idea suggested by Jordan, *op. cit.*, pp. 190 ff.

[90] *Epid.* 11.

[91] This passage comes into the context of *A.h.* IV. lxiv.1 (Stier. IV. xxxix. 1) abruptly, and is somewhat obscure; cf. V. i. 1 (Stier. ibid.) with its assertion that God, in His dealings with man, must also preserve his freedom, and V. viii. 1–2 (Stier. V. viii. 2) on the resemblance of the wicked man to the animal. Strangely enough this passage on self-destruction is seldom expounded; cf., however, J. A. Robinson's suggestions, "Notes on the Armenian Version of Irenaeus' *Adversus haereses*," in *J.T.S.*, 1931, p. 377.

awaits the resurrection of the dead, the physical miracle. The Christian believer's participation in Christ consists as much in the willingness of the mind to obey Christ's commandment of love, as in the enjoyment which the body has in the bread and wine of the Eucharist. If the sharp distinction between physical and ethical, which was at one time customary in the history of dogma, is applied to Irenaeus, the result does not tend to clarify, but rather to confuse. All this, of course, is by the way,[92] and we may now return to what Irenaeus has to say about man as a child.

It is significant that in his description of the Fall of Adam Irenaeus can co-ordinate two separate expressions: one, that the first man lost through sin his natural character and his child-like mind, and the other, that he lost the garment of holiness which he possessed by the Spirit.[93] The same thing is expressed in both of these statements. The gift of the Spirit is *child-likeness*. When Irenaeus deals later with the concept of the Church there is, therefore, an indissoluble connexion between the Spirit and sonship. The Spirit, bestowed by Christ, makes us anew the children of God. It is, therefore, hardly correct to speak, as Brunner does, of man, in the view of Irenaeus, as being sealed by his condition as a "child" in such a way that his distinctive mark is *innocence, not righteousness*.[94] If we set innocence and righteousness over against one another, then we must necessarily think of righteousness as being the sum of a series of righteous works. But righteousness is rather the unbroken receiving of life from the "hands" of the Creator; it is man's acquiescence in his own creation and not his self-willed resistance to God. Righteousness is involved in man's

[92] On the problem of *physical* and *ethical* in the early period in general see Brunner, *Der Mittler*, 2nd edn. Tübingen 1930, pp. 219–33, Eng. trans. *The Mediator*, London 1934, pp. 249–64, in which Irenaeus is specially dealt with, Folke Boström, *Studier till den grekiska teologins frälsningslära*, pp. 1–97, and in particular Ragnar Bring, "Till kritiken av Harnacks syn på den gammalkyrkliga frälsningsuppfattningen," in *S.T.K.*, 1933, pp. 232 ff., in which a penetrating criticism of both Brunner and Boström appears.

[93] ". . . quoniam indolem et puerilem amiserat sensum, et in cogitationem pejorum venerat . . . Quoniam, inquit, eam quam habui a Spiritu sanctitatis stolam amisi per inobedientiam," *A.h.* III. xxxv. 1 (Stier. III. xxiii. 5). On the struggle against the flesh see the parallel in v. ix. 2 (Stier. ibid.).

[94] Brunner, *Man in Revolt*, p. 84, n. 1. Compare, however, the meaning of *child* in *Epid.* 96.

status as a child, for righteousness can scarcely be anything other than the "garment of righteousness," which the child possesses "by the Spirit."[95] God's act of creation and His continuing activity among men are implied in the concept of *νήπιος*.

We have just seen that for Irenaeus man's growth is an immediate consequence of God's act of creation. The cessation of man's growth would be the same as the cessation of God's creativity, and we should be left with a powerless, passive and unmoved God. A direct corollary of the concept of sonship is the concept of *growth*. It is a distinctive characteristic of the child that he grows and becomes. This is exactly the same idea as the one which we saw above: man is created in the *imago* and *similitudo* of God, but he is not God's *imago* and *similitudo*—only the eternal Son is that, and only He possesses the whole of God's fulness in Himself. Man is created for the Son, and he attains to his perfection in the Son. His destiny was realised only when the image of God took human life in the Incarnation and took up into Himself the man who had been created in the image of God. The Incarnation and its benefits had no reality when man was first created: man, therefore, is a child, a son, whose goal and objective is full growth. In this idea of growth, however, we are not to discern any trace of the suggestion that man's initial condition, his life as a child, was in any way inherently sinful; it was characterised simply by the fact that man is *created*, and being created he lacks the divinity and perfection of the Son.[96]

[95] The statements in *A.h.* III. xxxv. 1 are sometimes understood as an extenuation of the Fall, as though Adam were not wholly responsible. Irenaeus does not attempt to diminish Adam's guilt, but what he tries to show is that Adam is not unrepentant. The final destruction will fall on the Serpent, but not on Adam. Cf. Stoll, *Lehre des hl. Irenäus*, pp. 11 ff., 25.

[96] *Εἰ δὲ λέγει τις· οὐκ ἠδύνατο ὁ Θεὸς ἀπ' ἀρχῆς τέλειον ἀναδεῖξαι τὸν ἄνθρωπον; Γνώτω, ὅτι τῷ μὲν Θεῷ, ἀεὶ κατὰ τὰ αὐτὰ ὄντι, καὶ ἀγεννήτῳ ὑπάρχοντι, ὡς πρὸς ἑαυτὸν, πάντα δυνατά· τὰ δὲ γεγονότα, καθὸ μετέπειτα γενέσεως ἀρχὴν ἰδίαν ἔσχε, κατὰ τοῦτο καὶ ὑστερεῖσθαι δεῖ αὐτὰ τοῦ πεποιηκότος· οὐ γὰρ ἠδύναντο ἀγέννητα εἶναι τὰ νεωστὶ γεγεννημένα . . . Καθὸ δὲ νεώτερα, κατὰ τοῦτο καὶ νήπια*, *A.h.* IV. lxii (Stier. IV. xxxviii. 1). On the text, however, see Karl Holl, *Fragmente vornicänischer Kirchenväter*, Leipzig 1899, pp. 64 ff. The concept of *νήπιος* is introduced here from the contrasting ideas of Creator and created, a concept which later on in this chapter of *A.h.* is of primary importance. Irenaeus passes at once to growth and to Christ. Cf., however, Hugo Koch in *Theol.*

Since Irenaeus sees man's goal lying in his conformity to the image of God, that is, to Christ, a conformity to which man attains only in the eternal Kingdom, the whole of the Christian life becomes a pilgrimage towards this goal. That which God presents to man through Christ is perfect in itself, but the man who receives it and incorporates it into himself is imperfect and in the process of growth. Whatever man may be given, and however high and holy may be everything that the Church bestows on him, yet, anything that man takes into himself is *eo ipso* limited and finite—man is "on the way," not at his destined goal. It has to be clearly remembered throughout that in the Irenaean concept of growth there is first and foremost an emphasis on the smallness of man and the greatness of God—but on the greatness of God as Creator, that is, the bestower of inexhaustible gifts. Man's growth has its source in the power of God. There is a gulf fixed between God and man, but this gulf is transformed into an increasingly close relationship, not because man is what he is, capable of increase and growth, but because God is what He is, good and powerful. The modern concept of a growth that is entirely from within the growing self, while benefits are bestowed from outside, is alien to Irenaeus. His concept of growth is well conveyed by the words which Paul uses of the grain: "But God gives it a body as he has chosen" (I Cor. xv.38). Any growth from the grain is the *creation of God*, the gift of God. The power to bestow growth lies beyond man and beyond the grain of wheat, in "God who gives the growth" (I Cor. III.7).

Man's growth is thus not simply a work, a consequence of God's act of creation, but actually *is* God's act of creation, exactly the same reality as God's creation, though seen from a different angle.[97] When theologians of a later period speak of

Stud. u. Krit. 1925, p. 201, where the contrast between natural and supernatural somewhat obscures the line of thought, and also Karl Prümm in *Scholastik*, 1938, p. 221, where the term *plasma* in Irenaeus and the idea of growth are investigated (see too p. 222); Prümm shows how closely held together these concepts are in the New Testament. Cf. also *A.h.* II. xxxvii. 3–xxxviii (Stier. II. xxv. 2–4) and II. xli. 1 (Stier. II. xxviii. 1) on man as created and continually coming into being.

[97] "Et hoc Deus ab homine differt, quoniam Deus quidem facit, homo autem fit: et quidem qui facit, semper idem est: quod autem fit, et initium, et medietatem, et adjectionem, et augmentum accipere debet. Et Deus quidem bene facit, bene autem fit homini. Et Deus quidem perfectus in omnibus, ipse sibi aequalis et

man's spiritual growth, his inward progression is generally understood as a development of the latent powers of the personality, and the consequence of this particular view is the conception of old age and death as being, by their own evidence, the cessation of this growth. Irenaeus speaks of death in this simple and natural kind of way as standing somewhere in the middle of man's growth, in his exposition of the adoption as sons which is given to us through Christ. There is nothing of an idealistic development of personality in this expression of Irenaeus: the personality *dies*, man dies, just as the grain in the earth dies in order to "grow," to rise, to be created by God, and as Christ was crucified and put to death in order that He might rise from the dead as the Prince of Life. Irenaeus conceives of man's growth, that is, as a growing together with Christ, who is the image of God. By this he does not imply that there is any imitation of the life which Christ led and His development of the life He lived within the compass of the years He spent on earth. Rather, Irenaeus would have us keep our attention fixed on the two quite definite points of Christ's *death* and His *Resurrection*, the two points which have shattered the modern immanent and romantic idea of Jesus, and which transfer man's goal from the development of his personality to the resurrection of the dead. For this reason, therefore, growth

similis; totus cum sit lumen, et totus mens, et totus substantia, et fons omnium bonorum; homo vero profectum percipiens et augmentum ad Deum. Quemadmodum enim Deus semper proficiet ad Deum. Neque enim Deus cessat aliquando in benefaciendo, et locupletando hominem: neque homo cessat beneficium accipere, et ditari a Deo," *A.h.* IV. xxi. 2 (Stier. IV. xi. 2, wrongly numbered in Stier.). In the passage immediately before this Irenaeus based the idea of growth on Gen. I. 28: *Crescite et multiplicamini*. We find the same relation between God and man in *Epid.*; cf. L. T. Wieten, *Irenaeus' geschrift 'Ten bewiize der apostolische prediking,'* henceforth cited as *Irenaeus' geschrift*, Utrecht 1909, p. 184 f. On the idea of continued growth and "training" in the Son's Kingdom after the resurrection of the just, see *A.h.* V. xxxv. 1 (Stier. ibid.). Cremers in *Bijdragen*, 1938, pp. 60 ff., tries to maintain that this "millenarian" idea is incompatible with what Irenaeus says elsewhere. See, however, Hugo Koch's comparison (which he made as early as 1925) of Irenaean passages on the "training" in *Theol. Stud. u. Krit.* 1925, p. 199 f., n. 1. In *Theophilus von Antiochen*, published in 1930, Loofs can occasionally reveal great understanding of how the idea of growth unites different aspects of Irenaeus's thought which are otherwise difficult to harmonise (see, e.g., p. 59 f., n. 3, where Loofs is fairly positive in his criticism of Koch's interpretation), while at other times he directly opposes such an understanding of Irenaeus (see e.g. p. 284, n. 2, and p. 372). It may be that these and similar discrepancies are found in Loofs because of the fact that his work was published posthumously.

takes place at the time of martyrdom, when Christians are torn in pieces by wild animals or burned to ashes. It is at the point of martyrdom that man is formed in the *imago* and *similitudo* of God, brought into communion with the dead Christ, and his participation in the Body of Christ becomes a reality.[98]

In the view of growth which we have here put forward there are several conceptions, the examination of which we must put off till later, since there is involved in them the idea of the growth which sinful and fallen man resumes again because of the sustenance he derives from Christ, the Incarnate one. It would, however, be appropriate even at this point to say a few words about this whole idea, since only so will the significance of the concept of "child" become perfectly clear. But the point at issue is that as long as man had not yielded to the Serpent's temptation to disobey God, there was no sin in the world, and therefore no death. In this section, however, we are dealing only with the starting-point of growth in God's Creation, with man as an innocent, though at this initial stage living, child.

In order that we may have some understanding of what follows later, there is one other subject which we must at least mention, and that is one aspect of Irenaeus's doctrine of free-will. The essential principle in the concept of freedom appears

[98] Cf. *A.h.* IV. lxiii. 3 (Stier. IV. xxxviii. 4), in which Irenaeus interprets Ps. LXXXII. 6–7, with *A.h.* V. xxviii. 3 (Stier. V. xxviii. 4), which deals with the significance of martyrdom, and with III. xx. 3 (Stier. III. xix. 3) on man's death and resurrection in the Body of Christ as His body in the resurrection. We must bear these passages in mind when we are evaluating the statement in V. xxix. 1 (Stier. ibid.): *Creation is made for man's sake, not man for Creation's*—a passage which is otherwise easily misinterpreted. Man has been created for eternal life: this is his distinctive characteristic in Creation. This is the primary concept, and from it we may also understand quite readily *A.h.* IV. viii (Stier. IV. V. 1) and IV. xxv. 3 (Stier. IV. xiv. 3), passages into which we might otherwise be inclined to read the later doctrine of a special "supernature"—a doctrine which is not to be found in Irenaeus; cf. what Irenaeus says about the destruction of Jerusalem in a parallel passage in *A.h.* IV. v (Stier. IV. iv. 1) which helps to clarify the point at issue. There has been a lengthy discussion on the question of the place of man in the theology of Irenaeus, and whether he was given a place in the centre of Creation that competed with God. It is better to start from *A.h.* IV. xxxiv. 6–7 (Stier. IV. xx. 6–7). I hope to be able to take up the examination of this discussion later on. For the present all we need do is to emphasise the fact that man's growth is not a development of his personality within this world, but that his essential moments in time are death and resurrection (cf. Rom. VI and Phil. III). The superficial and optimistic description of growth which we find, e.g. in Montgomery Hitchcock, *Irenaeus of Lugdunum*, pp. 52–64, is in any case wrong.

first in Christ's status as the sovereign Lord, because for Irenaeus man's freedom is, strangely enough, a direct expression of God's omnipotence, so direct, in fact, that a diminution of man's freedom automatically involves a corresponding diminution of God's omnipotence. This fundamental emphasis in Irenaeus's doctrine of freedom is bound up with his attack on the Gnostic classification of men, according to which the "pneumatics" are saved, while the "hylics" are destroyed, on the basis of their respective substances—God is powerless before this predestination from below, and can only watch passively while man's substance divides itself according to its own inherent quality into worldly and unworldly, spirit and matter. This Gnostic heresy provides us with the background of Irenaeus's characteristic statements about freedom, by which he makes man's freedom a direct expression of God's saving power, God's power of using man's freedom to break through all classifications of men and in Christ to free every man who believes. But this main aspect of freedom must not occupy our attention here, for it is another side of freedom with which we are concerned at this point, namely freedom as a condition for temptation and defeat.

Man is free because he has been created by the power of God to be free. He cannot be driven to take one course of action or another by some external, mechanical force or compulsion, as though he were simply an object or a creature, but has rather to will what he does from inside himself; in so far as he does so he resembles God, his Creator, whose nature is freedom. This human freedom corresponds closely to God's dealings with men both through the Commandment which was given at the very beginning of Creation, and through the Gospel which was given at the Incarnation, and which, before Christ, existed in the form of the promise. The intent of the Law is free obedience, while the intent of the Gospel or the promise is free faith, and also obedience to God's will. But man's freedom is also expressed in the possibility that he may reject both the Commandment and the promise in his disbelief or disobedience.[99] Time and time

[99] Many historians of dogma have held that the Irenaean doctrine of freedom is a deviation from Paul, and they have unfavourably criticised it. See, e.g., Ernst Luthardt, *Die Lehre vom freien Willen*, Leipzig 1863, pp. 15 f.; Klebba, *Anthropologie*

again we find the stress in Irenaeus on the fact that whole of God's revelation has this open and unconditional character. It is a revelation to *all* Creation, and on the day of Judgement, when the whole world, in spite of the fact that God's revelation has been disclosed to all, is divided and assigned to blessing or to curse, those who have rejected His revelation will be held responsible. In this regard there are consequently two related ideas involved in Irenaeus's concept of freedom, first, the idea of revelation for all in the time of grace—whether it is in Creation, in Moses, or in Christ, God's revelation is everywhere open and has been universally proclaimed—and second, the Last Judgement, in which every man will be judged by the clear revelation which God granted to him, whether that revelation was complete or limited. God's judgement is just because man is free, and man's disobedience involves guilt. His ultimate destiny is not determined from within himself by his inalienable substance.

We might well look at the comparisons and problems which Irenaeus avoided, such as, for instance, the contrast between free will and grace, and his attempt to detail their respective contributions in the deliverance of man from the power of his superior enemy. Man is held captive by the Serpent, and Christ alone bruises the Serpent's head. Besides this, Irenaeus has also refrained from putting the speculative question of how the Fall might have originated, and then solving the problem with the

des hl. Irenaeus, pp. 137 ff.; Dufourcq, *Saint Irénée*, p. 167; and Aleith in *Z.NT.W.*, 1937, p. 72 f. The following passages in *A.h.* are important for a proper treatment of this question: IV. vii (Stier. IV. iv. 3), IV. xi. 2–5 (Stier. IV. vi. 3–7), IV. xxvi. 2 (Stier. IV. xv. 2), in which Irenaeus maintains that freedom is the ground of justice in God's judgement; and IV. xlv (Stier. IV. xxix), a passage on Pharaoh's hardness of heart, with Irenaeus's insistence that nonetheless God is not the author of evil; IV. lx–lxi (Stier. IV. xxxvii. 2–7), in which he denies emphatically God's use of force, and of which the most important passage is IV. lxi. 1 (Stier. IV. xxxvii. 6) with its striking introduction: "Qui autem his contraria dicunt, ipsi *impotentem introducunt Dominum* . . ."; and also IV. lxiii. 3 (Stier. IV. xxxviii. 4) on free will as the basis of growth and therefore as being synonymous with the status as *child*; IV. lxiv. 3 (Stier. IV. xxxix. 3–4) and V. xxvii. 1–xxviii. 1 (Stier. ibid.) with its echo of the passage on judgement and faith in Jn. III. 18 f., but also V. xxviii. 2 (Stier. ibid.) on Antichrist as one who acts by his own free will, *and yet who has been sent by God* who has foreknowledge of all things and who governs all things. Cf. *Epid.* 11 and 55. On this main problem see Nygren, *Commentary on Romans*, pp. 368–70, and especially what is said on p. 369 on "predestination from below." Lastly in this connexion, cf. Wolfgang Schmidt, *Die Kirche bei Irenäus*, Helsingfors 1934, p. 159.

help of free will. As we saw earlier on in describing the omnipotence and inscrutability of God, Irenaeus quite clearly and expressly avoids putting the problem in this way. He proceeds from man's actual temptation and establishes as a fact man's actual defeat, and farther on proceeds from man's actual bondage to Satan and establishes his actual deliverance through Christ. Man who falls and is delivered has been created by God. He is a free man. He was not forced, mechanically, into sin, but rather allowed himself to be dragged into sin; nor is he forced, mechanically, out of his imprisonment by the victory of Christ, but rather is freed from his bonds and can now go anywhere he wants—out into freedom in Christ, or back into bondage to the Devil. But since through all that happens to him, from Creation to the Last Judgement, he remains *man*, he has the responsibility for everything that he does from first to last. However he may deprive himself, God retains His power. God alone possesses power, and this is demonstrated by the fact that at the moment man turns from being the child of God to being the captive of the Devil he moves from life to death. Man's new lord is stronger than himself, but he is not strong enough to be able to create. He has only one thing to offer—death.

CHAPTER II

DEFEAT

The Devil

It is something of a surprise to note how Irenaeus "pauses" in dealing with the Devil in almost the same way as he does when he comes to deal with God in the course of his discussion. He poured ridicule on every attempt by the Gnostics to set up an independent principle in the universe which was in opposition to God, maintaining that any god which had a second power opposed to itself demonstrated by the very fact of the actual existence of the second principle that it itself was not "God." And yet when Irenaeus came to deal with the Devil's struggle against God in his various writings, it seemed that all such affirmations about God's demonstrable sovereignty were to be forgotten. For Irenaeus Satan is a real enemy of the Creator, and the cost of defeating this adversary of God was the blood and death of God's own Son.

And yet it is at this very point that God's unlimited supremacy over the Devil is to be found. The freedom of the Evil One is bounded by a period of time that is limited and appointed by God Himself. The Devil was created by God.[1] The life, which the prince of evil has now, has been permitted to him by his present enemy—God. Yet it is only God who creates: the Devil can only prey on what God produces. He can destroy, he can put to death, but he can never create. For this reason Irenaeus frequently describes the contrast between God and the Devil in the same language as he describes the contrast between Life and Death.[2] All life comes from God. He is the only source of

[1] "Nihil enim in totum diabolus invenitur fecisse, videlicet cum et ipse creatura sit Dei, quemadmodum et reliqui angeli," *A.h.* iv. lxvi. 2 (Stier. iv. xli. 1).

[2] E.g. *A.h.* v. xii. 1 (Stier. ibid.) and *Epid.* 31 and 37. On the passage from *A.h.* cf. the whole context on flesh and spirit from v. ix onwards (Stier. ibid.).

life. Before the fall of the Devil and his subsequent hostility to God he had no independent life whatever, since he himself had been created by God, and when his period of free activity comes to an end and Christ returns again in power, he will be destroyed. God, who has control of every event and is the Lord of history, has lordship over the Devil, in spite of the relative power which he enjoys within the compass of the present age.

Having said this, however, we must emphasise as strongly as possible that all that is regarded in modern thought as the history of mankind occurs within this age, within the period of the activity of the Devil. From the time of the first man, mankind was *fallen* mankind, subject, captive, and bound, and will remain in this unnatural condition until the resurrection from the dead. The chief adversary of the Devil is God. But God is never subject to evil—it is *us* whom the Devil has defeated, and we are in his power right up to the time when Christ will come and undertake the fight which we are unable to maintain. Here on earth a struggle rages between good and evil. The defeat of the Devil will be ultimately certain, but until it is achieved there will be a continual struggle—Christ's fight and victory.[3] The necessity of taking seriously the power of the Devil is demonstrated by the fact that Christ was tempted, delivered, crucified, and put to death.

The anti-speculative aspects of Irenaeus, which we mentioned above, denote that he restricts himself to dealing with man's actual situation and the present condition of human existence. Sin is a present reality in conflict with God. Man stands in the middle of the line of conflict as the cause of the contest between God and the Devil. The ontological contrast between God and Satan is not for a moment eliminated by our knowledge that, since Christ has delivered the decisive stroke, the outcome is certain.[4] Christ has triumphed and in his due time the Devil

[3] *A.h.* III. xix (Stier. III. xviii), III. xxxvi (Stier. III. xxiii. 7) and V. xxi–xxiv (Stier. ibid.). On this *motif* of struggle and victory, which we intend to treat more fully in connexion with the work of Christ, see Gustaf Aulén, *Den kristna försoningstanken*, Stockholm 1930, pp. 38–69, and Jean Rivière, *Dogme de la rédemption*, pp. 95–145. The last sections of *A.h.* about Antichrist, from V. xxv (Stier. ibid.) are also part of this double perspective.

[4] Cf. Oscar Cullmann, *Christ and Time*, p. 141 f. What he says here on the significance of *time* is particularly applicable to Irenaeus, as Cullmann himself brings out in another passage: "Therefore also no theologian of antiquity grasped so clearly

will be destroyed, but in the meantime sin has sufficient power left to draw men into destruction. To imagine that Irenaeus held that the sovereignty of God abolished the contrast between God and Satan would be to interpret his writings on the assumption that it was timeless truths they dealt with. In Irenaeus, however, time is determinative. For this reason the struggle between God and the Devil exists naturally and simultaneously with His supremacy over the Devil. Both facts are equally real. The struggle continues, but the issue is decided. This is a fact we must bear in mind in passing from the description of God the Creator and His omnipotence in the previous chapter to the account in the present chapter of the defeat of the man whom God created and his captivity to the Devil. We now turn to the discussion of the sinful reality which stands in opposition to God, the Devil, the enemy of God, and from this point onwards our discussion will be of the Devil alone in his hostility to God without continually bringing the question of God's omnipotence to bear on this hostility.[5] In due time it will be seen that God has power over darkness. The victory has been won in Christ.

In their exposition of the theology of Irenaeus theologians have tended to minimise the comparison which he makes between God and the Devil. From time to time they have asked questions concerning the reason for the Fall and have attempted to find references to it in Irenaeus, but they have omitted to mention that Irenaeus himself said that there was no possible answer to this question.[6] By referring to Ps. cx.1, a verse which

as did Irenaeus the radical opposition which emerges between Greek and Biblical thinking as to this point, namely, the question of the conception of time" (p. 57). In spite of this Cullmann maintains the belief (see above) that Irenaeus deviated from early Christianity by his futurist interpretation of Christ's work of deliverance. His grounds for this belief may perhaps be the difficulties which Irenaeus (*A.h.* v. xxiv. 1; Stier. ibid.) put in the way of his own "christological" interpretation of Rom. xiii. 1 ff. See Cullmann, pp. 56, n. 9 and 196 f. It is, however, remarkable that Cullmann has no place for a discussion of the *Law* in his analysis of the history of salvation. His christocentric conception of the State may be related to this.

[5] When we are describing a war, for instance, we do not normally suppose that the battles are any less hard because the end of the war will mean victory for one of the sides. What happens is, rather, that victory comes because one of the sides has proved itself to be stronger in these very battles.

[6] See Böhringer, *Kirche Christi*, vol. ii, p. 477 f. and Klebba, *Anthropologie des hl. Irenaeus*, p. 50. P. Beuzart, *Essai sur la théologie d'Irénée*, pp. 69–73, has a good discussion on the problem of sin without becoming too involved in his analysis.

the early Church repeatedly related to Christ, Irenaeus cut short the question of why the Devil, in spite of being God's creation, rebelled against God and dragged man headlong with him in his fall, and in so doing he referred to the *time* when the answer will be given—it is when Christ's enemies are made His footstool that the problem of the Fall will be answered.[7] Interpreters of Irenaeus have sometime taken their starting-point in the statement that sin, the death of Christ, and the Devil's hopeless struggle and ultimate destruction, are part of God's plan of salvation, and that evil cannot overturn God's purpose of salvation, but on the contrary is forced to serve it. There has accordingly been a tendency to regard the opposition to God as a *fiction*, as though the whole thing were a theatrical performance: the play must, of course, be put on, but in actual fact nothing is changed, and the real condition of the universe is the same before the beginning of the performance as it is at the end. Such an interpretation of Irenaeus would mean also that man transcends time.[8] For Irenaeus, however, such an interpretation would be quite impossible, since he holds that opposition to God, sin, and rebellion, imply that there are many who become *eternally* lost and accompany the Devil, when at the last time he is cast into destruction.[9] This opposition to God means also, however, that the Son of God has to die in order to be victorious. Such obstructive hostility to God is no fiction. For Irenaeus, the Devil's struggle with God in the time allotted to him, however long it may last, is a fight to the death.

Irenaeus does not go into very much detail in his description

[7] "Similiter autem et causam propter quam, cum omnia a Deo facta sint, quaedam quidem transgressa sunt, et abscesserunt a Dei subjectione; quaedam autem, imo plurima, perseveraverunt et perseverant in subjectione ejus qui fecit: et cujus naturae sunt quae transgressa sunt, cujus autem naturae quae perseverant, cedere oportet Deo et Verbo ejus, cui et soli dixit: Sede a dextris meis, quoadusque ponam inimicos tuos suppedaneum pedum tuorum," *A.h.* II. xliii. I (Stier. II. xxviii. 7). Cf. too, e.g. Kunze, *Götteslehre des Irenaeus*, p. 28 f.

[8] We find that there is a strong tendency to make this kind of misinterpretation in the article by D. B. Reynders, "Optimisme et théocentrisme chez saint Irénée," in *Recherches de théologie ancienne et médiévale*, 1936, pp. 242 ff.; and also by Escoula in *N.R.T.*, 1939, pp. 390–9, although in other respects Escoula has a very close knowledge of Irenaeus. Surprisingly enough, there are similar tendencies in Cullmann, *Christ and Time*, p. 57, n. 10, at the beginning.

[9] Cf. *A.h.* III. xxxii. 2 (Stier. III. xxiii. 3), at the end, and v. xxvi. 2–3 (Stier. v. xxvi. 2).

of the fall of the devil. In the two passages where his account of the Devil's fall is clearest, it is the Devil's envy, *invidia*, which is central. Man was, in fact, created for a higher life than the angels themselves, and though only a child, was superior to the angels, despite the fact that they were full-grown and not ordained by God to "increase" yet farther.[10] Envy of man seized one of the angels "who are set over the spirit of the air" (cf. Eph. II.2), and in his envy this angel, the Devil, was even as early as this separated from God and exalted against God. "Invidia enim aliena est a Deo."[11] With the intention of depriving man of the life which he lived in accordance with the *imago* and *similitudo* of God, of wresting from him his superiority and his destiny, the Devil tried to entice man into disobedience to God's Commandment. Temptation is a temptation to anticipate the end which God has set as an objective, by holding out the promise that the child will not have to wait to grow and increase, in order to become like God.[12] The child violates the will of God at the forbidden tree, and by that act is ensnared in disobedience.

Thus the Devil falls himself, and causes man to fall with him. Man is drawn into association with the Devil, and is made captive to evil.[13] Irenaeus thinks of the mastery of sin in particular as bondage, an unnatural occupation, through which the whole of human life is laid under the tyranny of the op-

[10] *Epid.* 12.

[11] *A.h.* v. xxiv. 4 (Stier. ibid.). The other passage where this is clearly seen is *Epid.* 16. Cf. also *A.h.* IV. lxvi. 2 (Stier. IV. xl. 3). With regard to the part played by envy in this connexion cf. W. E. Crum, "Texts attributed to Peter of Alexandria," in *J.T.S.*, 1903, p. 396 f., especially n. 3. See too *A.h.* IV. lxvii. (Stier. IV. xli. 2).

[12] Gen. III. 5. See Bonwetsch, "Der Gedanke der Erziehung des Menschengeschlechts bei Irenäus," in *Zeitschrift für systematische Theologie*, henceforth cited as *Z.S.T.*, 1923–4, p. 639. Note that when, through the recapitulating work of Christ, man regains life, it means that he "rises above the angels," when he is made *secundum imaginem et similitudinem Dei*, *A.h.* v. xxxvi (Stier. v. xxxvi. 3). This means that the work of Creation is completed. Cf. on this point Jean Hering, *Die biblischen Grundlagen des christlichen Humanismus*, henceforth cited as *Biblischen Grundlagen*, Zürich 1946, pp. 24 ff.

[13] To maintain, as Sven Silén does, *Den kristna människouppfattningen intill Schleiermacher*, p. 72, that universal sinfulness does not stem from Adam's sin but in a "fall of the angels" (Silén bases this on *Epid.* 18) is to go against the whole of Irenaean theology. The passage referred to by Silén in Harnack's statements on *Epid.* (Texte und Untersuchungen edn., p. 58) does not seem to offer any grounds in support of this theory.

pressor. The Devil who fell from heaven is continually at war with the Spirit who was also sent from heaven, with the consequence that man on earth has both his Advocate, the Spirit, and his Accuser, the Devil, Satan.[14] Very often, too, Irenaeus uses the term *Serpent* in describing the evil power which dominates mankind. When the Fall took place, the Devil was concealed in the Serpent.[15] In accordance with Biblical usage, Irenaeus uses the different names interchangeably (the Devil, the Serpent, and Satan), without making any real distinction between them.

God is completely and utterly opposed to His enemy, and this opposition cannot be lessened, but must culminate in fighting and in ruthless and eternal judgement. For the Devil, the foremost opponent of God, there is no turning back. He is forced to submit to the eternal fire, and nothing can save him. It will be otherwise for those whom he has won over to himself by untruthfulness and with specious promises, and who do not properly belong to him. Irenaeus vigorously maintains that there is no section of humanity which is rejected, not even the Gnostics, and he continued his controversy with them in the hope that they might be convinced and come to believe, in order that thereby they might be delivered from the power of Satan. The eternal fire is prepared primarily for the Serpent, but also for his followers. The number of these followers, whom the Serpent has misled, may become smaller than it is at present. The purpose in preaching the Gospel is to rescue men from the clutches of the Devil, so that, if possible, the Devil alone is overwhelmed in the irrevocable end that awaits him.[16] Irenaeus insists that it was the Father Himself who prepared the eternal fire, according to the version of the passage in Mt. xxv.41 in the text which he used.[17]

[14] *A.h.* III. xviii. 2 (Stier. III. xvii. 3).

[15] *Epid.* 16. Irenaeus also attempts here to make a distinction of meaning between the words *Devil* and *Satan*. But he clearly states that the three expressions, the Devil, Satan, and the Serpent, refer to exactly the same evil reality.

[16] See *A.h.* III. xxxiii. 2–xxxvii (Stier. III. xxiii. 3–8) and also V. xxvi. 2–3 (Stier. V. xxvi. 2); and particularly on the Gnostics as not being finally lost, III. xlii. 2 (Stier. III. xxv. 7).

[17] The quotation from the Gospel "Discedite a me maledicti in ignem aeternum, quem praeparavit Pater meus diabolo et angelis ejus," *A.h.* IV. lxvi. 1 (Stier. IV. xl. 2);

In treating the Devil as harshly as this, in destroying him, God is dealing with the Devil *justly*. The position which the Devil has in relation to man is one which he has acquired *unjustly*. Irenaeus repeats these simple points time and time again. They are of no great importance, but if we compare these statements in Irenaeus with later theology which, with the purpose of emphasising man's guilt, stressed rather the Devil's right to man, the individuality of Irenaeus becomes quite pronounced.[18] The theme which underlies his discussion of God's right and the Devil's usurpation is his belief in Creation. It is God alone who has created man, while the Devil has abducted him. Evil, as evil, is at the same time unnatural. Emerging from Irenaeus's belief in Creation is his view of the Law as God's Law, an expression of the will of God. The activity of the Devil is against Creation and against the Law, and its nature is disobedience and rebellion, a rebellion into which man is drawn.[19] And when man is seduced into rebelling against God it is by lies and false promises that he is beguiled (Gen. III.5). Even in the course of the continuing struggle to gain hold of man, e.g. when the Devil tempts Jesus in the

cf. what Harvey says in his note 3 on the passage. With regard to the question of the form of the New Testament text which Irenaeus used, only references can be offered. See e.g. Souter in *Novum Testamentum Sancti Irenaei*, pp. cxlviii ff., 1–103, which just gives us the New Testament text and collected fragments, and also the essays mentioned above by H. J. Vogels and John Chapman in *Rev. Bén.*, 1924, and B. Kraft, *Die Evangelienzitate des heiligen Irenäus*, also published in 1924, in particular pp. 107, 111, in which he states that there was a Greek harmony of the Gospels, now lost to us, which as early as this had influenced the Greek text of Irenaeus. August Merk takes a sensible and moderate position, "Der Text des Neuen Testamentes beim hl. Irenaeus," in *Z.K.T.*, 1925, pp. 310–12 and other passages: Irenaeus wrote in a harmonising period, but his versions do not spring from any actual harmony of the Gospels.

[18] Cf. Aulén, *Den kristna försoningstanken*, pp. 54–7, where Aulén criticises this aspect of Irenaeus's theology. Rivière, *Dogme de la rédemption*, p. 95, rightly groups all that Irenaeus has to say on this under the general heading of *La "justice" envers le démon.*

[19] *A.h.* III. xxxii. 2. (Stier. III. xxiii. 1), v. ii. 1 and v. xxi. 3, and most clearly in v. xxiii. 1 and also v. xxiv. 4 (all these refs. are the same in Stier.). In the next section I intend trying to show that *man also* has *no right*, i.e. he stands in absolute guilt before God. The man whose guilt is complete, however, may be either unrepentant (like the Devil) or repentant (like Adam). This distinction does not by itself affect the question of guilt, and yet it is of importance for faith and salvation. Repentance is faith, lack of repentance disbelief. The Gospel is preached for the *sinner*, and is received in *faith*.

wilderness, the enemy of God never ceases using lies, whereas the Son of man in His struggle against the Devil never employs any other weapon than the truth. The power of the Devil resides in rebellion, abduction, and untruth; it is born of envy and ends in death. The power of God is based on Creation itself. It is the outpouring of life from its source—Love. And since this power of God, as distinguished from the power of evil, has been in existence from all eternity, and will continue for ever, it has no need of untruth but only truth. The work of Satan, on the other hand, springs from unrighteousness.

If God acts rightly in His treatment of the Devil, He is being merciful to men in His very dealings with the Devil, and the blow which strikes the Serpent simultaneously releases the Serpent's victim. And this deliverance is unearned, since man became subjugated by wrongful assault, and, misled by the promise of gaining some advantage, shared voluntarily in an act which openly transgressed the distinct commandment of God. The whole of our salvation through Christ, the vanquisher of the Serpent, is pure grace and divine goodness. Man stood between obedience and disobedience, and he freely chose disobedience.[20] Since Adam and man are not two separate entities but one, these statements about the Fall consitute a description of the actual behaviour of all men. If man is free and there is no external compulsion over him, in seeking to get something he wants he goes his own way. He is indifferent to the commands which God has addressed to him until it is too late, and he finds that his irrevocable transgression of God's commandment is now behind him. For those who are in such a condition, imprisoned under sin, Christ has suffered death, being Himself set in the same ethical struggle—the story of the Temptation—without yielding, even when confronted by crucifixion. Christ recapitulates the history of Adam in the opposite direction and with the opposite result: Adam yielded to temptation, and because he did so he fell from life to death; while Christ resisted

[20] *A.h.* IV. lxiv. I (Stier. IV. xxxix. I) and IV. lxvii–lxviii I (Stier. IV. xli. 2–3). The Devil's conquest is made easy because man is a "child." Irenaeus makes this point clear. But it does not follow from this that there is sin in the status as "child" in which God has placed man in Creation. Sin is continually committed against God, but no one will ever know fully how it came into being.

temptation, and because He did so, rose again from the dead. Through Him salvation has been won.[21]

The statements in Irenaeus about Christ's work of deliverance as a recapitulation in reverse of Adam's fall are most instructive even from the point of view that his description of salvation in that way becomes immediately a description of sin and man's defeat and bondage. Christ moves triumphantly forward over the battle-ground where previously—in Adam—the battle had surged in the opposite direction, when the Devil, who has now been defeated in Christ and loses his captives, himself advanced and conquered. For Irenaeus, the analogy between the defeat of Adam and the victory of Christ is a striking proof that the God of Creation and the Law is also the God of salvation, and that the God of the Old Testament is also the God of the New. The whole of the course of evil must be reversed, in order that man may return behind the Fall to the uncorrupted and undestroyed Creation.

This is perhaps most clearly expressed symbolically by Irenaeus when he sets the act of Mary, her obedience, against the act of Eve, which was her disobedience, and compares what Eve did with the tangling of wool into knots. The only thing to be done is to unravel the wool and untie the knots, and this is what Mary did when in faith she obeyed God and bore her son into the world, the perfect Man, the primary cause and purpose of Creation.[22] Since man was created in order to "increase," Irenaeus understands this movement backwards as being at the same time a movement forwards, a struggle to bring something new into being, to bring something into existence which has never existed before, a man of flesh and blood upon the earth, who is an image of God and like God. Christ's own struggle against temptation is a continuation of

[21] *A.h.* III. xix. 5 (Stier. III. xviii. 6) says of Christ: "Luctatus est enim, et vicit: erat enim homo pro patribus certans, et per obedientiam, inobedientiam persolvens: alligavit enim fortem, et solvit infirmos, et salutem donavit plasmati suo, destruens peccatum. Est enim piissimus et misericors Dominus, et amans humanum genus." See too the immediately succeeding passage in *A.h.* as well as III. viii. 2 (Stier. ibid.).

[22] *A.h.* III. xxxii. 1 (Stier. III. xxii. 4) and V. xix. 1 (Stier. ibid.) and *Epid.* 33. On the difference between the Gnostic view and that held in the early Church of the mother of mankind in comparison with the Mother of Jesus, cf. W. Staerk, "Eva-Maria," in *Z.N.T.W.*, 1934, pp. 97–104.

the same movement backwards: in taking His stand against the Devil, he forces His way through the Fall and emerges on the other side in God's sinless Creation—but the place of His emerging is in fact His Resurrection on the third day. This was the consummation which, through all His struggles, as though in darkness, He strove to reach. The life of the Resurrection without death is in fact the life of Creation without death. Between these two worlds of light, each with the same new and uncorrupted life, there lies a zone of death where the battle is waged. The entrance to this region of darkness is the Serpent's conquest of man; the way out is Christ's victory over the Serpent.[23]

The point to be noted here is that the Devil's essential nature is defection, revolt, and apostasy, not primarily death. Sin, the source from which death arises, is first. And like sin, death is an unnatural thing, an abnormality which has forced its way into Creation. Consequently, it is not something *super*natural which is given to us in Christ, but rather it is in the victory and whole work of Christ that this "health" which we have been discussing is to be found—here is the life of perfect health and the absolute and faultless completion of Creation. We might almost describe it as nature that has come to full maturity. The gift which Christ bestows surpasses the first Creation, not in the sense that the supernatural surpasses nature, but rather in the sense that the fully developed and mature life surpasses the undeveloped and immature, or as a man is stronger than a child. And the reason that Irenaeus can see the life of Creation and of salvation, and indeed the life of the Resurrection as belonging together, as being Life, is that he conceives of existence not as something which increases in value as it develops, but as a struggle against an enemy. And this dynamic or movement is not the ascent of a climber but the labour of the one who struggles for life against the powers of

[23] Cf. *A.h.* v. xvi. 3 and from v. xxi. 1 (Stier. ibid.) where we read ". . . uti quemadmodum per hominem victum descendit in mortem genus nostrum, sic iterum per hominem victorem ascendamus in vitam." (The "defeated man" is Adam, the "victorious man" is Christ). See also v. xxi. 2 (Stier. ibid.) and v. xvii. 4 (Stier. ibid.); on this latter passage cf. Loofs, *Theophilus von Antiochien*, p. 254 f. Loofs sees an allusion in this text also to Gen. I. 26. A similar theme is touched upon in *Epid.* 34.

destruction—*Satan* stands against Life, and *Death* stands against Life. In his childhood man has received an injury; he has been wounded by sin and death; and since the healing of his injury is salvation, life before the injury (i.e. at the Creation), and life after the healing (i.e. in the Resurrection), are the same life.[24] When one finds difficulty in holding together the ideas of Creation and Resurrection and the idea of an injury is not in fact accepted, but human life is rather treated as being essentially intact—intact, that is, though not sufficiently "spiritual"—salvation or "religion" in this case represents an addition to what is earthly, something which is over and above man's natural condition. This scheme, however, is alien to Irenaeus.[25]

The contrast or dualism between God and Satan is a primary factor in the theology of Irenaeus, and one to be borne in mind in any question which we are discussing in Irenaeus. Christ's work corresponds to the Fall of man, and is diametrically opposed to it. Since sin, and as a consequence of sin, death, have gained control over man through the victory of the Serpent, Christ's victory over the Serpent must, if it is to be a victory at all, mean the complete defeat of both sin and death—not one or the other, but both. And to a certain extent the same sequence is to be found in Christ's victory over the Devil—first, the overpowering of sin, and then the annihilation of death. Since this too is a characteristic feature of Irenaeus's understanding of the nature of God's adversary, I shall add a few words on this subject.

Death forms a barrier to sin. God thus uses one of His enemies, death, as an instrument by which to weaken His other enemy, sin. When man's body is dissolved in the earth, man ceases to serve sin, and this dissolution of man's earthly body is

24 "Dolor autem plagae est, per quam percussus est homo initio in Adam inobediens, hoc est, mors, quam sanabit Deus resuscitans nos a mortuis," *A.h.* v. xxiv. 2 (Stier. ibid.); the words are an exposition of Is. xxx.26.

25 Those who have previously assumed the scheme of *nature–supernature* elsewhere and automatically think in these terms will certainly read their own ideas into what Irenaeus says about "increase," as though it were supernature which grew from nature. Those who impose this scheme on Irenaeus, however, usually begin to make complaints, sooner or later, about the "obscurity" of Irenaeus, the confusing use of language in the sources which he used, and the inconsistency of his terminology, etc. For similar reasons Roman Catholic theologians and liberal neo-Protestants usually find Luther obscure and inconsistent.

the beginning of his living to God.[26] The destructive powers in existence can be transformed by God and the power of the Devil thereby weakened if these powers are turned by God so as to destroy the evil nature and self-will within us.[27] By sharing in the death of Christ man also follows Him into the Resurrection. In so doing, the defeat of sin becomes the defeat of death. Death is the last enemy. When man, that is, when Adam, is roused to eternal life, death is crushed and its work rendered ineffectual. Creation is purified, and freed from its poison.[28] In the Creation which Christ has restored man does not grow old. Old age, which is in fact simply a form of death, has no place in heaven and in the renewed youth of the humanity which "forgets to die."[29] The continuation of life is in itself a witness to the newly-acquired freedom of Creation, and a sign that sin, the will which rebels against God, is ended. The Devil is primarily an evil will which opposes God. Death is not an independent reality in the power which is in opposition to God, but because Satan sets himself against God in disobedience, everything that he does is marked by death, since he stands against the Creator who is the source of all life. In his envy he defies the one power who controls Life, and by this defiance is overcome by death together with all his captives. Through sin death has come into the world.[30]

The Corruption of Man

As we began our discussion of Creation with God in order to proceed to a special study of man who has been made by God,

[26] Irenaeus says of God, "Prohibuit autem ejus transgressionem, interponens mortem, et cessare faciens peccatum, finem inferens ei per carnis resolutionem, quae fieret in terra; uti cessans aliquando homo vivere peccato, et moriens ei, inciperet vivere Deo," *A.h.* III. xxxv. 2 (Stier. III. xxiii. 6). On his dependence on Theophilus at this point, see Klebba, *Anthropologie des hl. Irenaeus*, p. 65 f.

[27] Cf. Escoula in *N.R.T.*, 1939, p. 396 f.

[28] Irenaeus links the idea with I Cor. xv. 26, 54. "Domino igitur vivificante hominem, id est Adam, evacuata est et mors," *A.h.* III. xxxvi (Stier. III. xxiii. 7). The identification of Adam and man is particularly noticeable, and is consecutively developed.

[29] ". . . et renovato homine, et vigente ad incorruptelam, ut non possit jam veterascere," *A.h.* V. xxxvi (Stier. V. xxxvi. I), ". . . obliviscetur mori jam," *A.h.* ibid. (Stier. V. xxxvi. 2); the quotation in this latter passage is again from I Cor. xv. 26. *A.h.* V. xxxv. 2 (Stier. ibid.) is linked with Rev. xx.14.

[30] See e.g. *Epid.* 15 f. and *A.h.* V. xxi. 3, V. xxiii. 2 (Stier. ibid.).

so we shall now start our analysis of defeat with the Devil, in order to focus attention on what the Devil has imposed on man, and therefore with *man's corruption*, the heading of this particular section. Man who is bound by evil is identical with the man who has been created by God. But what is the relationship between Creation and sin in regard to man's actual status? What is man's condition in his bondage to death? It is on questions such as these that our investigation will turn in the present section.

Man's "growth" is destroyed through the circumstances of his attachment to evil, and the "child" ceases to progress towards his destiny which has been appointed by God—this is one of the main aspects of the discussion with which we are dealing at present.[31] Man is created in order to conform to the *imago* and *similitudo* of God, but in actual fact he fails to achieve his destiny. It is the opposite which he achieves—disobedience to God's will and enmity with God—allied as he is with God's chief enemy. Since the true *imago* and *similitudo* of God in Creation is the Son, the Word who effects Creation, man's thraldom to the Serpent is a departure from the Son, and therefore a kind of alien status before the coming Christ, in whom he would otherwise, were he wholly and entirely human, see a true expression of his own nature and being. His humanity has been spoiled, and he cannot clearly see what it means to be man. Man's immaturity and the enormous gulf between him and Christ is therefore due not to his having been created by God as a "child," and to that extent imperfect, for there is no sinful defect in God's Creation, but is rather something for which man is responsible—it brings guilt in its train. If sin had not entered man's life he would have increased and progressed from his status as a child to the age of manhood, since God creates and gives, and therefore those who are in communion with Him increase and receive His gifts.[32] But it is this very

[31] Cf. Bonwetsch, *Theologie des Irenäus*, pp. 79–81, although his comments on the statements of Irenaeus, e.g. what he says on repentance on p. 79, may be disputed.

[32] Hugo Koch in *Theol. Stud. u. Krit.*, 1925, p. 188, observes that in the Fall man loses his *future* which God has set out in prospect, because he loses his *destiny* (cf. Koch, *op. cit.*, at the foot of p. 197 and n. 1 on p. 212). For this reason Koch rejects the division which Böhringer, Wendt, and Harnack make in Irenaeus's way of thinking (Koch, *op. cit.*, pp. 183–5). Sometimes, however, someone like

communion with God which is broken and severed by reason of man's disobedience. Man is cut off from the source of his life.

There is a certain tendency evident in writings on Irenaeus to isolate the Fall from his other theological points. In connexion, for instance, with the relationship between anthropology and Christology, scholars have analysed the relation between man "in his original condition" and man who has faith in Christ, but they have failed to discuss the ideas of destiny and defeat (sin, that is), and so have deduced that the Irenaean concept is of a level and undisturbed advance from Creation to the Incarnation. Alternatively, other scholars have worked out the scheme that the Fall represents something lost, while salvation represents something which has been added. Advocates of this particular view maintain that this line of loss and addition is secondary, and incompatible with the progressive line of development, and as unlike Irenaeus in its "undisturbed" character as the latter. But the general view which we find in Irenaeus is not this, and in either the first or progressive line, or the second "representational" line the idea of a demonic power or some active and evil power of the Devil which is the source of constant disturbance is to be found in his writings.[33] In Irenaeus every page, and almost every sentence, conveys the idea of a struggle, a never-ending contest, between the two active powers, God and Satan, and to make any assertion about man, without taking into account the fact that he is caught up

Böhringer can demonstrate remarkably clearly how the basic concept in Irenaeus of man as a growing child in Creation achieves a unity of terminology and thought; see, e.g., Böhringer, *Kirche Christi*, VOL. II. p. 469 f. He fails, however, to make this fundamental concept the basis of his exposition of Irenaeus. Cf. too his anlysis of Irenaeus's Christology on pp. 541–5, where he makes useful suggestions in each connexion. For a discussion of Hugo Koch's theory, cf. Loofs, *Theophilus von Antiochien* p. 59 f., n. 3.

[33] The approach of Wendt, *Christliche Lehre*, pp. 20–30, is typical. Wendt maintains that there is in part an evolutionary line in Irenaeus, but that on the other hand there is also a line of subtraction (i.e. the Fall) and addition (i.e. recapitulation), so that the conclusion is almost identical to the starting-point, and therefore there is no increase or ascent. But in Irenaeus we find that the concepts of growth (the first line according to Wendt) and of injury and cure (Wendt's second line) are interrelated. If we bear in mind that it is the living man, and not a theological product, who has been mortally wounded and is now being made whole, this confusion should not be so hard to understand. *There are not two lines in Irenaeus but only one.* It is a pity that even Bonwetsch, *Theologie des Irenäus*, p. 102, does not make this completely clear. See, however, Prümm in *Scholastik*, 1938, pp. 342, 344.

in the midst of this contest, is meaningless. Any analysis of Irenaeus's doctrine of God's creation of man should be as determined as the attempt to outline the upheaval which is wrought in the process of Creation by the power of evil.[34]

If we hold together the Irenaean analysis of man as having been created in order to grow and his view of evil as an injurious activity which deprives men of their freedom, we shall understand the interconnexion between Christ and the original Creation, and how the Incarnation is the victory of the Creator over death, which penetrated into human existence through envy. Christ cleanses humanity by being Himself a man and securing His victory, but the cleansing and restoration of a living being which God has created in order to grow means giving this person, whom God has made, freedom for new growth—in other words, it means that Creation is begun anew. The divine power which created the world and man dwells in the crucified and risen Lord, the giver of life who pours out His Spirit over the arid and dead world of men.[35] Behind the work of the Creator and the work of Christ there is God, one and the same in His gracious activity, and the source of all life, and we see more clearly the uniform divine activity in both these spheres if we look also at the opposite of God, the Devil, whose work of destruction in his evil activity sweeps over the whole of Creation, the place of God's action. We see selfish envy against God's generosity, death and atrophy against life and strength. We see the temptations in the wilderness before Jesus began His life-work, which were an attempt to thwart the work of God in His incarnate Son and to lure Him from His mission. We see finally the Crucifixion and the death of Jesus, the final but ineffectual thrust at God. In all of this, Irenaeus maintains, we trace a single power which comprises both sin and death, both ethically evil will and physical decay—the power of Satan.

[34] Aulén has without any doubt broken away from a stereotyped interpretation of Irenaeus with his dualistic perspective, and has put into the centre of discussion a topic which all readers of Irenaeus had accepted, but which none of them had chosen to deal with, namely, the struggle between God and the Devil. It is true, of course, that there are other subjects such as Creation and the Law which require further treatment than Aulén has given to them. But by stressing this pattern of struggle and victory Aulén has pointed to an aspect of Irenaeus which is quite fundamental. See *Den kristna försoningstanken*, pp. 48 ff.

[35] See e.g. III. xviii. 2 (Stier. III. xvii. 3) and III. xxxviii. 1 (Stier. III xxiv. 1).

But against Satan there stands likewise a single power—God, the Lord of all physical life and the source of all life, but who also declares His will in the commandments which enjoin righteousness and love, and who is Himself what He commands in His Word, that is, in Christ.[36]

Man's corruption is therefore both "ethical" as well as "physical" in character, involving both sin and death. Man's corruption is primarily his sin, his disobedience, that is, based on his selfishness and his attempt to anticipate the gift which God wills to give to man, but which man himself refuses to wait for, and therefore it is an assertion of his independence and his defiance of God. In actual fact man's rebellion against God does not mean his independence and freedom, but his bondage to the Lord of rebellion and the father of apostasy—the Devil. There is no neutrality in the conflict between God and Satan. If man does not belong to God, he is not free, but is bound to submit to the power of the Serpent. We have already discussed whether man receives the Spirit in Creation (before the Fall) or whether he is first given the Spirit in Christ. But it is the same with the Spirit as with the *imago* and *similitudo* of God which we have already discussed. Man is destined for the Son and for the Spirit. Man does not achieve the whole of his destiny only in being created by God for he is to grow in a certain direction. There is no sin implied in this fact of his undeveloped state. But man's failure to possess the Spirit is due to his Fall. He is to be accused on the grounds that, unlike Christ in His incarnate life, he does not possess the Spirit, as he may also be accused of having failed to attain to God-likeness, and both these accusations reveal that man has betrayed his

[36] In present-day terms one might express this by saying that vitality and truth have the same source. The modern tendency to regard communion with God as a religious province in an otherwise profane life would be interpreted by Irenaeus as a new version of Gnosticism—Creation has one Lord and the "religious" have another. The unity of ethics and vitality gave early Christianity a unique power. In dealing with the violation of God's law Irenaeus realised that he was dealing with something that was under condemnation and corruptible and cut off from this vitality. On the other hand, the martyr of the Church who shed his blood in witness knew that in his very martyrdom he was coming to the point of the renewal of his life, and was one with Christ who was put to death upon the Cross and who rose from the dead. The martyrs of the Church fought not simply for ethically unimpeachable ideals, but were in union with the source of physical life, and knew that their own bodies would have their life renewed in the resurrection of the dead.

destiny, that his growth has come to a standstill, and that he is ruled from within by his evil nature. This turning aside from the *imago* and *similitudo* of God, as well as from the Spirit and the Son, is implied in the rebellion of the first created man against God. For the Son and the Spirit are from everlasting God.[37] Through his sin, Irenaeus holds, man loses the Spirit as well as his likeness to God.

It is not, however, simply the opposition of the human will to the divine will which is here involved. The Spirit is not only the Spirit of love, the Spirit is also the principle of life against death: the Spirit is indestructibility. The resurrection body which is at some point to be bestowed on man has been snatched from death because it is a "*spiritual* body." To lose the Spirit as a result of yielding to the Devil is the same thing as to die.[38] Man *is* mortal, but he ought not to be so, and God does not purpose to leave him helpless in the clutches of death. The wound which Adam received when the Serpent attacked him

[37] The Spirit "increases" too—man is trained and disciplined in how to receive the Spirit. The purely technical question of whether the Spirit was originally in Creation or came only at the Incarnation is not one which Irenaeus asks. See *A.h.* IV. xxv. 2 (Stier. IV. xiv. 2). When Irenaeus states in *A.h.* III. xxxv. 1 (Stier. III. xxiii. 5) that Adam lost the garment of righteousness which he had been given by the Spirit he is not going against the concept of growth into communion with the Spirit as an end for mankind. It was this gradually developing life which he lost, but his destiny remains clear, and his life is started again in Christ. See especially *A.h.* III. xviii. 1 (Stier. III. xvii. 1): the Spirit descends on the Son of man and "accustoms" himself to dwell in mankind, in men who are renewed "a vetustate in novitatem Christi" (in this latter passage the ideas of growth and transformation into the *imago* and *similitudo* of God are taken up again). See also Bonwetsch, *Theologie des Irenäus*, pp. 66–9, and Prümm in *Scholastik*, 1938, p. 218 f. (unfortunately Bonwetsch later in the same work goes on to make a comparison between the Spirit and the "supernatural" which is contrary to Irenaeus's own terminology). In *Epid.* 56 Irenaeus discusses the devout in the Old Testament, who awaited the coming of Christ, as the bearers of the Spirit. Hugo Koch goes too far in insisting on man's lack of the Spirit in his primal state (*Theol. Stud. u. Krit.*, 1925, pp. 206 ff.) as does also Slomkowski, *État primitif*, p. 44 f. (in his debate with d'Alès). The opposite approach to the question which we find in Klebba, *Anthropologie des hl. Irenaeus*, p. 33 f., also goes too far. Klebba regards the Spirit as a *donum superadditum*, which is later removed from man in the Fall.

[38] See *Epid.* 14 and 15 together with *A.h.* v. xii. 2–3 (Stier. ibid.). That Adam's death was due to his sin is stated directly in the latter part of v. xii. 2: *Ὡς οὖν δ' εἰς ψυχὴν ζῶσαν γεγονὼς, ῥίψας ἐπὶ τὸ χεῖρον, ἀπώλεσε τὴν ξωήν.* But God has foreknowledge of everything, and His purpose in regard to the giving of the Spirit is achieved in the midst of man's opposition to Him. It does not follow from this that the opposition of man can be excluded from our interpretation of Ireneaus. *A.h.* v. xii used to be the corner-stone of the misinterpretation of Irenaeus.

will be healed in the Kingdom of Christ.[39] The complete healing of the wound which man has received in his defeat is the resurrection to eternal life. When man becomes so healed, the "physical" gift which is given to him is not separate from the forgiveness of his sins, but rather the forgiveness of sin and the removal of his guilt issue in the coming of health to his body. The passage in Mt. IX.1–8 about the paralytic demonstrates the interconnexion between forgiveness and healing, in the description of how Jesus raised up the afflicted man. Jesus first says, "Your sins are forgiven," and afterwards, "Take up your bed and go." Irenaeus notes, "The paralysis was a consequence of sin."[40] The primary factor is sin; and therefore the removal of sin is the primary factor in the healing. Irenaeus regards death as a whole in the same way—it is a sign, that is, of the dominion of sin. The graveclothes on the hands and feet of the dead Lazarus (Jn. XI.44) are a symbol of man's bondage in sin.[41] Irenaeus defines it thus—"disobedience to God brings death."[42]

In his *History of Dogma* Adolf Harnack has argued that the consequence of the Fall was physical death alone, and that the Fall had no ethical aspects.[43] If we are to form a correct judgement of this theory, we must bear in mind the relatively high estimate which Harnack had of the Gnostics.[44] There is, too, the further generally recognised fact that Harnack was a professed advocate of the position taken by Marcion, though he had made quite meaningless reservations in defending this attitude.[45] This significant approach of Harnack's, which is bound up with the almost complete lack of a belief in Creation in modern Protestant theology and what we might call its "inwardness," makes it clear that he held that there was something unethical in the emphasis on *death* as a consequence of sin which we find in Irenaeus. The statements which Irenaeus makes about death can be understood only in relation to his belief in the *Creator*—

[39] Cf. also *A.h.* v. xxxiv (Stier. ibid.).

[40] *A.h.* v. xvii. 2 (Stier. ibid.); cf. the whole context.

[41] *A.h.* v. xiii. 1 (Stier. ibid.). On the man who was blind from his birth cf. v. xv. 2–4 (Stier. ibid.).

[42] ". . . . inobedientia autem Dei mortem infert," *A.h.* v. xxiii. 1 (Stier. ibid.).

[43] *History of Dogma*, VOL. II, p. 271 f.

[44] *Op. cit.*, VOL. I, pp. 227 ff.

[45] Harnack, *Marcion: Das Evangelium vom fremden Gott*, 2nd edn., Leipzig 1924, pp. 228–35.

communion with the Creator of life has been broken by sin, and so death has the mastery over the man who is disobedient to God. Irenaeus himself makes the character of such a man's guilt quite clear.[46] It is ridiculous that we should allow ourselves to be guided in our historical judgements by the standards of the Gnostics, on the assumption that would lead to a weakening of the ethical to believe in the first article of faith. We must turn to Irenaeus as we meet him in his own statements and attempt to understand how he sees sin and death as being interrelated—a task which Harnack has never even taken up, and which he therefore cannot imagine he has solved.[47]

We have seen above that death acquired its supremacy by reason of sin, and that sin is primary, while death is an effect of sin and a consequence of the rupture of man's communion with God.[48] I propose now to look in some detail at the guilt which is connected with death and the *judgement* which is involved in our transience. In Irenaeus *judgement* and *to judge* imply separation, sifting, and division. He thus safeguards the primary meaning of *κρίσις*.[49] Those who, in the judgement, have passed over to life are separated from those who have turned away from God.[50] Judgement and death are thus immediately related to one another, and are both conceptually and terminologically coincident. Irenaeus connects this with the Johannine passage: "He who believes in him is not condemned, but he who does not believe is condemned already" (Jn. III. 18). It is said of those who have been saved that they are not condemned, i.e. they are not separated from God—they are united to God in faith.[51] Those who are condemned in the Judgement are those who are

[46] Cf. on this point Klebba, *Anthropologie des hl. Irenaeus*, p. 53, and the passages which he cites. Of interest too in this connexion is Osmo Tiililä's *Das Strafleiden Christi*, Helsinki 1941, p. 125, a work which disputes Aulén's position.

[47] See Harnack, *History of Dogma*, VOL. II, p. 247. In the earlier period the study of the history of dogma seldom investigated any inner connexion in a given line of theological approach, but rather the function of this theological attitude in the formation of dogma.

[48] In addition to passages which have been referred to earlier, see *A.h.* v. xii. 5 (Stier. v. xii. 6) and the significance which is there attached to *malitia*; on the term itself cf. the latter part of III. xxxiii. 2 (Stier. III. xxiii. 3).

[49] See the whole of *A.h.* v. xxvii. 1–xxix. 1 (Stier. ibid.), and cf. *Epid.* 97.

[50] *A.h.* v. xxvii. 2 (Stier. ibid.).

[51] "Qui credit in me, non judicatur, id est, non separatur a Deo: adunitus est enim per fidem Deo" (ibid.).

separated from God, and their condemnation is identical with their separation from God which they have freely chosen.[52] But Irenaeus defines death in exactly the same way: "Separation from God is death, and separation from light is darkness."[53] Since Irenaeus never thinks of life as being narrowed down or having independent existence in human organisms, but always understands it as proceeding from God the Creator—a human being lives because God creates—separation from God is identical with death. But death means to be condemned. And to be condemned means literally to be separated, to be sifted, or to be rejected.

Faith, thankfulness, and patience bind men to God in such a way that they may continually be created, moulded, and formed by God's hand and remain living creatures with "gentle and submissive hearts." Faithlessness and ingratitude create a gulf between God and man in such a way that man becomes hardened, pushing aside the hands of the Creator—he "flees from His hands"—and by this rejection is at the one time both dead and evil.[54] The man whom God creates in faith is also created in the corruptibility of his physical life and is perfected as God's masterpiece in the resurrection. The man who has grown hardened in his unbelief is separated from God, i.e. he is condemned, and the Last Judgement can only reveal his death. God is continually working and continually giving, but different men receive Him differently. The thankful man is a vessel which gathers up His divinity. The ungrateful one is a vessel which can be filled only with God's wrath and condemnation.[55] The former may look forward to imperishable life, but the latter has forfeited his inheritance and has no eternal inheritance to receive.[56] Death is the lot of sin.

[52] Ibid.

[53] *Χωρισμὸς δὲ τοῦ Θεοῦ θάνατος· καὶ χωρισμὸς φωτὸς σκότος*; cf. the Latin text (ibid.). The condemned resemble men who have put out their eyes. Cf. *A.h.* IV. lxiv 2–3 (Stier. IV. xxxix 2–3) where the same metaphor occurs in connexion with statements about God's continuing work of creation among men.

[54] The expressions sound surprisingly modern but are actually in Irenaeus. See *A.h.* IV. lxiv. 2. Cf. IV. xxi. 2 (Stier. IV. xi. 2).

[55] *A.h.* IV. xxi. 2.

[56] Cf. *A.h.* IV. lxviii. 1 (Stier. IV. xli. 3). What is lost through sin is not supernatural goodness as Klebba suggests, *Anthropologie des hl. Irenaeus*, p. 71 f., but life in its entirety.

The "physical" aspects of the thought of Irenaeus are a corollary of his belief in Creation and do not weaken the "ethical" aspects any more than the ethical relationship between parents and child is spoiled by the fact that the children are also given food and clothing in their home. If a man does anything which is wrong, the guilt of his act does not become any the less if it can be shown that disease, destruction, and death follow from the wrong action. That the Irenaean unity of "physical" and "ethical," i.e. the unity of God as Creator and as holy and perfect will, is not a common feature of writings on Irenaeus, is to be explained by the fact that this inadequate grasp of his theology is based on the meaningless system of separating two distinct lines of thought in interpreting his theology. According to this particular approach, the ethical features which are characteristic of Irenaeus may not be confused with the so-called physical contrast between life and death, which is derived from the belief in Creation, since his ethical concepts belong, it is maintained, to "another line of thought," i.e. the moralistic line which Irenaeus took over from the Apologists and which is determined by such concepts as freedom of the will, progressive development, an optimistic view of mankind, etc. This particular line of thought is developed in another direction in which sin is regarded as having no disastrous effects at all, in which there is no need of Christ as Saviour, and from which all the "physical" concepts are excluded. Accordingly, this approach becomes quite simply a moralistic one rather than ethical—purely moral, that is, and with no need of any re-creation or re-birth.[57] What happens when we

[57] Aleith, in *Z.NT.W.*, 1937, pp. 72 ff. enumerates the points at which Irenaeus diverges from Paul, and on p. 72 f. maintains that in the first place Irenaeus's doctrine of free will is one of these. Farther on we read (p. 73): *Daneben läuft eine andere Linie. . . .* The subject under discussion here is the consequences for the human race of Adam's Fall. Here too Irenaeus diverges from Paul—the really serious consequence of Adam's Fall for him is death, not *die grundlegende etische Verderbnis*. If we make this distinction we shall see that when we come to the idea of *guilt* in Irenaeus we are carrying over the concept of free will which appears in the first line of thought. The concept of guilt, which ought to have a bearing on the "physical" aspect and be dealt with in the discussion on death, is never connected with the second line of thought, and simply confirms that what we have called the moralistic line is in fact moralistic. Cf. Harnack, *History of Dogma*, VOL. II, pp. 267–75, and especially p. 270, n. 1: Harnack frequently describes the

adopt this particular approach is that we are splitting a unitary way of thinking into two quite distinct parts, and then complaining that the first part excludes the ethical, and that the other is simply moral and nothing more, whereas we only need to relate the two distinct parts to one another to find that both reasons for complaint would lose their substance and that Irenaeus would emerge as a perfectly intelligible theologian.

Man who has been defeated by Satan is thus at one time both evil and subject to death—that is, he is "ethically" as well as "physically" bound. As we have seen above, however, God does not cease to retain his sovereignty over the Devil. This supremacy of God is also expressed in many respects in man who is captive to the Devil. For instance, the fact that death itself can be used to serve God as a barrier to sin is one such evidence of the power of God in the midst of man's bondage. The will of the Serpent is that man should live in transgression of God's Commandment, but through death God bring man's transgression to an end, with the ultimate purpose of bringing death itself in His own time to a final end in the resurrection.[58] This latter purpose means the victory of life and the restoration of Creation; between Creation and the resurrection, however, there has been the fact of sin, and, as a further demonstration of God's sovereignty, even the disruptive fact of sin itself between the Creation and the resurrection has directly served the purposes of God. As Jonah was swallowed by the monster not in order to be killed, but that he might become a better instrument in God's hands than he was previously, God likewise allows the monster of evil to swallow man, in order that he should be freed from his imprisonment by Christ, and understand the meaning of grace and come to praise God.[59] Even if man had been unaffected by sin and had lived for ever in Paradise, his eternal life would have been a gift from God, since

moralistic line, but notes that, having been misled by the text of Irenaeus, he has by now begun to speak of death as being over all the children of Adam, and so he adds in a footnote: "This view belongs properly to the second line of thought." But perhaps the one who should decide which concepts are related in Irenaeus is Irenaeus himself! The two-line system leads to difficulties of interpretation, and so should be done away with.

[58] *A.h.* III. xxxv. 2–xxxvi (Stier. III. xxiii 6–7).

[59] *A.h.* III. xxi. 1 (Stier. III. xx. 1) and the conclusion of v. xxi. 3 (Stier. ibid.).

man's life is always the creation and the gift of God.[60] But man had not realised that this was in fact the case. It is through his bondage to sin and his salvation in the Incarnation that he discerns the source of all goodness and his proper relationship to God. Even man's sin has a part to play in the development of man and in confirming him in his relation to God. The factor which initially impedes man's development may ultimately direct his development along the proper course.

In his occasional use of the expression, "Man is free," Irenaeus is dealing with precisely the same question. The concept of freedom in Irenaeus has many aspects, of which this is one. Man is not changed as a result of his defeat simply into an inanimate being which lacks any power of action. He is indeed a captive, but if his fetters are loosed he can take independent action if he chooses to do so. It is a characteristic of Irenaeus's doctrine of bondage and free will to connect the idea of captivity with the idea of the possibility of independent action which is still preserved in man, though it is bound. It would be difficult to give a positive indication of what this means in relation to the ability of fallen man to do what is good, but it is quite obvious that Irenaeus finds no difficulty in the idea of all men in their general conduct being able to follow certain divine Commandments.[61] In connexion with the question with which we are dealing it would appear to be of greater importance that captive man can wait in hope for the One who is to release him from his captivity, and that even before the Incarnation there is therefore a patient expectation of Christ. In the same way as we believe in Christ after He has come, one may believe in Him while His coming is still delayed. Both before and after the Incarnation love is very closely connected with faith.[62]

[60] For a helpful treatment of this connexion between life and God, cf. *A.h.* v. iii. 3 (Stier. ibid.).

[61] Cf. *A.h.* IV. xxiv. 1 (Stier. IV. xiii. 1) and IV. xxv. 3 (Stier. IV. xv. 1) and my article in *S.T.K.*, 1940, pp. 134 ff.

[62] As far as the Old Testament is concerned, see *A.h.* IV. xxvii–xxviii (Stier. IV. xvi), and for the New Testament, *Epid.* 87 and 95. Many other passages could be quoted. In Irenaean theology freedom on the whole has such a close connexion with Christ as the One who liberates that it cannot be dealt with in full until we come to Christ's work of salvation. This should be considered in relation to the question put by Klebba, *Anthropologie des hl. Irenaeus*, pp. 154 ff. Even in a passage like IV. lxiii. 3 (Stier. IV. xxxviii. 4) it is the victorious *Christ* who is in the history

Freedom, of course, is implied in this connexion, a freedom which before Christ had its source in the work of Christ which was yet in the future but absolutely certain to come. The Son is Lord even of those who have lived before His coming to earth as man.

It is striking that if we make a list of the passages in Irenaeus which describe God's continuing sovereignty over man in spite of his fall, the same primary factor is to be discovered in every case—God's lordship resides in the promised and coming Christ who is to trample the Devil underfoot. Man is a prisoner, but since the Christ who is awaited is yet stronger, his tyrannical lord has no power to retain his hold on him. Man has access by hope to new life, despite the fact that by his own fault he has fallen from the state of health ordained by the Creator, and allowed the powers of death to set to work within himself. Man as we know him is in actual fact determined both by God and Satan, both by Creation and sin.[63] Two powers, in mutual conflict, have chosen man as the area of their struggle against one another, and it is by their conflict and not by any one or other of these powers alone that man's actual situation is defined, until one of these powers, the usurper, has once and for all been expelled. But it is quite clear what comes from God as it is what comes from the Devil. From God man receives life and righteousness; from the enemy of God he receives death and unrighteousness.

In the section that follows we shall be dealing at greater length with the characteristics of human life since Satan's

of man from the freedom of Creation, and man's position as a child which he is then given, through the Fall and death, to the resurrection with its realisation of the *imago* and *similitudo*. It is strange that Bousset, *Kyrios Christos*, does not see how that idea of the Fall and sin as forming an integral part of *God's design*, or "evolution" (pp. 437–40), quite clearly makes the commonly accepted concept of free will untenable. Where God gives man freedom he has freedom, and where God denies him freedom, he has no freedom. A human freedom such as this can never, as some have suggested, come into conflict with God's grace.

[63] There is a tendency in writings which deal with Irenaeus to dismiss the idea of man as being determined by an evil power which is in opposition to God, as though it were only within himself that man has certain evil "consequences" of the Fall, such as death and sin. It is impossible to understand Irenaeus if we fail to realise that the most important "consequence" of man's defeat by the Devil is his dependence on an evil and destructive power outside of himself which is objective in the same way as God is objective.

defeat of man and man's hopeful expectation of the birth of Christ and His work of deliverance. We must, however, before we actually introduce this section, emphasise once more that man who is in bondage is one who is *burdened with guilt* and not merely sapped by his frailty and mortality. Man has lost his child-likeness and innocence. The whole of Irenaeus's description of Adam after the Fall is dominated by the idea of Adam's penitence and contrition and not of his physical affliction.[64] For this reason it is a characteristic of life which is lived under the power of sin that God, before the coming of Christ, uses the *Law* in nurturing and disciplining man.

The Conditions of Bondage

We have just mentioned the two main points with which we have to deal in this present section. One is the promise of salvation, and the other is the corrective work of the Law. We shall have occasion to analyse here Irenaeus's view of the Old Testament as containing in part prophecy about Christ and in part instruction by means of strict and repressive laws, i.e. in the first case promise, in the second, Law. In the disciplinary function of the Law in regard to man there is also a preparation of man for the coming of Christ in its work as man's tutor so that he may receive the freedom of the Gospel. The dominant and most important aspect of the Old Testament is therefore the expectation of Christ.[65] Man's bondage is marked by his expectation of the coming Christ.

We shall begin with Irenaeus's doctrine of the Law. In using the expression *lex* Irenaeus generally means something which corresponds to sin in man, and which has therefore a bearing on human bondage and has offset his bondage. Irenaeus's use of *lex* is distinct from his use of the expression *praecepta*, Commandments, by which he as frequently signifies the commands

[64] *A.h.* III. xxxv. 1 (Stier. III. xxiii. 5). The question of death and life comes later. In Irenaeus contrition and repentence usually point forward to Christ, who is the hope of new life. But on the other hand it is quite unlike Irenaeus to suggest that there is any righteousness in Adam's repentance which might neutralise and excuse his sin. After his fall Adam is unable to grasp his freedom out of the power of the Devil, and can only wait in hope for the coming of the vanquisher of evil. Cf. also Stoll, *Lehre des hl. Irenäus*, pp. 11 ff., 25.

[65] In both of its distinctive aspects, the Law and prophecy, the Old Testament is pointing to something which was to come only with the Incarnation.

given by God which are permanently valid, even in man's freedom, and which are received by man with a willingness to obey. The "Law" appeared at a certain point in history and disappeared at a certain point in history. The Law was given for men in bondage. It appeared in history after man was defeated as a means of attacking the Devil, and has as its task the bringing of man into compulsory obedience as far as the external and purely physical is concerned, in such a way that man is dragged as though by chains into obedience to God's Commandments. Later on, when Christ comes and frees man, his chains will be removed. The Law in its proper sense may then disappear, since then it has accomplished its pedagogic task, and man will "follow God without bonds."[66] The contrast between bondage and freedom, in which freedom is identical with the work of Christ in His Incarnation—salvation—is the predominant one in this section of Irenaeus. The Law is a counterpart to sin—when sin gains control the Law is interposed against sin, and when the power of sin is broken in Christ, the Law is removed.

In addition to this, however, there is another factor in Irenaeus which has just been suggested, namely, the natural laws. These were in existence before the Law—while he was still in Paradise and uncorrupted and free from sin man stood under God's Commandments—and also continue and have validity in Christ. I propose to deal more closely with the particular features of these "Commandments of freedom" later on, when I shall try to describe what it is that characterises man in the Church in relation to the ethical aspect of his situation. It is sometimes maintained that these *naturalia praecepta* have the same content as the Decalogue.[67] There are some, too, who

[66] "Etenim Lex, quippe servis posita, per ea quae foris erant corporalia animam erudiebat; velut per vinculum attrahens eam ad obedientiam praeceptorum, uti disceret homo servire Deo: Verbum autem liberans animam, et per ipsam corpus voluntarie emundari docuit. Quo facto, necesse fuit auferri quidem vincula servitutis, quibus jam homo assueverat, et sine vinculis sequi Deum," *A.h.* IV. xxiv. 2 (Stier. IV. xiii. 2); see Harvey's commentary on the passage in n. 4. See, too, the passage in *A.h.* up to and including IV. xxix (Stier. IV. xvii. 5).

[67] ". . . per naturalia praecepta, quae ab initio infixa dedit hominibus, admonens eos, id est per Decalogum . . ." *A.h.* IV. xxv. 3 (Stier. IV. xv. 1); cf. the remarks on *virtus decalogi* in IV. xxvii. 3 (Stier. IV. xvi. 3). On the passage quoted cf. Lundström, *Studien*, p. 130.

emphasise that all who partake of life or salvation live in conformity with these Commandments.[68] Their sum total amounts to *faith* in God and *love* to one's neighbour. Christ has not abolished the command to have faith and love but rather has emphasised and extended it (e.g. by His insistence upon a right motive and love of one's enemy). By renewing man's heart the Lord makes man willing at the same time to do the will of God from within. In this sense Christ has abolished the Law for man, not merely the ceremonial law, but quite expressly also the Ten Commandments.[69] But such freedom from all the laws of God exists only in the sphere of faith and love, i.e. where the whole of the Law is realised. Irenaeus is always concerned to stress that the Law is fulfilled in the very fact of its abolition and in the actual transgression of its externals by Christ and His disciples—in showing themselves to be lords of the commandment about the Sabbath they are thereby displaying the law of love, and have thereby fulfilled the Law. The breaking of the Law corresponds to the Law which is to be in force only for a prescribed time.[70] When the Spirit is poured forth, man's bondage comes to an end. Faith and love thus exist in freedom.[71]

The contrast between bondage and freedom also lies behind the distinction which Irenaeus makes between the two "testaments." In Irenaeus the word "testament" means *covenant*—it is not a collection of writings, but a condition in which man lives, and an arrangement or ordering made from God's side.

[68] *A.h.* IV. XXV. 3 (Stier. IV. XV. 1) parenthetically; the expression *salus decalogi* in *A.h.* IV. XXVI. 2 (Stier. IV. XV. 2) is more obscure.

[69] On the relationship to God and one's neighbour see *A.h.* IV. XXVII. 3–XXVIII. 1 (Stier. IV. XVI. 3). The emphasis on the Decalogue and indeed its extension in the Gospels is most clearly dealt with in *A.h.* IV. XXIV. 2–3 (Stier. IV. XIII. 2–4), where the idea of free will is also expressed in a remarkably lucid way. In *Epid.* 96 Irenaeus asserts the application of freedom even in the laws of the Decalogue. Cf. Wieten, *Irenaeus' geschrift*, p. 187 f. On this whole aspect of Irenaeus see the very fine exposition in Reinhold Seeberg, *Lehrbuch der Dogmengeschichte*, 3rd edn. Erlangen 1922, VOL. I, p. 432 f., and also the illuminating historical comment made by Friedrich Karl Schumann, "Bemerkungen zur Lehre vom Gesetz," in *Z.S.T.*, 1939, p. 213, n. 1. Stoll, who wrote in 1905, and was therefore unaware of the *Epideixis*, which had not by that time been discovered, exaggerates the distinction between "ceremonial law" and "moral law," e.g. *Lehre des hl. Irenäus*, pp. 41, 87.

[70] *A.h.* IV. XVI–XVII (Stier. IV. VIII. 2–3).

[71] See too in this connexion Harnack, *History of Dogma*, VOL. II, p. 310, n. 1, and Bonwetsch, *Theologie des Irenäus*, p. 88 and also p. 139 f.

What we refer to as the New Testament is translated by a double expression in Irenaeus as "the Gospel and the Apostles," and the Old and New Testaments together (in our sense of the word) he calls "Scripture," ἡ γραφή, *scriptura* (often in the plural also). When the Spirit came on the first day of Pentecost, entrance was thereby given to the people of God to the new covenant, of which the sign is freedom, in the same way as the Old Testament had as its characteristic bondage.[72] Irenaeus sometimes states that there are four covenants—God's covenant with Adam and Noah, His covenant given through Moses, and His covenant in Christ—but even then the covenant in the Son is absolutely unique, the only one which gives salvation and life to men.[73] All God's purposes for the human race after the defeat of Adam and before the victory of Christ are stamped by the fact that evil remains dominant and unconquered, and merely checked, circumscribed and limited by the Law. Christ defeats evil and bestows the Spirit who turns those who are in bondage into children who are free.[74]

The distinction between the old covenant and the new is thus at all points conditioned by the fact that Christ Himself has come to end the old and initiate the new. Before Christ appeared in human form the old could not end nor the new begin. Irenaeus does not conceive of two separate groups of writings which are identical in their basic proclamation, but rather thinks primarily in terms of, first, an old, anticipatory, and forward-looking "testament," secondly, Christ Himself, and, thirdly, a new "testament" in which the Gospel is proclaimed which concerns that which has come to pass and has been accomplished. Christ appears between old and new in Scripture, and He alone brings unity to the old and the new. The Scriptures can be held together only by having Christ as their

[72] *A.h.* III. xviii. 1 (Stier. III. xvii. 2), IV. lv. 5 (Stier. IV. xxxiii. 14) and in a very marked way in the latter part of III. xii. 17 (Stier. III. xii. 14). See J. Hoh, *Die Lehre des hl. Irenäus über das Neue Testament*, henceforth cited as *Lehre des hl. Irenäus*, Münster 1919, pp. 1–4, 62 f., 75–8, 200–2.

[73] *A.h.* III. xi. 11 (Stier. III. xi. 8); the Greek text names instead Noah, Abraham, Moses, and Christ. As we shall see, Abraham occupies a unique position. *A.h.* IV. xxxix (Stier. IV. xxv).

[74] See *A.h.* IV. xlix. 2 (Stier. IV. xxxii. 2), and IV. lviii. 2 (Stier. IV. xxxvi. 2). Cf. Prümm in *Scholastik*, 1938, p. 349.

centre.[75] In the old covenant men look forward, and in the new they look backwards, to a perfect work, while between the two there stands the incarnate Lord.

There are two observations made by Harnack: first, that from the appearance of the law given in their bondage through Moses up to the time of Christ it is the people of Israel alone with whom Irenaeus is concerned, and second, that these same people of Israel forfeit their exceptional position after the Incarnation and completely cease to represent humanity as to a certain extent they had done before Christ.[76] There is a quite clear and conscious understanding in Irenaeus at this point that the Church is Israel. God first created man and the whole universe, but later, when sin disrupted God's creation, He selected Israel and directed His continuing work, which was to prepare for the Incarnation, at this single people, Israel. It was within these narrow bounds that Christ lived as man. These limits were then shattered by the Spirit, who was bestowed upon the Gentiles as well, and yet the concentration was still maintained, and there was still this narrow base for God's dealings with the world. The old Israel began to disappear, but a new Israel, the Church, the Bride and possession of Christ, became the dwelling-place of the Spirit. This widening out towards the whole of humanity is the object of God's activity through the Church, as it was the object of God's activity through the old Israel, and therefore the Church must constantly aim beyond itself to the salvation of the world, though this broad aim will be obtained only in the resurrection of the dead, the Last Judgement upon all men, and the fulfilment of Creation.[77]

[75] *A.h.* v (preface) (Stier. ibid.), *Epid.* 86, and Reynders, "Paradosis," in *Recherches de théologie ancienne et médiévale*, 1933, pp. 186–8.

[76] Harnack, *History of Dogma*, VOL. II, pp. 305 f., 309 f.

[77] In *A.h.* III. xviii. 2 (Stier. III. xvii. 3) Irenaeus interprets Judges VI. 36–40 as follows: the Spirit falls first upon Israel as the dew upon the fleece, while later it falls upon the Church, "upon all the earth beside." In the new covenant the fleece is dry, it is Israel deprived of the Spirit, Israel which has rejected its own Messiah. In *A.h.* IV. v–vi (Stier. IV. iv. 1–2) Jersusalem is compared to the stalk which is to bear the ear of corn and later wither: "sic et Hierosolyma, quae jugum in se *servitutis* portaverat, in quo domitus est homo, qui antea non subjiciebatur Deo cum mors regnabat, et domitus habilis factus est ad *libertatem*, adveniente fructu *libertatis*," v (Stier. iv. 1). In several places Irenaeus lays a great deal of emphasis on the fact that Jesus belonged to the house of David; see e.g. *A.h.* III. xvii. 1–3 (Stier. III. xvi. 2–3). In his *Christ and Time*, pp. 108 ff., Cullmann has a very good

Evil will have then been destroyed and nullified, the Spirit will be reunited with Creation, and mankind's affliction healed. This "narrowness" of Israel, or the narrow line of the Church and the gulf between the Church and the world, is something which is bound to be and cannot be annulled in this present age. Nevertheless the Body of Christ must be aware of itself as being in solidarity with all men and involved in a "growing up" to *become* humanity in the world of the resurrection. Mission, the life of service to society, and the hope of the resurrection, are inseparably linked.

If it is said that the Law is to hold man in bondage, we are explicitly saying that sin is man's master. God's will in Creation is free, generous, and indulgent, when man, as he does when Creation was uncorrupted, obeys and follows His will in creation, but this same will of God in Creation becomes the Law when man resists it in setting up his will against God's in sin. Then God's purpose for man, that he should become like God, presses heavily upon him and binds him, though formerly this purpose of God was consistent with man's free development and was recognised as being a gift from God. In so far as man appropriated to himself the work of God, the work of God in Creation became man's own growth towards the object of his own existence, which is likeness to God. But now instead man as an evil being resists God. At the same time, however, the Law is a present reality with its demands which could all be summarised as a summons to man to become like God

exposition of the line of redemptive history from Creation—Israel—Christ—the Church—to Creation again, according to the view held in the early Church. If we are judging Cullmann's terminology from outside the writings of Irenaeus it is certainly inappropriate to refer to the Incarnation as the "middle" of history. Christ has come at the last period, at the end; see *A.h.* I. iv (Stier. I. x. 3), and cf. on this point Scharl, *Orientalia*, 1940, p. 393, n. 3, and also (though our investigation here should be critical) Martin Werner, *Die Entstehung des christlichen Dogmas*, Berne and Leipzig 1941, pp. 84 ff. See too *A.h.* IV. xxxix (Stier. IV. xxv. 1) and V. xviii. 2 (Stier. V. xviii. 3). In the *middle* there lies the time of the *Law*, the time of bondage between Creation and the Incarnation: "Circumcisio vero et Lex operationum media obtinuerunt tempora," *A.h.* IV. xxxix; and also *Epid.* 8: ". . . In the end of the times He opened up the covenant of adoption; but . . . in the intermediate times, when men forgot God and departed and revolted from Him, He brought them into subjection by the Law." It would appear that Irenaeus can seek support for such language in the New Testament. With his peculiar Christocentricity Cullmann hardly gives himself room to discuss the Law. See Cullmann, *op. cit.*, p. 138, the one short reference in n. 3.

(cf. Lev. XIX.2 and Mt. v.48). Since God is love, this means that man is to be love. The law of bondage in the law books of the old covenant contains very much, it is true, which lacks this objective and ethical significance which is rooted in Creation, but these rules for men who are in bondage have rather the function of disciplining and training them up to obedience and submission to God, in order that they may be able to receive the subsequent work of the Creator—their liberation in the Son, grace, and new birth.[78] The final aim of Creation is and will continue to be that God's purpose that man may attain to the *imago* and *similitudo Dei* may be realised and that he may thereby obey God and love his neighbour. The obstacle to this is sin, the power of self-will over man. As death prevails because of sin, so the law prevails because of sin. The disobedience to God of apostasy is the primal evil.

In certain respects the Law is in itself a prophecy of Christ since Christ is the *imago* and *similitudo Dei*, the fulfilment and end of the Law. The Law might therefore be said to prophesy about its own abolition. The Son, the *Verbum*, spoke to Moses; the Law was given through Him who afterwards became incarnate, and who in the Incarnation has power over the Law.[79] Christ is already active in the old covenant before the Incarnation. Irenaeus finds no more difficulty in thus conceiving of Christ as being active before the Incarnation than he does in imagining that the Spirit is at work before Pentecost, or even before the appearance of Jesus, for Jesus alone is Christ or Messiah, i.e. the One who is anointed by the Spirit.[80] And yet

[78] There is a detailed description of the relationship between Creation, the Law, sin, and finally salvation, in Irenaeus, with fairly full references to sources, in my article in *S.T.K.*, 1940, pp. 137–43.

[79] "Utraque autem testamenta unus et idem paterfamilias produxit, Verbum Dei, Dominus noster Jesus Christus, qui et Abrahae et Moysi collocutus est, qui nobis in novitate restituit libertatem, et multiplicavit eam, quae ab ipso est, gratiam," *A.h.* IV. xviii (Stier. IV. ix. 1). Ragnar Bring has expounded the relationship between the Law and Christ according to Paul in a way which is very much reminiscent of the basic Irenaean view; see "Till frågan om Pauli syn på lagens förhållande till tron," in *S.T.K.*, 1945, pp. 37 ff.: the proposition that Christ is God's only righteousness is further strengthened by the emphasis which we find in Irenaeus on the unity between Creation and Christ, a stress which we do not find at all in Paul. The righteous Creation arises again in Christ; the Law is merely "intermediary," a correlative to sin.

[80] E.g. *A.h.* III. xii. 9 (Stier. III. xii. 7).

the Spirit is speaking even through the prophets and all the writers of the books of the Old Testament in the same way as the translation into Greek of these same books has been effected by the inspiration of God through the Septuagint translators.[81] From the Creation onwards the Spirit and the Son are the hands of God through whom the world was created, and they cannot be made to discontinue their activity simply because man has fallen into sin. They do not enter into the human race in their full strength until the Son is made man and the Spirit makes His dwelling-place in man, that is, in Jesus Christ, but even before His birth in Bethlehem the Son and the Spirit are at work with man. The Spirit "accustoms" itself to dwelling in the human race by working in the prophets and patriarchs who also have faith since they trust in God's promise. Grace (which is connected with the Spirit and with faith) is not therefore to be understood as being non-existent between the Fall and the Incarnation, but grace can also increase and "become greater": God is gracious in the old covenant, although grace does not for that reason abound as it does in the new covenant.[82]

External Creation already witnesses to the Creator and reveals God's power and divinity.[83] Mankind's first parents had knowledge of God without having the Scriptures, the same knowledge which was afterwards communicated by the word which was written and spoken by men.[84] The world and all creatures and living beings have come into existence because the Creator spoke, came into existence, that is, through the Creative Word. This *Verbum*, which is the Son, also speaks through the prophets to whom the Word "comes" in order to

[81] *A.h.* III. xxiv (Stier. III. xxi. 2–3); the Septuagint is here specially discussed. On the question of Irenaeus's view of the inspiration of Scripture cf. Montgomery Hitchcock, *Irenaeus of Lugdunum*, pp. 192–4, W. S. Reilly, "L'Inspiration de l'ancien testament chez saint Irénée," in *Revue biblique*, 1917, pp. 489–507; the author makes a distinction in the nature of inspiration between the Old Testament and the New; Hoh, *Lehre des hl. Irenäus*, p. 94 f., who is more cautious (he has no "mantic" conception of inspiration); and also Herrera, *S. Irénée de Lyon exégète*, pp. 66, 70, and Seeberg, *Lehrbuch der Dogmengeschichte*, VOL. I, p. 370. The last-mentioned finds Jewish influences: ". . . die ganze jüdische Anschauung von dem heiligen Buchstaben."

[82] See Bonwetsch, *Theologie des Irenäus*, pp. 66–9, 86 f., 143 f.

[83] *A.h.* II. iv. 5 (Stier. II. vi. 1) and II. viii. 1 (Stier. II. ix. 1). Cf. Harnack, *History of Dogma*, VOL. II, p. 305 f., and Escoula in *N.R.T.*, 1939, pp. 551–67.

[84] Bonwetsch, *Theologie des Irenäus*, p. 33.

go out to men through them. The *Verbum* was not yet incarnate, but nonetheless it was at work with power among men and the world which was created through the same *Verbum*. The difference between the Word before it was incarnate in the old covenant and the incarnate Word in the new covenant is vividly seen in the typical introductory formulae in the two "Testaments"—in the prophets it is "Thus saith the Lord"; in Christ, "But I say unto you" (Mt. v). The new covenant is within this "I." But now the Word is in man, it has been given form and has become flesh, it is the *Verbum incarnatum*. The Spirit, which laid hold on the prophets, dwells in Jesus who is the Anointed, the Christ. And just as the Spirit and the Word in the Old "Testament" took the prophet into their power in order to reach Israel, the people of God, through him, so the Spirit and the Word are in Jesus Christ in order to be proclaimed to men through Him, and poured out upon the people of God, the Church, the Israel of the New "Testament."[85]

The Son of God thus stands before the Incarnation in a certain relationship with the holy men and women of the old covenant. It is characteristic of Irenaeus that he refuses to regard the frequent "theophanies" of the Old Testament as the visitation of angels, but on the contrary sees them as signs of the immediate presence of the Son, the manifestation of the *Verbum*

[85] There has been a great deal of discussion whether Irenaeus has also the philosophical conception of *logos* or whether by *logos* or *verbum* he always means *spoken word*. On the discussion see Kunze, *Gotteslehre des Irenaeus*, pp. 30 ff.; Montgomery Hitchcock, *Irenaeus of Lugdunum*, p. 141 f.; Seeberg, *Lehrbuch der Dogmengeschichte*, VOL. I, p. 406; Loofs, *Theophilus von Antiochien*, pp. 208, 347 f. (Loofs's basic theory is that what Irenaeus says here has been drawn from several authors); and Lietzmann, *Church Universal*, p. 209 f. There is fairly general unanimity on Irenaeus's "unphilosophical" character. On Christ in the Old Testament see *A.h.* II. xlvii. 2 (Stier. II. xxx. 9), the comprehensive section in III. ix–xii (Stier. ibid.), III. xxxii. I (Stier. III. xxii. 4), the particular emphasis in IV. iii. I (Stier. IV. ii. 3) and IV. xviii (Stier. IV. ix. I), and also IV. xl. I (Stier. IV. xxvi. I) in which Irenaeus says that Christ is hidden in the ancient writings like the treasure in the field; and finally, e.g., IV. lv. I (Stier. IV. xxxiii. 10), on the Old Testament prophets as the "members" of Christ, *membra Christi*. It is next to impossible to make a list of all that Irenaeus says on these lines. Practically the whole of the *Epideixis* is dominated by this particular line of thought (see esp. *Epid.* 6). On the Word and the Spirit as proceeding through the incarnate Christ to men, and so passing on into the preached Gospel and thereby issuing in the salvation of men, see *A.h.* III. x (Stier. III. ix. 3). To say that the Word and the Spirit are in Christ is the same as saying that Christ nourishes and sustains His Church. With regard to the formula *Haec dicit Dominus* and *Ego autem dico vobis*, cf. *A.h.* IV. lviii. I (Stier. IV. xxxvi. I).

Himself, the *Logos*.[86] It is on account of this hidden presence of Christ in the Old Testament witnesses that Abraham is given this peculiar double position in Irenaeus as first parent and type of both Testaments, of the covenant both of bondage and of freedom, of both the Law and the Gospel, one through circumcision, the other through faith. Irenaeus links up with the line of thought in Paul at this point. In Abraham faith comes first, before circumcision, and through faith he prefigures the covenant of freedom and adoption. Circumcision, on the other hand, is an expression of the testament of the Law and bondage. Strangely enough, however, in the actual redemptive history it is the latter which comes first: Moses precedes Christ, as Tamar's first son was born after her second (Gen. xxxviii. 27–30).[87] The promise is earliest, before the Law, and likewise is last and definitive. In Christ the primal condition re-emerges, and man is given his free position as a child again. Bondage "intervened" and was transient, as the domination of sin was transient.

Redemptive history is the history of the repulsion of sin and the recovery of the dominion which the Devil has occupied. It is in this cosmic perspective that we must see God's dealings with men in the two Testaments and the means of access to eternal perfection through the bondage of the Law and the freedom of the Gospel. But it should be remembered in addition to this that the part of God's Creation to be occupied by the Devil was first of all *man*, the world of men, humanity. It is only secondarily and through man that the Devil has obtained possession of animate and inanimate nature. It was primarily man whom the evil angel took with him in his fall. Therefore it is primarily man who has to be rescued and recovered. It is for this reason that the Son became man, and in this evil area of conflict, in the form of sinful flesh, took up the struggle against Satan. Before the coming of the Son, the world of men could do no more than toil and await His coming—toil under

[86] J. Barbel, "Christos Angelos," in *Theophaneia*, iii, 1941, pp. 63 ff., and his summary on p. 68. *Epid.* 44 f., e.g., is typical.

[87] *A.h.* iv. xxxix (Stier. iv. xxv). On the faith of Abraham, cf. iv. x (Stier. iv. v. 3–5), iv. xii–xiii (Stier. iv. vii. 1–2), iv. xv (Stier. iv. viii. 1), and iv. xxiv. 3 (Stier iv. xiii. 4); and also *Epid.* 24 and 35 in addition. See too Åke V. Ström, *Vetekornet*, Stockholm 1944, pp. 179, 265: Abraham is the father of the Church.

the Law and hope in the promise as a captive lives in captivity, looking forward to his deliverance, the Christ for whom he waits.[88]

In the time of the old covenant, therefore, Christ has not yet come. He lives, He speaks, and His spokesmen are heard, but He himself has not come. His arrival is delayed, and He is unseen and hidden. In the same way as an occupied country may await in an attitude of expectancy its coming liberator, and yet be quite aware that this liberator-to-come has not yet arrived, and that the day of his arrival is unknown, so as early as the Old "Testament" there is a relationship of faith and hope in Christ Himself through the promise and through prophecy, though Christ is not actually present, that is to say, He is not yet incarnate. The hidden presence of Christ in the old covenant is not such that He is, as it were, "sufficiently" present, and does not need to be "any more" present, but rather points forward to the Incarnation and means that the futurist prophecy is invested with a deeper significance.[89] Irenaeus puts it this way: if a king's herald announces that his master is to enter a certain country, something completely new happens when the king, bringing with him freedom and his other gifts as well, actually arrives, however detailed may have been the description which his servants gave of him.[90] The king does not become

[88] See *A.h.* IV. iv. 2 (Stier. IV. ii. 7). Cf. *A.h.* IV. v (Stier. IV. iv. 1).

[89] When Irenaeus comes upon a "type" of the new covenant in the old, he maintains that it contains a *reference to what is to come*—it is *prophecy*, or promise, and the uniqueness of the Incarnation is never lost by his thinking thus in terms of "type." The Passover in Egypt prefigures the death of Christ, but this means that the Jewish Passover was unfulfilled until Christ suffered death: "Et non est numerum dicere, in quibus a Moyse ostenditur Filius Dei: cujus et diem passionis non ignoravit, sed figuratim praenuntiavit eum, Pascha nominans: et in eadem ipsa, quae ante tantum temporis a Moyse praedicata est, passus est Dominus *adimplens* Pascha," *A.h.* IV. xx. 1 (Stier. IV. x. 1); cf. *Epid.* 25. It is one of Irenaeus's principal objects to prove that the prophetic assertions of the Old Testament are unfulfilled until Christ fulfils them. See several references in *Epid.* between 52 and 86, and 90–94; and also the whole concluding passage of *A.h.* on the fulfilment of the prophecies in the *regnum*.

[90] *A.h.* IV. lvi. 1 (Stier. IV. xxxiv. 1). In this passage freedom is spoken of as being something which has been given by the king who has arrived. *Libertas* is mentioned frequently in *A.h.* IV. lvi, and by it is meant the distinctive mark of the new covenant or the Church. The essence of the Church is the Gospel and freedom, just as the sign of the old covenant is the Law and bondage. On what was completely new in the Incarnation, in spite of prophecy, cf. *Epid.* 92.

king on that very day, but it is on that day that he invades that particular part of the country with power. There was no freedom in the world as long as Christ had not appeared on earth as man. The disciplining and education of men achieve their object when they lack the justification for their existence. The old covenant is fulfilled in being abrogated; and it is abrogated in being fulfilled. Man's bondage points forward to its own dissolution in Christ.[91]

We may use an analogy in connexion with Irenaeus's own exposition in order to explain how it is that the faithful men and women of the Old Testament both have and do not have Christ at one and the same time. Faith in Christ's dominion over the world in the new covenant in which we are now set means an eschatological hope for the future. In the resurrection and the Last Judgement Christ will be visible king over the world, and the Spirit will obtain power even over men's bodies, i.e. over matter. But this is not the actual situation at the present time, and is therefore something which we cannot adequately represent. When it takes place, it will be something new and immense. And yet even in the present time faith grasps this prospect, and actually in a sense faith even now possesses the future, since it has Christ, and the resurrection from the dead is Christ's future work. In the same way, Abraham trusted in the promise about Christ, and thereby saw beforehand the Incarnation, the day of Jesus Christ, even although his conception of the birth and work of Jesus were not exactly as they later occurred.[92] In believing in the promise Abraham actually possessed Christ as He then was, thereby grasping the Incarnation, since the future work of the Word or Son was the Incarnation. Abraham had essentially the same kind of faith as we have.[93]

[91] Bonwetsch, *Theologie des Irenäus*, pp. 88–94.

[92] Cf. Prümm in *Scholastik*, 1938, p. 350.

[93] Irenaeus interprets Paul's words on Abraham in Gal. III. 6–9 thus: "Ob quae non solum prophetam eum dixit fidei, sed et patrem eorum qui ex gentibus credunt in Christum Jesum, eo quod una et eadem illius et nostra sit fides: illo quidem credente futuris quasi jam factis propter repromissionem Dei; nobis quoque similiter per fidem speculantibus eam quae est in regno haereditatem, propter repromissionem Dei," *A.h.* IV. XXXV. I (Stier. IV. XXI. I). Cf. how in *A.h.* IV. XXXIV. 10 Moses, Elijah, and Ezekiel saw "parables and prophecies" of a future glory, and the description of *lineamenta rerum futurarum* in IV. XXXIV. II (Stier. IV. XX. II beginning and end.)

Every phase of Christ's redemptive work means that something completely new occurs, but provided men live completely in the conditions of faith, the terms of faith are the same.[94] The basis of faith is always the promise of God's word, and the promise always relates to Christ.[95]

By being defeated by sin man, who is God's created child and who ought to be the image of the Son, fell into captivity. There is no way by which he can revoke his bondage by himself. His whole salvation lies in the hope that Christ will come and release him from his destruction. His progress so far has been from life to death, and if he is left alone, he will remain in death. It is only if the tyrant who holds him prisoner is defeated by one who is stronger than he that man can be brought from death to life.

[94] Cf. *A.h.* IV. xlix. 2 (Stier. IV. xxxii. 2).
[95] *A.h.* IV. xxxvi. 2 (Stier. IV. xxii. 2).

PART II

CHRIST

CHAPTER I

BECOMING MAN

Recapitulatio

FOR Irenaeus, the One who is master over evil has lived, died, and risen again, and now rules at the right hand of the Father. His whole conception of Creation and man's defeat is influenced by his belief in Christ. It was clear in Part I that we were continually coming to discuss the work of Christ in spite of the fact that this rather formed the proper discussion of this present section. It was impossible, of course, to separate the work of Christ from His becoming man and His victory. In spite of our failure to do so in Part I, we shall now undertake a comparable task. As far as possible, the whole of this middle Part II, which has the general heading of "Christ," will deal with the redemptive work of Christ without dealing with the Church or the Consummation.[1] We shall look only at Christ. It will be impossible to achieve this fully, because Christ, as Irenaeus says, is nothing by Himself, but what He is, He is for other people, for other men—for *man*. In Part III we shall reconsider the idea of man in bondage in order to understand how he is freed by Christ's victory. In this middle section, however, we shall be dealing only with the incarnate Christ Himself—as far as any such definition is possible. After that we shall be dealing with His becoming man as such, i.e. with the fact that God became man. This will give us the opportunity of opening the discussion on the concept of *recapitulatio*, even although this cannot be more than a partial glimpse at the idea of recapitulation in the present connexion. If the whole ques-

[1] In Part III, "From Death to Life," the two chapter headings are "The Church" and "The Consummation." We shall there see how fallen man receives Christ and all that He has won for us in His Incarnation and victory.

tion is to be thoroughly elucidated, there are several other aspects which will have to be considered.[2] But the main point for our present consideration is first of all this: through the birth of Christ Creation returns to its purity, the original form of Creation is revealed in its perfectly developed form, and in Him Life enters into the world of Death.

Even although the actual words ἀνακεφαλαίωσις or *recapitulatio* had been found in Justin, and, as was quite likely, had been borrowed from Justin by Irenaeus, we are unable with our present knowledge to derive this far-reaching doctrine of recapitulation which we find in Irenaeus from any source earlier than Irenaeus himself. The use of the terms ἀνακεφαλαίωσις and *recapitulatio* is an attempt by Irenaeus to embody the whole of the Biblical proclamation about the work of Christ in a single word.[3] A passage in Book IV of the *Adversus haereses* provides the basis of the theory that Justin was the initiator of the doctrine of recapitulation who was closely followed by Irenaeus. Irenaeus quotes from the lost *Syntagma* of Justin against Marcion: "Justin well states that . . ." he writes, and then there follow some sentences in which, amongst other things, it is stated that the only-begotten Son recapitulates His creation. We cannot, however, say whether this last statement is an actual part of the quotation, or whether the passage from the *Syntagma* had stopped before this point, and Irenaeus was merely continuing the line of thought with his own ideas.[4] Bousset and Armitage Robinson—the latter has devoted a special study to the problem of this quotation—both hold that the quotation ends farther back and does not include the part

[2] From *A.h.* III. xvii. 6 (Stier. III. xvi. 6) it is clear that Christ's progression through His birth, passion, resurrection, coming again, and the Last Judgement in its entirety, is *recapitulatio*. Of the work of recapitulation there still remain the *parousia*, the resurrection of the dead, and the judgement of the world. Christ awaits the proper time for this part of ἀνακεφαλαίωσις as He sits now as Lord and Head of the Church, *caput Ecclesiae*. Cf. W. Schmidt in *Teol. tidskr.*, 1934, p. 188 f., and Escoula in *Nouvelle revue théologique*, 1939, p. 399 f., n. 11. In the present chapter we shall be analysing only the first part of recapitulation—Christ's becoming man. We shall postpone the discussion of the relevant literature until we can offer a more detailed picture.

[3] Cf. Eph. I. 10: ἀνακεφαλαιώσασθαι τὰ πάντα ἐν τῷ Χριστῷ, τὰ ἐπὶ τοῖς οὐρανοῖς καὶ τὰ ἐπὶ τῆς γῆς.

[4] *A.h.* IV. xi. 2 (Stier. IV. vi. 2).

about the Son as the One who recapitulates His creation.[5] Loofs and Scharl, on the other hand, suggest that the passage from Justin includes the statement about Christ's work of recapitulation, and that Justin is therefore the initiator of this idea of recapitulation which is widely found in Irenaeus.[6] This latter opinion seems a possible one, and I doubt if we can get nearer to the true facts than this. It is quite a hopeless task to isolate, as Loofs does,[7] the doctrine of ἀνακεφαλαίωσις from the rest of the teaching which we find in *Adversus haereses*, and then to erect a limited and specific theology of recapitulation which is characteristic of Justin and "Irenaeus selbst," but which is unrelated to the principal sources of which *Adversus haereses* is composed, and which do not have the concept of *recapitulatio*. In point of fact it is *recapitulatio* which creates unity in the theology of Irenaeus, whatever the source of this concept may be.

Recapitulation means the accomplishment of God's plan of salvation, and this accomplishment is within history, in a time-sequence, and is not an episode at one particular point of time. It is a continuous process in which the οἰκονομία, *dispositio*, of God is manifested by degrees.[8] First, and most important of all—and the basis of our whole salvation—is the event of the birth of Jesus when the Son of God became an actual man. Many other things are consequent on this basic fact—the conflict, death, and Resurrection of Christ—but from one aspect what follows the primary event is simply a development of the resources of the power which was brought into the world through the child in Bethlehem. If we keep to the metaphor of conflict which we employed earlier, we might put it this way, that after

[5] Bousset, *Kyrios Christos*, p. 432, n. 1; J. Armitage Robinson, "On a quotation from Justin Martyr in Irenaeus," in *J.T.S.*, 1930, pp. 374–8. On the general problem of Justin and Irenaeus cf. Bousset, *Schulbitrieb*, pp. 307 f., and A. Nussbaumer, *Das Ursymbolum*, Paderborn 1921, pp. 82–5.

[6] Loofs, *Theophilus von Antiochien*, pp. 225–7, 359; Scharl, *Orientalia*, 1940, p. 400 f. Cf. Harnack, *History of Dogma*, VOL. II, p. 220, n. 1, who maintains the same view.

[7] See Loofs, *op. cit.*, pp. 359–64, 371 f. Loofs's attempt fails because of the technical impossibility of marking *unknown* sources off from one another.

[8] On the term οἰκονομία, see the tabulated analysis by A. d'Alès, "Le mot *oikonomia* dans la langue théologique de saint Irénée," in *Revue des études grecques*, 1919, pp. 1–9; Bonwetsch *Theologie des Irenäus*, p. 69, n. 1.

a power stronger than the occupying power has invaded the enemy-occupied territory, the sequel of this primary event, i.e. the defeat of the enemy, is often a *fait accompli*, but it is a sequel which is accomplished in conflict—victory ensues in a series of events, and not timelessly as a logical consequence of the fact that the invading power is stronger than the power of the enemy. The historians of dogma who maintain that in Irenaeus salvation is achieved through the physical Incarnation, and that from this view Christ's ethical struggle has no significance, are in complete error. There are so many references in Irenaeus to Christ's fight against temptation that we shall have to devote a whole chapter in this present section which deals with Christ to His conflict and victory alone. In doing so we shall come upon a new aspect of what is involved in recapitulation, i.e. that it is, to be perfectly simple, everything that Christ has done or is doing, from His birth through His Passion, death, and Resurrection, the Church and the Consummation, up to the time when He shall have "delivered up the kingdom to the Father" for eternity (1 Cor. xv.24).[9] Christ alone is the subject of recapitulation, and there is nothing which He does from His birth until the End which is not an integral part of recapitulation—everything is a part of the *ἀνακεφαλαίωσις*.

Recapitulation thus begins with the birth of Jesus of the Virgin Mary. The Son of God does not come into being at that point, for the world was created in Him, and He has been working in the old covenant, but before the time of His birth of Mary He has not been active as *recapitulator*.[10] It is only the Incarnate One, the One who has been made flesh, who recapi-

[9] Cf. Scharl, *Orientalia*, 1940, pp. 389, n. 2 and 407. Scharl's "intentional" recapitulation has almost the meaning of *predestination to recapitulation*, but Scharl himself admits on p. 389 that Irenaeus does not refer to the movement of Creation towards its destination in Christ by the term "recapitulation." It is only Scharl's "real" recapitulation which has the true Irenaean significance, and it is clearly connected with the Incarnation. The distinction between real and intentional recapitulation is not be to found in Irenaeus, and is due to Scharl's dependence on d'Alès, who in his own time made a separation between a "logical" and a "cosmic" recapitulation. See d'Alès, "La doctrine de la récapitulation en saint Irénée," in *Recherches de science religieuse*, 1916, p. 188, and Scharl, *op. cit.*, pp. 377, 379. On the use in the early Church of this particular term cf. d'Alès, *op. cit.*, p. 188 f. The Irenaean references are brought together in footnotes in d'Alès.

[10] Cf. *A.h.* IV. xxxiv. 8 (Stier. IV. xx. 8). Prophecy places *recapitulatio* in the future.

tulates.[11] All that Christ does from His birth at Bethlehem until the judgement of the world He does as the One who was incarnate. His humanity, His flesh, is part not only of His Passion and death, but also of His Resurrection and dominion over the world—He never gives up the humanity which he bore during the days of His earthly life. "He will come and reveal the glory of the Father in the same flesh in which He suffered."[12] While Christ is active, recapitulation continues "till he has put all his enemies under his feet" (1 Cor. xv.25) and "himself be subjected to him" that God may be "all in all" (1 Cor. xv. 28).[13] If the universal lordship of Christ is incomplete, His *recapitulatio* is incomplete. We must study every part of this whole time-process in which Christ is active before our picture of recapitulation is complete. But at this point let us turn our attention to the first section—Christ's becoming man.

It is characteristic of Irenaeus's exposition of the meaning of Creation that he understands the world and man as having been created in the Son and the Spirit. The separation and the contrast between God on the one side and the world together with man on the other is due not to any distinction which has been in existence from the beginning between spiritual and material, but rather is attributable to the victory which evil has gained over man, the destruction of the order established by God by His enemy, and the effective rupture of man's relationship with God. In the Incarnation there is to be seen the One in whom the world and man were created. In the birth of Jesus the

[11] It should be mentioned too that Irenaeus can use the term *recapitulatio* in its general sense, and say, for example, that a fuller passage of Scripture is recapitut lated in a summary, etc. Several such passages are quoted in Scharl, *Orientalia*, 1940, 378 p. f. Irenaeus also holds that Antichrist "in himself recapitulates the apostasy of the Devil," *A.h.* v. xxv. 1 (Stier. ibid.). In none of these instances, however, could Irenaeus have employed the term ἀνακεφαλαίωσις or *recapitulatio* withou-qualifying his use of the word. If a present-day theologian were to write a book on the work of Christ with the title *Deliverance* he would still be quite justified in using the word "deliverance" in its ordinary everyday sense. But it is merely confusing to introduce sentences into an analysis of the basic concept of a theologian such as Irenaeus which have merely the *word* and not the sense. In Irenaeus, *recapitulatio* —without any addition to qualify its meaning—invariably refers to the incarnate Christ. We shall return later to the question of Antichrist or the "beast" as the one who recapitulates evil.

[12] *A.h.* III. xvii. 8 (Stier. III. xvi. 8). Cf. *Epid.* 38 f.

[13] R.S.V. "everything to everyone." Cf. *A.h.* v. xxxvi (Stier. v. xxxvi. 2–3). In this latter passage man is perfected after the *imago* and *similitudo* of God.

source of life is made manifest in a world which had separated itself from the source of life and no longer was aware of its origin. Irenaeus holds Creation and the Incarnation together.[14] The same force underlies both. In Creation the whole of the universe comes into being, while in the Incarnation it is a single, hidden human being who comes into existence, but in this one man there is to be found the purity which the whole world has lost. The need of the world which God has created is to be liberated from sin, and sin has no power over the Man whom Mary bore. Men need only come to acquire what the incarnate Son possesses to be delivered from their bondage and return to the wholeness of Creation. And it was precisely to bestow upon men the life which He Himself possessed that Christ was born into the world.[15]

Since Creation appears in its unspoiled state through the Incarnation, there is therefore a similarity between Adam and Christ. Christ clothes Himself in the flesh of Adam. Adam has in fact been created in order to become like the Son. In the Incarnation the Son enters His Creation—He assumes flesh, and the flesh is Adam, who was created for Him, i.e. man. When God becomes incarnate, He becomes *man*. He gives His life, which is uncorrupted by any sin, to the human being, to man, who from the very beginning was destined to live eternal life without sin. Man therefore receives his fulfilment when the Son of God becomes through His human birth a man like us, or like Adam, with a human nature and lot, but without any

[14] See *A.h.* II. xxxvii. 1 (Stier. II xxv. 1), III. xi. 9 (Stier. III. xi. 5) (on this passage cf. Loewenich, *Johannes-Verständnis*, p. 133 f.); IV. xi. 1–2 (Stier. IV. vi. 2), IV. xi. 5 (Stier. IV. vi. 7—on the text at this point cf. Loofs, *Theophilus von Antiochien*, p. 381 f., note), and the somewhat obscure language of *A.h.* IV. lvi. 4 (Stier. IV. xxxiv. 4); and also *Epid.* 43.

[15] "Ostenso manifeste, quod in principio Verbum exsistens a pud Deum, per quem omnia facta sunt, qui et semper aderat generi humano, hunc in novissimis temporibus secundum praefinitum tempus a Patre, unitum suo plasmati, passibilem hominem factum, exclusa est omnis contradictio dicentium: Si ergo tunc natus est, non erat ergo ante Christus. Ostendimus enim, quia non tunc coepit Filius Dei, exsistens semper apud Patrem; sed quando incarnatus est, et homo factus, longam hominum expositionem in seipso recapitulavit, in compendio nobis salutem praestans, ut quod perdideramus in Adam, id est, secundum imaginem et similitudinem esse Dei, hoc in Christo Jesu reciperemus," *A.h.* III. xix. 1 (Stier. III. xviii. 1). Parallels in Irenaeus to the expression *in compendio* will be found in Loofs, *Theophilus von Antiochien*, p. 354, n. 5.

evil contamination. Irenaeus quite explicitly states that in this connexion recapitulation is integrally related to Adam, the first created man.[16] That which occurs in the Son's assumption of Adam ought to have taken place already in Creation—in Jesus Christ there appears the One who possesses everything that man as a creature ought to have, and nothing of what Adam brought upon himself as a result of his yielding to temptation. In the very centre of this connexion between Adam and Christ there is the profoundest contrast. Christ's connexion with Adam is in relation to Adam as a created being. His contrast with Adam is in relation to Adam as a fallen creature, as one who has been defeated by Satan.[17] For Christ assumes the "substance of Adam," though He is free from sin, undefeated, and unbound. As we shall see, however, it is in His human life that He confronts His enemy—in the temptations and the crucifixion—without, however, being defeated.

Not to receive Christ in His incarnation in faith means consequently to be part of destroyed Creation and not of unspoiled Creation, and the lack of those who so fail to receive Christ is not simply that they lack the "supernatural," but that they do not even live a "natural" life. They are "in Adam," who was defeated and who forfeited the life which matched his own nature. In other words, they are in Death, and fail to see that the form of human life which they value so highly has already been broken by the fetters of death, and that any who desire to receive life that is whole and unspoiled may do so freely and without cost, without depravity of the will and without corruption, in the new Man, the recapitulated Adam, the Son of Mary.[18] The Son of God has become a human being, and life has thereby entered our mortality and brought healing to the whole of the world. Irenaeus interprets the New Testament title of Son of Man so as to include the idea of Christ's becom-

[16] "Et antiquam plasmationem in se recapitulatus est . . . : ita recapitulans in se Adam ipse Verbum exsistens, ex Maria quae adhuc erat Virgo, recte accipiebat generationem Adae recapitulationis"; and cf. the following passage, *A.h.* III. xxx–xxxi. 1 (Stier. III. xxi. 9–10). See v. ii. 1 (Stier. ibid.) and *Epid.* 32.

[17] Both the contrast and the connexion are to be seen very clearly in *Epid.* 31 and also *A.h.* v. xiv. 1 (Stier. ibid.). On the translation of this latter passage, cf. Scharl, *Orientalia,* 1940, p. 394 f. See too Stoll, *Lehre des hl. Irenäus,* p. 51 f., who compares Irenaeus with Paul on this point.

[18] This is made quite clear in *A.h.* v. i. 3; cf. v. xxi. 1 (Stier. ibid.).

ing man—the Saviour is a son of a man.[19] It was in a human body that Christ was to endure His struggle, since sin had got its power in man. The Son of God had to invade humanity at the point where His enemy had gained a foothold, and there take up the struggle. Only if the Word was made flesh could the work of liberation be achieved.[20] The concept of becoming man in Irenaeus develops immediately and naturally into the concept of conflict and victory. We cannot dispense with either of these concepts and maintain that one comprehends the whole meaning of both, nor can we play one against the other and maintain that any subsequent line of thought could contain both. The two ideas are inseparably related, and if they are isolated from one another they are both inadequate and incomplete.

Irenaeus lays a very great deal of emphasis on the fact that it is the Son from all eternity, and therefore *God Himself*, who assumes human flesh in Jesus. The One who has created everything from nothing enters into His corrupt Creation in the Incarnation in order to renew it. Irenaeus is no less vigorous in his consistent emphasis that the eternal Son of God became a *man*, and that there is nothing lacking in His humanity. The divinity of Christ does not for a moment imply any diminishing of His humanity. If we isolate and analyse the natural characteristics of a human being, and then turn to Jesus Christ in order to see if any of these natural endowments are absent from Him, we discover that according to Irenaeus there is not a single part of humanity lacking in Him. If there were, it would mean that the sinless One had not wholly entered the sphere from which sin was to be expelled.[21] Sin is never in itself any-

[19] *A.h.* IV. li. 1 (Stier. IV. xxxiii. 2). Cf. also III. xi. 1 (Stier. III. x. 2), III. xvii. 2 (Stier. III. xvi. 3) and IV. lxiii. 1 (Stier. IV. xxxviii. 2) which has a special nuance: . . . *συνενηπίαζεν Υἱὸς τοῦ Θεοῦ, τέλειος ὢν, τῷ ἀνθρώπῳ*. . . .

[20] "So *the Word was made flesh*, that, through that very flesh which sin had ruled and dominated, it should lose its force and be no longer in us. And therefore our Lord took that same original formation as (His) entry into flesh, so that He might draw near and contend on behalf of the fathers, and conquer by Adam that which by Adam had stricken us down," *Epid.* 31. Cf. Rom. VIII. 3. We shall have a fresh opportunity of discussing the relation between Adam and Christ in the next section on *imago* and *similitudo*.

[21] *A.h.* III. xxxi. 2 (Stier. III. xxii. 2) and V. i. 2 (Stier. ibid.), and also III. XIX. 3 (Stier. III. xviii. 3). There is no contradiction to these passages in *A.h.* III. XX. 2–3

thing human, but on the contrary is the Devil's destruction of man as God made him. It is no limitation of Christ's humanity that He has no sin, but on the contrary His very freedom from sin qualifies Him for achieving the thing which is truly human, but which no other human being is capable of doing, for the whole of humanity is bound, captive, and unnatural.[22] Christ is God, and He is also man—these are not two irreconcilable truths. Very God and very man in one, with no separation between His divinity and His humanity—this is salvation: the presence of life in the world of death.[23]

We have seen above that the *Spirit* is life. The two hands of God at the Creation of the world were the Son and the Spirit, and when man estranged himself from God by reason of his sin, he cut himself off from God's hands. But in the Incarnation the hands of God lay hold of man again. The Son becomes flesh, and the Spirit makes His dwelling-place in a human body and soul. For this reason Jesus is called Christ, the One who is anointed with chrism, the anointing of the Spirit, just as a king is anointed for his rule over his people.[24] Jesus Christ means the anointed Jesus, the anointed One, the One who is filled by the Spirit, Jesus Messiah. We notice here how far Irenaeus is from Hellenistic thought with its tendency to define human and divine as two mutually opposed substances or natures, and how close he is to Hebraic thought, of which it was a characteristic that the Son and Revealer of God was descended from the house of David and was born of an earthly dynasty. For Irenaeus, the name of Christ had very much the meaning of its Hebrew equivalent, Messiah—a man who was anointed as king. Christ's kingdom is a spiritual kingdom, and He is anointed with the Spirit. There is no distinction between His

(Stier. III. xix. 2–3) despite Harnack, *History of Dogma*, VOL. II, pp. 284 ff. Harnack does not take into account sin as a factor which destroys what is human, nor growth as that which continues the development of what is truly human.

[22] There is a good definition in *A.h.* v. xiv. 2 (Stier. ibid.): "... *justa* caro recon ciliavit eam carnem, quae in *peccato* detinebatur, et in amicitiam adduxit Deo." Adam and Christ are the same flesh in the possession of two different powers, that of Satan and that of God (cf. Col. I.22). The latter part of *A.h.* III. xxv. 2 (Stier. III. xxi. 4) has the same essential meaning.

[23] Cf. how the divine and the human in Christ go together in the work of salvation in *A.h.* v. xvii. 3 (Stier. ibid.).

[24] See *Epid.* 47. Cf. Acts x.38.

humanity and His anointment, between Jesus and Christ, but the Spirit is incarnate in Jesus—in fact, we may say that the Spirit is incarnate in the same way as the body will be made a spiritual body in the resurrection, a σῶμα πνευματικόν.[25] The man Jesus possesses the Spirit, and gives the Spirit, i.e. Life, to men.[26] We shall see the point being discussed more clearly if we turn our attention to a different aspect of the idea with which we are dealing, i.e. to the idea of Christ as the *Verbum incarnatum*.

We find the same fundamental idea here too, for the *Verbum* is understood as a word which is spoken by God. The spoken word is never inactive or in equipoise between speaker and hearer. Simply because it is a *word*, it *issues* from someone and it is *received* by someone: Christ joins God and humanity together because He is the Word which God addresses to man. Irenaeus has an identical understanding of the Spirit in Christ —the Spirit is given by God to mankind in the anointed One, Jesus, and mankind is thereby united with God. The Spirit is like the Word in that both must proceed from the Saviour to men, since both are creative—they are the hands of the almighty God, and they must be continually active. The Spirit proceeds from God in the Incarnation, and moves directly to the Church, while the Word is addressed to men by God in the Incarnation, and nourishes the Church. We cannot say anything about Christ without also describing the Church, for

[25] The body which rises is wholly a *body*, despite the fact that it is spiritual. The change to such a "spiritual body" belongs to the Consummation. In the birth of Christ the movement was in the opposite direction. The Spirit became embodied. But the assumption in both cases is the same: the body and the Spirit are not opposed. The enemy of the Spirit is Satan, who is able to create great havoc in the body and "possess" it, but who in that very act of usurpation reveals himself to be an interloper who has no claim on the body.

[26] ". . . Jesum ipsum esse Filium Dei testificatus est, qui et unctus Spiritu sancto, Jesus Christus dicitur. Et est hic idem ex Maria natus," *A.h.* III. xii. 9 (Stier. III. xii. 7). See the whole of the previous section in III. xii, and also III. x (Stier. III. ix. 3): "Non enim Christus tunc descendit in Jesum; neque alius quidem Christus, alius vero Jesus; sed Verbum Dei, qui est Salvator omnium, et dominator coeli et terrae, qui est Jesus, quemadmodum ante ostendimus, qui et assumsit carnem, et unctus est a Patre Spiritu, Jesus Christus factus est." On the giving of the Spirit to men, see *A.h.* III. xviii. 1 (Stier. III. xvii. 1) and *Epid.* 53. Cf. Lk. IV.18. It is through the Spirit that the Church is begotten. The most interesting chapters in Loofs, *Theophilus von Antiochien*, pp. 182–210, also 269 f. (on Aphraates), deal with the Spirit-Christology; cf. p. 444. Loofs's theory of the Source IQA on pp. 234–57 is criticised by Hitchcock in *Z.NT.W.*, 1937, pp. 35–8.

Christ confers what He possesses, and the Church must extend. But I propose to postpone the analysis of Irenaeus's view of the Church to a later part of this present study. For the moment it is of greater importance to notice how the Irenaean concept of the *Verbum incarnatum* makes any distinction between the divine and human natures of Christ impossible.[27]

The *Verbum* is God's and is divine, but it comes to man through being spoken by Jesus Himself and being heard as every other human word is heard. A man moves among his fellow-beings, speaks to them, and has dealings with them. In the case of the divine Word—the *Verbum*—there is no progression to a certain point at which it assumes human substance and then communicates the divine to mankind. Rather, the concept of the *Word* shatters the concept of substance, and a function or dialectic movement between God and men appears in place of the two static natures, and it is the spoken and heard Word which unites man to God. God is in His Word, His Son, and the Word, that is the divine Word, is operative in His divinity because it is heard, i.e. because it is human, material, and corporeal.[28] If the humanity within the *Verbum incarnatum* were to be eliminated the divinity would simultaneously be lost. For Irenaeus, the same immediate relation exists between the Spirit and the man Jesus, the Anointed One.[29] It should be borne in mind that both the Word and the Spirit are the hands

[27] The starting-point of the discussion is the doctrine of the Word in the Prologue to the Gospel of St John, the doctrine of the Word which became flesh. See *A.h.* III. xi. 7–8 (Stier. III. xi. 1–3), v. xvi. 1 (Stier. v. xvi. 2), and v. xviii (Stier. ibid.) and also III. ix. 2 (Stier. III. ix. 1). It is in this way that Irenaeus interprets the term *recapitulatio*. Cf. Dufourcq, *Saint Irénée*, p. 183 f. Sanders, *Fourth Gospel*, p. 75 f. might also be mentioned.

[28] God addressed Adam in the cool of the day: "Where art thou?" (Gen. III. 9), and the same question will be addressed to man through the *Verbum incarnatum* at the last day, although man may have hidden himself in his sin. "Quemadmodum enim tunc ad Adam vespere locutus est exquirens illum Deus; sic in novissimis temporibus per eandem vocem visitavit exquirens genus ejus," *A.h.* v. xv. 4 (Stier. ibid.).

[29] It is for this reason that Irenaeus continually opposes those who "divide the Lord" into two substances, "ex altera et altera substantia dicentes eum factum," *A.h.* III. xvii. 5 (Stier. III. xvi. 5). Cf. II. xxx (Stier. II. xix. 4): ". . . sicut ipsi dicunt, contrarium esse terrenum spiritali et spiritale terreno." See also III. xviii. 3 (Stier. III. xvii. 4): ". . . alium autem Christum et alium Jesum intelligunt." This criticism of the Gnostics constantly recurs. Cf. H.-D. Simonin in *Rev. des sciences*, 1934, pp. 286 f.

with which God has created the heavens and the earth. Everything which exists has proceeded from the Son (the Word) and the Spirit (Wisdom). These creative hands are involved anew in creating in Christ, and in particular in laying hold on man in order to fashion him according to the decree of God, and in recapitulating the previous creation of Adam.[30] We shall understand this aspect of recapitulation better if we move on without delay to the concept of *imago* and *similitudo*.

Imago and Similitudo

We have seen from our study of Irenaeus's view of Creation that at the very beginning the Son is the *imago* and *similitudo* of God. When man is created in the *imago* and *similitudo* of God it means that he is created in the likeness of the Son and is destined for Him. In the Incarnation it is the eternal Son who becomes man and thus enters into Creation—into man who is destined for the Son from the beginning.[31] Such an assumption becomes inconceivable if our interpretation is based on a contrast between divine and human, and if we have set man and Christ over against one another. The relationship between Christ and man involves several complex questions. This present section as well as the following one which will deal with "God and man" will be devoted to such relevant questions in an attempt to be faithful to our intention to limit our discussion in this part at least to Christ Himself, and if possible to avoid discussing the Church, i.e. the significance of Christ for others. For the present we shall concentrate on Christ's own humanity, His own existence as man. When, in the next section on "God and man," we come to the core of Christology, this distinction will be seen to be impracticable, since it is part of Christ's

[30] Cf. *A.h.* III. xxx–xxxi. I (Stier. III. xxi. 10–xxii. I) with V. i. 2–3 (Stier. ibid.) and V. xiv. 2 (Stier. ibid.). On the Incarnation as the union of the Word with the flesh of Adam, see also *A.h.* I. i. 20 (Stier. I. ix. 3): *Σὰρξ δέ ἐστιν ἡ ἀρχαία ἐκ τοῦ χοῦ κατὰ τὸν Ἀδὰμ ἡ γεγονυῖα πλάσις ὑπὸ τοῦ Θεοῦ, ἣν ἀληθῶς γεγονέναι τὸν Λόγον τοῦ Θεοῦ ἐμήνυσεν ὁ Ἰωάννης* (Jn. I. 14).

[31] Cf. Klebba, *Anthropologie des hl. Irenaeus*, p. 24 f., where, however, the distinction between *imago* and *similitudo* is unjustified, and Loofs, *Theophilus von Antiochien*, pp. 253–6, 284, n. 2, and 386 with its instructive analysis in spite of its division of the sources; and finally P. Gächter in *Z.K.T.*, 1934, p. 511, and Scharl, *Orientalia*, 1940, pp. 390–2.

nature that he has been given for men. But it will help to clarify the point at issue to preserve this distinction for as long as it is possible.

It should, perhaps, be said by way of introduction that there has been a continuous debate in literature about Irenaeus on whether it is man who occupies the central place in his theology, or whether it is the work of God which has this position. There are many scholars who maintain that the basic thought of Irenaeus is marked by a strong anthropocentricity. Martin Werner vigorously asserts this point in his large work on the history of dogma published in 1941. He holds that the Irenaean doctrine of recapitulation is in fact an instance of the removal of eschatology in the post-apostolic period, and that what we find in him is a soteriology which is restricted to *man's* salvation rather than the great, eschatological cosmic drama, while God's activity is interpreted as being nothing more than an activity which ministers to the salvation of the believer.[32] It is quite incorrect to state, as Werner does, that redemptive history as an act of God in dealing with the cosmos is given a minor place in Irenaeus; on the contrary, most interpreters are in fact particularly offended by the largely naturalistic description which he gives in his account of the irruption of the end-period. And yet there is a certain justification in what Werner says, since the changing events of nature are quite definitely centred on that which befalls man, and man is the lord and central point of Creation—Creation exists for man's sake, and not man for Creation's.[33] In Irenaeus, however, the fact that redemptive activity is directed towards man is also related to the fact that the Devil's destruction of Creation is accomplished by way of man. Evil has man in its power, and it is in man that God's struggle against the Devil must be located. It is in this perspective that we have to look at the Incarnation, God's becoming man. When man is restored and receives eternal life God's decree for man is fulfilled, and it is fulfilled

[32] Werner, *Entstehung des christlichen Dogmas*, pp. 275, 390, 477 ff.

[33] "Et propter hoc conditio insumitur homini: non enim homo propter illam, sed conditio facta est propter hominem," *A.h.* v. xxix. 1 (Stier. ibid.); cf. the exegesis of Rom. VIII. 19–21 in v. xxxii. 1 (Stier. ibid.): "Oportet ergo et ipsam conditionem reintegratam ad pristinum, sine prohibitione servire justis." According to *Epid.* 11 the world has been created as man's dwelling-place.

against Satan,[34] for man is destined for *subjectio* to God and to be in a receptive relationship to God.[35] Werner's thesis must be rejected in the form in which it has been offered.

Other scholars insist on a completely different interpretation, and assert that everything in the theology of Irenaeus points to Christ and the accomplishment of God's eternal purpose—man has no significance at all in or by himself. Irenaeus has a passage in which he explains Paul's reasons for referring in Rom. v. 14 to Adam as "the type of the one that was to come," *τύπος τοῦ μέλλοντος*, *typus futuri.* This means, Irenaeus holds, that the Word, as the Creator of everything that is, foreordained the order of redemption to come for humanity *in Itself*, in the Word Itself which was to be incarnate in the future, in such a way that everything would culminate in Christ, who in Himself fulfils the decree of God in Creation. God fashioned psychic man (Adam) as one who was to obtain his salvation in the spiritual Man (Christ) (cf. 1 Cor. xv.45–49). "For since salvation existed beforehand, it was necessary that there should be created that which was to be saved, that salvation should not lack anything".[36] From this point of view man's history becomes quite secondary. The only reality of any significance is the Son. Moreover, this quotation from Irenaeus is by no means an isolated instance, as Hugo Koch points out in contradicting A. d'Alès, and there are other similar passages in the *Adversus haereses* which might be compared to it.[37]

[34] Cf. Montgomery Hitchcock, "The apostolic preaching of Irenaeus and its light on his doctrine of the Trinity," in *Hermathena*, 1907, pp. 328, 336 f.; Bonwetsch, *Theologie des Irenäus*, pp. 71–3. Man is drawn into the work of God; see *A.h.* III. xvii. 6 (Stier. III. xvi. 6) and IV. xxxiv. 6–7 (Stier. IV. xx. 6–7). Cf. also on this point Hunger in *Scholastik*, 1942, p. 171 f., and Prümm, "Zur Terminologie und zum Wesen der christlichen Neuheit bei Irenäus," in *Pisciculi F. J. Dölger dargeboten*, henceforth cited as *Pisciculi*, Münster 1939, p. 198.

[35] *A.h.* V. xxix. 1 (Stier. ibid.), in which *aeterna subjectio* is discussed in the middle of a passage which is apparently anthropocentric. *Subjectio* means submission and obedience to God.

[36] "Unde et a Paulo typus futuri dictus est ipse Adam: quoniam futuram circa Filium Dei humani generis dispositionem in semetipsum fabricator omnium Verbum praeformaverat, praedestinante Deo primum animalem hominem, videlicet ut a spiritali salvaretur. Cum enim praeexisteret salvans, oportebat et quod salvaretur fieri, uti non vacuum sit salvans," *A.h.* III. xxxii. 1 (Stier. III. xxii. 3). Cf. Harnack, *History of Dogma*, VOL. II, p. 265 f., and Böhringer, *Kirche Christi*, VOL. II, pp. 543 ff.

[37] There has been a lively debate in theological journals on the interpretation of the main passage which has just been quoted, especially among Roman Catholic

How is it possible that different interpreters can form such a completely different judgement on the same subject-matter? One important reason for the difference of opinion in this connexion might well be a theological misunderstanding of the nature of God as outgiving love. Anders Nygren's radical approach to Irenaeus has something to say to us at this point. God, he explains, is central, but God is *love*, and love is such that it gives to another than itself—and so unworthy man thereby comes into the centre. Christ does not compete with man to see which one of them is the more important, but He who was from eternity gives Himself in the uttermost humility in order to come to man and save him.[38] This is the basic view of Irenaeus, and if we forget it, all our subsequent discussion gets out of balance. We may afterwards emphasise in a certain context the eternity of the Son and God's purpose to sum up all things in Christ, or again emphasise man's need of redemption in some other context, but the central fact is God's love in Christ, a love which seeks evil man and aims at restoring him from his defeat. It seems as if we ought now to recognise more generally again that the movement of God's love to man is a truth to which the whole of the New Testament bears witness.[39] In Sweden, Einar Billing has long ago stressed this line of approach.[40] Irenaeus thus displays a primitive Christian line of thought, which cannot always be said about modern theologians who are attempting to free themselves from the liberal Protestant tradition by simply remaining silent about man, or being

scholars, but unfortunately with a somewhat distorted method of discussion derived from the Middle Ages (which might lead one to ask if the main question is really whether Irenaeus followed Thomas or Duns Scotus!). See d'Alès in *Recherches de science religieuse*, 1916, pp. 191 ff., in which the problem is put; Koch in *Theol. Stud. u. Krit.*, 1925, p. 210 f.; Prümm in *Scholastik*, 1938, p. 362; and Escoula in *N.R.T.*, 1939, p. 388 f., where this particular method of inquiry is finally terminated.

[38] See Nygren, *Agape and Eros*, pp. 392–412. Nygren's comprehensive view of Irenaeus puts many points in a new light, and brings order and continuity to the subject with which he is dealing. We shall be dealing with those aspects of his interpretation of Irenaeus which we can discuss (e.g. the "immortality of the soul" and "divinisation") in the final section of Part III when we are discussing "*Imago* and *similitudo*."

[39] See Hering, *Biblische Grundlagen*, pp. 15 ff.; and Cullmann, *Christ and Time*, pp. 108 f., 217–21.

[40] E. Billing, *De etiska tankarna i urkristendomen*, 2nd edn. Stockholm 1936, pp. 412ff. 431 f.

detrimental in their references to man. It was, however, a relatively new development for Irenaeus to take up, as he did, the direct exposition and analysis of the doctrine of man.[41] Whether, by so doing, he in fact separated himself from primitive Christianity is a question which has not yet been answered by anyone who has sufficiently dealt with the sources.[42]

The characteristic confusion of divine and human which we noticed earlier in Irenaeus's use of the concept of "*imago et similitudo Dei*" makes it possible for us to offer some kind of interpretation. We might expect that in regard to the incarnate Christ Irenaeus would say, first, that He is like God, that He is the image of God, and also that He is like Adam and had assumed the form of Adam—and these two diametrically opposed propositions ought, presumably, to be interchangeable, for Adam was created in the image of God, and therefore He who is the image of God ought *eo ipso* to be like Adam. In fact, the writings of Irenaeus confirm to a remarkable degree that this presupposition is justified. In this we are confronted with a major difficulty—are divine and human the same thing for Irenaeus, and is Christ true God *because* He is true man? If not, then what is the difference between divine and human? We shall be dealing with this problem presently, but in the meantime we shall first discuss the statements in Irenaeus about the likeness of the Incarnate One to God and His likeness to Adam.

It has been said that man's likeness to God is certainly mentioned in the account of Creation, but it is not "demonstrated,"[43]

[41] See, however, e.g., the *Epistle to Diognetus* (date uncertain), x. 2 (*Die apostolischen Väter*, ed. Bihlmeyer, Tübingen 1924, p. 147).

[42] In regard to the New Testament, cf. also Lohmeyer, *Briefe*, p. 55, with Col. i. 15 on the concept of *εἰκών*: "Das 'Bild' Gottes hat von allen diesen Funktionen nur die eine, ichbezogen zu sein. Es ist nicht zufällig, dass Menschen die Ebenbildlichkeit Gottes tragen oder zu tragen bestimmt sind; niemals heisst so die Welt als ganze."

[43] *'Εν τοῖς πρόσθεν χρόνοις ἐλέγετο μὲν κατ' εἰκόνα Θεοῦ γεγονέναι τὸν ἄνθρωπον, οὐκ ἐδείκνυτο δέ· ἔτι γὰρ ἀόρατος ἦν ὁ Λόγος, οὗ κατ' εἰκόνα ὁ ἄνθρωπος ἐγεγόνει· διὰ τοῦτο δὴ καὶ τὴν ὁμοίωσιν ῥαδίως ἀπέβαλεν. 'Οπότε δὲ σὰρξ ἐγένετο ὁ Λόγος τοῦ Θεοῦ, τὰ ἀμφότερα ἐπεκύρωσε· καὶ γὰρ καὶ τὴν εἰκόνα ἔδειξεν ἀληθῶς, αὐτὸς τοῦτο γενόμενος ὅπερ ἦν ἡ εἰκὼν αὐτοῦ· καὶ τὴν ὁμοίωσιν βεβαίως κατέστησε, συνεξομοιώσας τὸν ἄνθρωπον τῷ ἀοράτῳ πατρί*, *A.h.* v. xvi. 1 (Stier. v. xvi. 2). This is one of the few passages where *εἰκών* and *ὁμοίωσις* are distinguished. The text is debated in Loofs, *Theophilus von Antiochien*, pp. 250–4, and in Montgomery Hitchcock in *Z.NT.W.*, 1937, p. 37. We shall return to the discussion of this point.

for the *Logos*, in whose image man was formed, was not yet visible and had not been made flesh. It was for this reason too that man forthwith lost his likeness to God, and his yielding to temptation meant that evil had destroyed the image of God. But when the *Logos* became flesh, He secured the image and likeness by making the image of God visible and by Himself becoming what man, who had been fashioned after Him, was himself, and also by transforming man into the likeness of the invisible Father. Since the Son is a manifestation of God and at the same time an actual becoming real of the original man who was created in the image of God, the Incarnation presents a double aspect to us, or a double "demonstration": it is *God* who reveals Himself, but in this very act of His self-disclosure it is also revealed what *man* ought to be, and indeed what sort of man he actually is in his unfallen state. We can see in other words what in man's actual status is God's pure and uncorrupted creation, and what is the destruction or deterioration of that creation by evil. The Son is the image of the Father.[44] But the Son is also man's antetype, the model or pattern after whom man was formed, at the time when he was created from the dust of the earth. As the Incarnate One He reveals God for the very purpose of redeeming man. We do not possess God in His majesty by His becoming man in Jesus Christ, but we do have Him in His goodness and love.[45] It is not within the power of man to find out God, despite His participation in manhood, but Jesus gives man power to *believe*, and in so doing makes him the child of God. It was for this purpose that the Lord came—to establish communion between God and man.

Irenaeus is very emphatic that in the Incarnation Christ assumes the form of Adam, thereby recapitulating His image and creation.[46] Had he not done so, the man whom God at the beginning had destined for life would still be subject to death, in complete contradiction to the purpose of God. If man is to

[44] Cf. the somewhat obscure words of *A.h.* IV. xxx (Stier. IV. xvii. 6). Attempts to interpret the passage have been made by Robinson in *J.T.S.*, 1931, p. 160 f., and Hunger in *Scholastik*, 1942, p. 175. See, however, *A.h.* IV. xxxiv. 9, at the beginning (Stier. IV. xx. 9).

[45] *A.h.* IV. xxxiv. 3–5 (Stier. IV. xx. 4–5).

[46] *A.h.* V. xxi. 1 (Stier. ibid.), V. xvi. 1 (Stier. V. xvi. 2), and *Epid.* 22. On this latter passage cf. Scharl, *Orientalia*, 1940, p. 390, n. 2 (a quotation from A. Struker).

be saved, it is necessary that the first man, Adam, be brought back to life, and not simply that a new and perfect man who bears no relation to Adam should appear on the earth. God, who has life, must permit His life to enter into "Adam," the man who truly hungers and thirsts, eats and drinks, is wearied and needs to rest (Jn. IV.6), who knows anxiety, sorrow (Jn. XI.34) and joy, and who suffers pain when confronted with the fact of death.[47] The *Verbum* has assumed the old creation of Adam, infused it with God's undefeated life, and thereby renewed it.[48] No other life than that of God Himself could accomplish the miracle of this renewal, for in the original creation man was set over the angels, and there was no creature within creation who stood over man—and it was this pre-eminent life which Satan had succeeded in obtaining by false pretence and subjecting to death. If man were to be refashioned by anyone, it would have to be the Creator Himself, who has in fact done such a thing in the wholly divine creative activity of His eternal "hands." For the accomplishment of this particular task there was something required which had never before existed in Creation, viz. that God Himself should become man—not simply that He should create a living being *like* God, viz. man, but that He should actually *become* a man. Christ is God and Adam, true God and true man.[49] He brings us to God and God to us. In Him God is like man and man is like God.[50]

We shall be able to see the distinctiveness of Irenaeus's thought at this point if we isolate part of it for examination, and select, for example, the statements which we find in several parts of his writings on the Virgin Birth. In later periods the birth of Jesus of a Virgin was regarded exclusively as a sign of His divinity. For Irenaeus, on the other hand, the miraculous birth of our Lord testifies rather to His connexion with *Adam*—Adam was taken from the virgin soil and had no earthly father. God purposed to employ the same procedure in the restoration of man; in Jesus's birth there was to be a recognisable similarity to Adam's coming into existence, and man would thus come to

[47] *A.h.* III. xxxi. 2 (Stier. III. xxii. 2).

[48] Cf. *A.h.* III. xxxii. 2 (Stier. III. xxiii. 1) and V. i. 1–2. (Stier. ibid.). See especially III. xxxi. 1 (Stier. III. xxii. 1).

[49] *A.h.* IV. xi. 5 (Stier. IV. vi. 7). Cf. Nygren, *Agape and Eros*, p. 278.

[50] Scharl, *Orientalia*, 1940, p. 409 f.

be in accordance with the image and likeness of God, as it was written that he should from the very beginning.[51] Christ came to seek the lost sheep, and man was lost. The purpose in preserving this connexion with Adam in the Incarnation was to eliminate the appearance of any completely new factor in Creation, and to effect the rescue of what in fact was lost or old.[52] And in order to establish this contact with Adam, the Son of God received human form from the Virgin Mary. Both of these factors, the absence of a human father and the co-operation of the earthly mother, testify, according to Irenaeus, to the same fact—the recapitulation of Adam.[53] If God had taken the dust of the ground and formed a completely new and perfect man instead of allowing Jesus to be born, then Adam would not have been restored. His birth of the Virgin Mary testifies to Christ's humanity. If God had allowed Jesus to be born as the son of an ordinary husband and wife, as all the descendants of Adam were born, His birth would have been unlike Adam's, and would have had no similarity to the creation of man. Mary's virginity bears witness to Christ's resemblance to Adam, i.e. to His humanity.[54]

This does not, of course, mean that for Irenaeus the birth of Jesus had nothing of the character of a miracle. It is simply that his discussion of the miracle of Christ's birth was on a different

[51] *Epid.* 32; see Wieten's translation, *Irenaeus' geschrift*, p. 37. (Out of five translations which I have consulted there are not two which have exactly the same meaning. Each has its own distinct emphasis in translating this passage. Cf. *Patrologia orientalis*, VOL. XII, pp. 684, 772.) See also Bonwetsch, *Theologie des Irenäus*, p. 96.

[52] *Epid.* 33. Cf. *Epid.* 31.

[53] The stress in the doctrine of the Virgin Birth is still at this period on "born." Cf. *Epid.* 66. See Bousset, *Kyrios Christos*, p. 427, n. 2, and also W. Scherer, "Zur Mariologie des hl. Irenäus," in *Z.K.T.*, 1923, p. 122. It would perhaps be profitable to examine the function occupied by the doctrine of the Virgin Birth in various periods.

[54] *Εἰ τοίνυν ὁ πρῶτος Ἀδὰμ ἔσχε πατέρα ἄνθρωπον, καὶ ἐκ σπέρματος ἐγεννήθη, εἰκὸς ἦν καὶ τὸν δεύτερον Ἀδὰμ λέγειν ἐξ Ἰωσὴφ γεγεννῆσθαι. Εἰ δὲ ἐκεῖνος ἐκ γῆς ἐλήφθη, πλάστης δὲ αὐτοῦ ὁ Θεὸς, ἔδει καὶ τὸν ἀνακεφαλαιούμενον εἰς αὐτὸν, ὑπὸ τοῦ Θεοῦ πεπλασμένον ἄνθρωπον, τὴν αὐτὴν ἐκείνῳ τῆς γεννήσεως ἔχειν ὁμοιότητα. Εἰς τί οὖν πάλιν οὐκ ἔλαβε χοῦν ὁ Θεὸς, ἀλλ' ἐκ Μαρίας ἐνήργησε τὴν πλάσιν γενέσθαι; Ἵνα μὴ ἄλλη πλάσις γένηται, μηδὲ ἄλλο τὸ σωζόμενον ᾖ, ἀλλ' αὐτὸς ἐκεῖνος ἀνακεφαλαιωθῇ, τηρουμένης τῆς ὁμοιότητος*, *A.h.* III. xxxi. 1 (Stier. III. xxi. 10). In *ανακεφαλαίωσις* there is partly a connexion with what has gone before, and partly a new beginning. See also Ström, *Vetekornet*, p. 335 f.

level from the discussion of miracles which we generally find. For modern thought the appearance in history and the work of Jesus is something natural, i.e. it is something which has been fitted into an accepted picture of the ongoing movement of history. "Miracles" are isolated details which do away with or diminish the humanity of Jesus which He shares with other men. For Irenaeus, the primary miracle is that man is, that God has created him. In the second place, it is an even greater miracle that God, when man became bound and imprisoned in his selfishness, has allowed Christ to live as a man on earth, a perfect and uncorrupted man whom Satan failed to capture and corrupt. The great and the essential miracle is Christ's humanity, i.e. His renewal of Adam, His *recapitulatio* of the old Creation, and His representation of the *imago* and *similitudo* of God without blemish. God enters the world in order to re-create it by becoming man in Christ, and this divine miracle is effected, Irenaeus maintains, by way of the Virgin Birth; there are many passages in Irenaeus which demonstrate how it is that this birth from the Spirit of God constitutes the ground of Christ's own ability to give the Spirit to men, and to be active among men as the "Anointed" and bestow His life upon them.[55] But Christ's divinity is not to be set over against His humanity: on the contrary, it is by the power of His divinity that He can expel from men all that is evil and demonic, and in His earthly life, as a man among men, realise God's purpose for man.

But while Irenaeus maintains this profound connexion between divine and human, he also preserves the distance between Christ and man in the clearest possible way. Since man was created in the likeness of the Son, the Son therefore stands over him and is specifically distinct from him.[56] The definition of the Incarnation is that God has become man. There is in the Incarnation something that is essentially different from what

[55] *A.h.* III. xxvi. 2 (Stier. III. xxi. 6). Irenaeus lays stress on the fact that through His conception by the Holy Spirit Jesus is separate from men in general. Cf. *Epid.* 51, 53 and 57. In spite of the Virgin Birth Jesus is regarded as having come "of the seed of David." His descent is through Mary rather than Joseph. See *A.h.* III. xxvi. 1 (Stier. III. xxi. 5) and III. xxix (Stier. III. xxi. 9).

[56] *A.h.* IV. lii. 1 (Stier. IV. xxxiii. 4). Cf. Bonwetsch, *Theologie des Irenäus*, pp. 104–11, and the unusually large number of relevant texts which have been appended in the footnotes to these pages.

we find in Creation, even when Creation is at its most perfect. That which became a reality in the Incarnation is not present even as a potentiality in man. He is destined to be like God, but he has never been destined to be God.[57] Out of all mankind only Jesus Christ is God. When the eternal Son of God was born as man, what also took place was that, simultaneously with this event of God's becoming man, the actual human being whom Mary bore, and in whom the fullness of God dwelt bodily, was in his actual birth a pure being, free from sin, and therefore the perfection of humanity as such. And this fulfilment of humanity was due to the fact that God became man in Christ, a principle which is to be completely distinguished from any question of human perfectability as such, and He became man since only God can defeat the Devil, i.e. remove man's enemy from man. It is essential for any understanding of the relationship between the divine and the human in the Incarnate Christ that we should see that the contrast between God and Satan is one which is immediately related to our condition.[58] To emphasise the point which we are making more sharply: Christ is man because He is God, but other men cannot be true men because they are subject to Satan, the destroyer of our humanity.

In Christ we see the *imago* and *similitudo* of God. In the beginning man was created in the *imago* and *similitudo* of God, but man was only a child, and, even before the Fall, did not achieve the *imago* and *similitudo*. In the Incarnation man takes flesh and blood in accordance with the purpose which God has for him, and in Christ we see on earth man in his full maturity and development.[59] From one point of view Jesus is the

[57] See Bonwetsch, *op. cit.*, p. 157. Even Prümm concedes this, though in other respects he is inclined to err in his interpretation in the direction of later doctrines of deification. See e.g. *Scholastik*, 1938, p. 216, n. 20. Cf. Klebba, *Anthropologie des hl. Irenaeus*, p. 186 f.

[58] Bousset, *Kyrios Christos*, pp. 437–42, overlooks this. It must, in particular, be stated that the unwillingness to take the dualism between God and evil seriously in the systematic interpretation of Irenaeus has resulted in the failure on the part of certain scholars to have even an elementary understanding of the ideas and the relationships between these ideas in the *Adversus haereses*.

[59] Prümm in *Pisciculi*, p. 198: "Aber es ist eben doch die Menschheit des Herrn, von der das Abgeschlossen—und Vollendetsein ausgesagt wird, und sie ist als Eigentum und Gut der Gattung Mensch betrachtet. . . . In der gottmenschlichen Person Jesu des Herrn steht also Vollendung verwirklicht da suf der Ebene des Geschöpfes."

perfection of human nature. If man who had been created by God had developed in his unfallen condition as God intended, he would have become like the man Christ. In the humanity of the Incarnation we are confronted with a humanity which surpasses that of Creation, but which is nevertheless the humanity of Creation.[60] "Growth" links identity with change, progression, and development. The full-grown man is different from the child, and yet the same. We shall see more clearly how it is that Christ, as man, is the man whom God created in his developed and full-grown form if we try at the same time to bear in mind the contrast which we have stressed above between God and evil, Life and Death, the Creator and Satan. These two ideas—first, of growth, and second, of the conflict between God and His adversary—are to be clearly distinguished. Man is a living being, protected by the power of God from the onslaught of death, and a growing personality who is wounded by the adversary but protected by the Father. In the Fall man's growth and life are arrested; in the Incarnation they are triumphantly revived, for death must of necessity yield to God Himself, and God becomes man in Christ.

God and Man

Up to this point there has been a certain lack of precision throughout our study in defining the relationship between the divine and human in Christ, a lack which we have noticed in Irenaeus himself at this point, for there are times when he seems to be asserting Christ's divinity as over against His humanity while elsewhere he appears to reverse the process,[61] and we get the impression that if we were to insist on his providing us with a clear definition of Christ's divinity as distinct from His humanity, we should be forcing him into the position of having to set Christ's divinity and humanity over against

[60] Hunger in *Scholastik*, 1942, pp. 170–3. Hunger's clarity is to a certain extent marred by his being influenced by Scharl and his "intentional" recapitulation (see notes on p. 172 f.) which we find some difficulty in accepting.

[61] In works on Irenaeus it is sometimes said that Irenaeus confuses "nature" with "the supernatural," e.g. Hugo Koch in *Theol. Stud. u. Krit.*, 1925, pp. 194, 204, 207, 213; and Prümm in *Scholastik*, 1938, pp. 212, 347. Bonwetsch, *Theologie des Irenäus*, p. 74, also makes use of the same unhelpful terminology.

one another in order to give a sufficiently clear answer to our question, in so doing destroying what is central to his theology. It will be necessary to have a less sharply defined distinction between God and man if we are not to lose sight of the specifically Irenaean concept of "growth"—a continuity in history which has no distinct lines of division, and no break, distinction, or discontinuity, at any point of its line of progression. And yet this would be a misleading impression to convey of what Irenaeus is in fact saying, for he continually maintains a precise distinction between God and man, though the distinction is such that it does not force him to contrast the two substances, divine and human, but in actual fact rather clarifies his concept of "growth." Our present task is to analyse this distinction and to try to understand the uniqueness of humanity and divinity. For the most part we shall be able to keep to the references which we discussed in the earlier section, and shall not have to overload the pages with further quotations from the sources as much as we have done up to this point.

If we are going to deal with the problem in the proper order we ought to begin with the question of the relationship between the divinity of the Father and the divinity of the Son. In the first place Irenaeus notes here that we do not know how the Son proceeded from the Father.[62] Of this we have no knowledge, but we do know that, as God, the Son is eternal, begotten of the Father from eternity. The one concern of Irenaeus is to explain how God acts in Christ who was made man—God Himself is in Christ and offers His salvation in His incarnate Son, for only the Creator can save men from the Devil.[63] This does not mean that the Son was born from eternity as Son of the Father in order to be born in the Incarnation as son of man. If we were to ascribe such a finality to the eternal birth of the Son from the Father, defining it in terms, ultimately, of the Incarnation, we should then, as Harnack rightly pointed out, be expressing a speculative judgement on the impenetrable mystery of the eternal birth of the Son,[64] and in a manner foreign to Irenaeus be

[62] *A.h.* II. lii. 4 (Stier. II. xxviii. 6). Cf. Seeberg, *Lehrbuch der Dogmengeschichte*, VOL. I, p. 402.

[63] See Aulén, *Den kristna försoningstanken*, pp. 44–6; and Nygren, *Agape and Eros*, pp. 278 ff. Cf. Bousset, *Kyrios Christos*, pp. 429–32.

[64] Harnack, *History of Dogma*, VOL. II, p. 265 f. Cf. the whole section from p. 262.

virtually putting *man* into the centre of the divine life within the Trinity before the Creation of the world.[65] In this, as in other respects, Irenaeus limits himself to the facts. God has in fact revealed Himself in Christ, and through Him has entered human life, constrained by His very mercy and love to come to man in his helplessness.

If Christ is the visible aspect of the Father—as Irenaeus puts it, "the Father is the invisible aspect of the Son, the Son the visible aspect of the Father"—and His divinity is thus the same as that of the Father, it is no less true that Christ's humanity is the same as our humanity.[66] Christ has undergone every period and circumstance of human life without leaving anything outside Himself, i.e. without leaving anything in the possession of Satan.[67] The Incarnate One, it is true, is without sin, and in being sinless He lacks what is common to all men, but His lack is the lack of that which corrupts man's humanity. If Christ too had been bound in sin He would not have been more human than He in fact now is, but less human. And, moreover, if He himself had been defeated, He would not have had the power to liberate man. The humanity in which Jesus lived was the pure humanity which God had created, and over which evil had no hold. It was the humanity of the Adam whom God had created, not of the Adam who was defeated. Despite His righteousness Christ shared man's lot in the form of sinful flesh, and suffered even death, the fruit of sin, for it was through sin that death had come into the world. Death had no place in

[65] Such an erroneous view of Christology might thus provide a basis for the theory of the essential anthropocentricity of the theology of Irenaeus. This theory is, in fact, maintained by Werner, *Entstehung des christlichen Dogmas*, p. 390.

[66] " . . . invisibile etenim Filii Pater, visibile autem Patris Filius," *A.h.* IV. xi. 4 (Stier. IV. vi. 6).

[67] In *A.h.* II. xxxiii (Stier. II. xxii. 3–6) Irenaeus attempts to prove that Jesus lived to between 40 and 50 years of age, so that it might be said that He had lived through every age. It follows from this that the Crucifixion should have taken place under Claudius Caesar—as Irenaeus also maintains in *Epid.* 74. On this question see Hitchcock, *Irenaeus of Lugdunum*, p. 318 f. According to Hoh, *Lehre des hl. Irenäus*, pp. 160–6, 202 f., Irenaeus's position on this question was to be explained by Jewish influences (a rabbi ought to be at least 40). The theological connexion with the concept of recapitulation is apparent from *A.h.* II. xxxiii. 2 (Stier. II. xxii. 4) and III. xix. 6 (Stier. III. xviii. 7): "Quapropter et per omnem venit aetatem, omnibus restituens eam quae est ad Deum communionem." Cf. *A.h.* IV. lxiii. 1 (Stier. IV. xxxviii. 2): the Son becomes a human child.

God's Creation, but gained its mastery first through evil and in man's yielding to temptation. The oneness of the Saviour with fallen man extends to death itself and to the very depths of man's nothingness.[68] The *Verbum* of the Creator who alone brings forth all life in the universe, the Word of the Creator which became man, was encompassed by His enemy, Death, in order that He might break from within the hold which death had over man, and free him for new life and growth.

This is precisely what Christ is able to do because He is God, and has the power of God in His humanity. It would be quite obviously incorrect to hold that for Irenaeus Christ's divinity and His humanity are the same reality, or to maintain that Christ is God *because* He is man. It is possible in a sense to say the opposite, viz. that Christ is man because He is God. But such a definition is liable to be completely misunderstood if it is interpreted as an identification of divine and human nature, as though it were of little consequence how we designated a substance which in and by itself is uniform. To say that Christ is man because He is God would be correct only in the light of the dualism it implied. In his bondage to the Serpent man is incapable of realising himself, and he is impeded and powerless in his attempt to realise his humanity. One who is stronger than man must repel and bind man's tormentor and adversary. There is only *one* who is strong enough—God. And God is in Christ.[69] God, who has the strength to defeat Satan, is in humanity and expels Satan from humanity so that man is liberated to be himself and can be what he rightfully should be, viz. uncorrupted, as he was when he proceeded from God's hand in the state of innocence at the beginning of Creation. Man in Jesus is like that: He is man as he was at the beginning of Creation, man in his uncorrupted state, and His humanity is the pure humanity because His divinity is pure divinity, and sin must flee from it. The purpose of the Creator concerning humanity has been fulfilled, and in the humanity of the incarnate Lord man has grown to his full stature.

[68] Tiililä, *Das Strafleiden Christi*, p. 124 f., holds that Irenaeus lays stress on Christ's work *qua homo*. This is true, although it does not imply any support from Irenaeus for later theories of satisfaction.

[69] See the powerful exegesis of Mk. III. 27 in *A.h.* v. xxi. 3 (Stier. ibid.).

The theology of Irenaeus has two distinctive characteristics: first, the whole of his theology is marked by his contrast between God and the Devil, and the ceaselessly raging conflict between the two powers, a conflict which is fought out in the midst of our humanity; and second, this humanity, independently of the conflict we have mentioned, is continually in process of change, developing and altering its form, but never remaining in the same fixed pattern. In Irenaeus's thinking both processes are frequently interconnected, and it is hardly surprising if at times it is difficult to express precisely and in generally agreed terminology the difference and the connexion between the two concepts. The division of Irenaeus's writings into their respective sources and the unfortunate two-line system of interpretation have both arisen on the basis of inexactitudes and awkwardnesses in the *Adversus haereses*; and many of his so-called illogicalities are no more than alleged, and are in fact to be explained by the modern interpreters' inadequate acquaintance with the thought-world of Irenaeus. It cannot, of course, be denied that there are certain theoretical and terminological inconsistencies in Irenaeus, but for those who are seeking to understand what he says and what are his basic ideas, all these insignificant blemishes are lost in the general picture which his writings convey. We are hardly justified in referring to Irenaeus as one of the greatest thinkers of Christianity, but one fact is beyond dispute: none of the modern theologians who have broken up his theology into two or more sections comes anywhere near Irenaeus as a systematic theologian.[70]

The critical analysis of the *Adversus haereses* from the standpoint of the history of Dogma has in the main suffered from a peculiar inconsistency. On the one hand scholars have adopted a superior attitude to Irenaeus, as they have done to most ancient authors, and have disparaged his primitive exegesis and obscure ideas; but on the other hand it was inconceivable to them that the contradictions for which so muddle-headed a thinker as Irenaeus was responsible should be evident only at

[70] *A.h.* is characterised by great systematic power, *Epid.* not to the same extent. Ireneaus is one of those who need the stimulus of refuting false ideas in order to produce their best work. *A.h.* is polemical, but not *Epid.* Loofs, *Theophilus von Antiochien*, p. 434 f., has a completely different view of the difference between *A.h.* and *Epid.*

certain points in his writings, and they obviously thought that Irenaeus's inferiority should at least be consistent. Otherwise it was meaningless to assume two different sources, since two concepts, which they held to be incompatible, are to be found in the *Adversus haereses.* If it is a matter of dividing early writings into their sources, then many of the insignificant writers of the early Church will automatically be transformed into penetrating theorists who adopted a single, consistent line of thought, and their sources will fall apart with smooth precision according to the law of contradiction. We are nevertheless bound to admit that Irenaeus had the same human failings as characterise writers of the present day. In one place, for instance, he overstresses a particular idea which he has to balance elsewhere by a secondary idea derived from the first; minor inconsistencies creep in, and so on.[71] Unimportant details such as these will be best corrected if the reader takes the proper attitude to the book which he is studying. If it is put squarely before the reader that his responsibility is to comprehend the meaning and intention of the author, then minor imperfections in a good author become of no consequence at all. Irenaeus comes into this category. Our task is to try to understand his basic idea, though it is so markedly dynamic in character, with its two variable elements of conflict and growth woven into one another.

Having established that Christ's divinity makes Him one with the Father, and that His humanity makes Him one with us, we are now confronted with the main problem, viz. the relationship between the divinity and the humanity of Christ. By His Incarnation our Lord brought God down to men through the Spirit, and man to God by His assumption of human flesh.[72] It is quite clear that Irenaeus does not regard the divinity and

[71] From one point of view it can be said that Loofs's division of the sources of *A.h.* is based on an *overrating* of Irenaeus and especially, of course, of his logically defined sources. At the same time Irenaeus is very much underestimated; see Loofs, *Theophilus von Antiochien,* p. iii. The overrating is involuntary, and is expressed in the distinguishing of sources—a discrepancy in Irenaeus's own line of thought is presumably inconceivable!

[72] ". . . et effundente Spiritum Patris in adunitionem et communionem Dei et hominis, ad homines quidem deponente Deum per Spiritum, ad Deum autem rursus imponente hominem per suam incarnationem," *A.h.* v. i. 2 (Stier. v. i. 1). Cf. Scharl, *Orientalia,* 1940, p. 409 f.

the humanity of the Incarnation as being mutually exclusive concepts, and in his exegesis of the meaning of forgiveness the co-operation of God and man in Christ is markedly apparent. Only God can forgive (for only God has given the Law which we have broken), and when Jesus in fact forgives sinners, He is demonstrably the *Verbum*, the Word in human form, who has received power from the Father to forgive. He has this power to forgive as God and as man, and in the Saviour's enactment of forgiveness God and man are uniquely related when it is declared that as man He has compassion on us, or suffers with us, and that as God He has mercy upon us and forgives us our debts.[73] Divine nature is the antithesis of human nature only when we have conceived of a deistic, transcendent, and static God to whom the Incarnation is something alien. And it is clear that, if we define divinity by itself in such terms as these, the Incarnation will contradict our very conception of God, since it will be difficult to elicit the meaning of the Incarnation theoretically. Irenaeus, on the other hand, allows his conception of God—God is love—to be determined by the Incarnation, and this conception of God can admit the humanity of Christ—the Man with the word of forgiveness is the God who voluntarily impoverishes Himself and who seeks man whom He created.[74]

In works on Irenaeus it has been quite customary to start

[73] "Peccata igitur remittens, hominem quidem curavit, semetipsum autem manifeste ostendit quis esset. Si enim nemo potest remittere peccata, nisi solus Deus; remittebat autem haec Dominus, et curabat homines; manifeste quoniam ipse erat Verbum Dei Filius hominis factus, a Patre potestatem remissionis peccatorum accipiens, quoniam homo, et quoniam Deus, ut quomodo homo compassus est nobis, tanquam Deus misereatur nostri et remittat nobis debita nostra, quae factori nostro debemus Deo," *A.h.* v. xvii. 3 (Stier. ibid.; Stieren's text seems to be better than Harvey's at this point).

[74] The historians of dogma have discussed Christ's divinity and humanity at length: see, e.g., Böhringer, *Kirche Christi*, VOL. II, pp. 540–7; Harnack, *History of Dogma*, VOL. I, pp. 275–87; Bousset, *Kyrios Christos*, pp. 432–44; Seeberg, *Lehrbuch der Dogmengeschichte*, VOL. I, pp. 405–10; Bonwetsch, *Theologie des Irenäus*, pp. 94–112; and, in a powerful argument against an older generation of scholars, Brunner, *The Mediator*, pp. 249–64. The question of the "natures" is not always related to the simple concept which we find in Irenaeus of God's love or forgiveness, but the first three of the above-named scholars do so adequately. There is an interesting, though now obsolete, interpretation, coloured by Hegelianism, in I. A. Dorner, *Entwicklungsgeschichte der Lehre von der Person Christi*, 2nd edn. Stuttgart and Berlin 1851, VOL. I, pp. 480–96, Eng. trans. *History of the Development of the Doctrine of Christ*, Edinburgh 1861, DIV. I, VOL. I, pp. 314–26. Dorner finds in Irenaeus his own favourite theory of the growing unity between divine and human.

from a self-evident contrast between divine and human nature, God and the world, or heavenly substance and earthly substance. Scholars have begun their investigation of a particular problem, e.g. the doctrine of the Eucharist in Irenaeus, or his anthropology, with a general scheme—that God is opposed to man—which is inconsistent with Irenaeus's own general scheme, for God does not oppose man, but in fact gives Himself to man in love.[75] It is then, of course, that the actual text of Irenaeus begins to present difficulties. When we speak of "ethical" and "physical" as being two mutually exclusive lines of thought, this false antithesis is in fact merely a consequence of the fundamental unanalysed contrast between divine and human, for if we have defined divine and human nature as two incompatible substances, it follows that everything which is personal, or ethical, or has to do with will or conflict, is excluded from the idea of the Incarnation, which thus becomes no more than "physical," while the "ethical" is merely an accompaniment to this "dogma." Just as he refused to oppose divine and human, Irenaeus made no distinction between "physical" and "ethical."[76]

But if Irenaeus does not obliterate the difference between God and man, nor set an insuperable gulf between them, it remains for us to express positively how God and man can be inseparably united in Christ without confusion. As far as may be known, in fact, the functions which unite God and man must be essential to God as well as to man, so that they are united when God does what is divine and man in the same act does what is human, that is, when God and man are perform-

[75] With regard to the doctrine of the Eucharist, see the excellent contribution by H.-D. Simonin in *Rev. des sciences*, 1934, p. 283. Simonin considers that the idea of transubstantiation is derived from an un-Irenaean contrast between heavenly and earthly, and struggles to avoid this obstacle to the understanding of Irenaeus, but without success. With regard to anthropology, see the similarly informative article by P. Gächter in *Z.K.T.*, 1934, p. 530 f., which makes the traditional contrast between the two natures; awkward problems follow when this traditional contrast is applied to Irenaeus's writings, which then become intractable. The importance which Loofs attaches to "die Geistchristologie" in the early Church is balanced by a remarkable affinity with Irenaeus on this point; see Loofs, *Theophilus von Antiochien*, pp. 256, 274 f., 280 (the last-mentioned pages deal with Aphraates). Cf. Wieten, *Irenaeus' geschrift*, p. 187.

[76] There is an erroneous distinction made between ethical and physical in Loofs, *Theophilus von Antiochen*, p. 303 f. Prümm attempts to correct this in *Pisciculi*, pp. 209–12 (using other terms, "dynamic" and "ontic").

ing their respective parts. We shall see the connexion between God and man most clearly if now we leave the problem of the Incarnation altogether and examine instead the relationship between God and man in general. It is highly illuminating to see how Irenaeus understands *life*, the power of life, or the fact that man lives.

In a certain passage Irenaeus is involved in refuting the objections raised by the Gnostics against the resurrection, and in particular their objection that our flesh could not receive eternal life. Irenaeus refutes this by simply saying that our bodies have life *now*. To be living beings, like the Gnostics themselves, and say that our bodies cannot receive life is like holding a sponge full of water in one's hand and saying that it cannot absorb water.[77] The fact that we live testifies to two things: first, that God the Creator *wills to give* us life (for He gives us what is real), and, second, that we *are able to receive* life (for we have in fact life in our bodies). Life comes from the Creator and is within us. When our body lies motionless in death, it is still our body, although its life is gone. Life is something different from ourselves, something which is given to us, and which can therefore also be taken away from us. But when we receive it, the gift is not something which exists apart from us, but is one with us—*we live*.[78] In this simple fact of our being alive there are two completely different processes involved—*God gives*, and *man receives*. Life flows from the hands of the Creator and fills His creatures who live by the life which He gives them. The characteristic life of the body is a fulfilment of the word, "(God's) power is made perfect in weakness" (II Cor. XII.9).[79] The resurrection life means essentially the same thing: God gives and we receive.[80] We are weak, and God is strong, but

[77] *A.h.* v. iii. 5 (Stier. ibid.).

[78] *Ὅτι γὰρ ἐπιδεκτικὴ ζωῆς ἐστιν ἡ σάρξ, ἐκ τοῦ ζῆν δείκνυται· ζῇ δέ, ἐφ' ὅσον αὐτὴν ὁ Θεὸς θέλει ζῆν. Ὅτι δὲ καὶ ὁ Θεὸς δυνατὸς παρέχειν αὐτῇ τὴν ζωήν, δῆλον· ἐκείνου γὰρ παρέχοντος ἡμῖν τὴν ζωὴν* [sc. *ζῶμεν*], *A.h.* v. iii. 3. Cf. *A.h.* II. lvi (Stier. II. xxxiv. 2–4), v. ii. 3, and the end of v. xxi. 3 (Stier. ibid.).

[79] *A.h.* v. iii. 1. The following section v. iii. 2 (Stier. ibid.) is of great interest from the point of view of the concept of Creation.

[80] For Irenaeus, *life* in all its forms is a unity, a work of God's Creation and a miracle. The resurrection is a miracle, but it is also a miracle that we are alive. Cf. III. xviii. 1 (Stier. III. xvii. 2). All that Irenaeus says about the Eucharist is based on the assumption that our life is a unity.

strength and weakness are related to one another; they are not, however, competitive or antagonistic, but have their own particular tasks, even opposite tasks, and each retains its own specific function—power gives, and weakness receives. They are then united while being quite clearly distinguished from one another in function.[81]

In our analysis of the concept of growth in the above discussion we have several times based our argument on this unity of man's receiving and God's giving. Man's "growth" is simply one aspect of the fact that God creates. As long as man does not break this fellowship with the Creator, he is continually given power to grow from God who is the source and origin of all life, and this power is not something which is substantially different from man, but rather appears in his own free, organic, and natural growth towards his destiny. If God were to sustain humanity in indissoluble fellowship, without sin and without any hostility towards God on the part of man to disrupt the relationship, humanity would grow unimpeded towards its goal and become full grown. If we were to ask Irenaeus where pure humanity is to be found on earth, he would point to Christ, who is perfect human nature. Again, if we were to ask Irenaeus where God has become united with humanity, he would point to Christ, who is true God and true man. And the two things are distinct: humanity's growth towards Christ's humanity is one thing, and the unification of the divine with fully-developed humanity is another; but they are related, and the former is possible only on the basis of the latter. *When God who gives is in humanity, humanity grows.* But to say that God is united with humanity means that sin, which separates God and man, and creates enmity between them, is not in humanity.[82] The unity of God and man in Christ is in itself, as a unity of these two, as *Incarnation*, a blow struck at the power of Satan. In the midst of

[81] Cf. *A.h.* IV. lxiv. 2 (Stier. IV. xxxix. 2): "Facere enim proprium est benignitatis Dei: fieri autem proprium est hominis naturae. Si igitur tradideris ei quod est tuum, id est, fides in eum et subjectionem, recipies ejus artem, et eris perfectum opus Dei." On the same idea in *Epid.*, see Wieten, *Irenaeus' geschrift*, p. 185. *A.h.* IV. xxi. 2 (Stier. IV. xi. 2), which deals with man's growth, is also very striking.

[82] If there were sin in Christ's humanity, God would not be united with it, for this humanity would have set itself against God in active sinfulness, like everything else that is human and bound by the Serpent.

conflict there is growth. Satan turns away from man, and man grows in freedom and receives life from the hand of the present and creating God. All this is accomplished in Christ who keeps nothing for Himself, but lives for others—for us and for all men.

God is Creator, man is created. This difference between God and man will never be abolished. For this reason there will be a difference between Christ and man until the Consummation in eternity. Christ gives to man, and we receive from Christ. Man is never transformed into God in such a way as to become Creator. But man and God are one when God creates and man is created. In the union which is achieved by Christ in His re-creation and reconciliation man is changed into the likeness of God, without actually becoming God.[83] What happens in this transformation is simply that man's creation is made complete, or that man has been created in the likeness of God (Gen. 1.26.f.). In the resurrection of the dead and the Consummation of all things man's creation will be brought to its fulfilment. But even then man will be only man, though his humanity will have been restored through Christ's work of salvation.

As will be evident from the chapter heading, the aspect of the work of Christ which we have been considering up to this point is His becoming man. We have not yet dealt with the life, death, and resurrection of Jesus, but we shall now proceed to consider them without further delay, and the chapter heading of "Victory" will be quite appropriate for the discussion of these subjects. All that we have said here about Christ's becoming man corresponds to what we said about Creation in Part I of the present study. Unblemished Creation reappears through the birth of Christ, and the primal state returns in new and more perfect form. As the chapter on Creation was followed by that on Defeat, so the present chapter which deals with Christ's becoming man will be followed by that which deals with

[83] When Christ recapitulates the creation of Adam in the Incarnation, it is something *created* which Christ assumes. By being the new Adam Christ becomes non-creative. Adam could never create, even in his absolute purity and sinlessness. Adam could only be created, i.e. grow. The one who creates is God in Christ. Divinity and humanity remain distinctly apart. Only thus can ἀνακεφαλαίωσις be effected.

Victory. And all that we shall be saying about Victory will correspond to what we have said about Defeat in Part I of our study, except that the movement is reversed, for then it was man who faced Satan and went astray, whereas now it is Christ who faces Satan and triumphs over him. From this point of view Christ's becoming man is an invasion at a point where battle is about to begin, though not indeed on enemy coast, for "He came to His own home" (Jn. I.11), but on enemy-occupied territory, in which God's enemy has wrongfully gained control.[84] Christ has been born and has assumed manhood, and the battle begins. Man has fallen from life to death as a result of his defeat, but he will be removed from death to life through the victory of Christ.

Before concluding the present section on God and man in Christ we should consider, in preparation for what follows, a point which we have already stressed above—divinity does not imply the least limitation of humanity. It is easy to say this, but it is difficult for us today to take it seriously. When, for instance, we speak of a great artist who has been afflicted by a terrible misfortune, but who in the midst of his afflictions has been attentive to the inspiration of his genius and has given the world a work of perfection, we can well see that his gifts did not lessen his human need but rather increased it. It would be quite correct to say that if anyone is thus gifted he can do such things. No comparable work of art is produced when a man with no out of the ordinary gifts comes up against the same extreme suffering. The talent must be present, and talent is innate. But if the conclusion which is drawn from this undeniable fact is that there was therefore no great achievement in producing the work of art, then such a conclusion is manifestly absurd. The talents of the artist bore fruit not in being unaffected by his sufferings but in being bound up with his fate in life. Genius and agony together produced the artist's work, taxing his resources in the effort. Genius and suffering do not counteract

[84] See *Epid.* 31 in particular, but also 37. Cf. *A.h.* III. xix. 5–6 (Stier. III. xviii. 6–7); at the end of this passage there are the familiar words, "Deus, hominis antiquam plasmationem in se recapitulans, ut occideret quidem peccatum, evacuaret autem mortem, et vivificaret hominem . . ." On this point see Aulén, *Den kristna försoningstanken*, pp. 42 ff. This is one of the most important passages in Aulén.

each other, so that suffering becomes of less importance and genius of greater.[85]

Irenaeus speaks similarly and quite naturally of Christ as God without His humanity being thereby lessened. God is in the Incarnate, and it is for this reason that Christ defeats Satan and has power to create. But God is in a *man*, who is tempted in the wilderness and trembles in Gethsemane. The agony which He has to endure was not easier than ours because of His Godhood, but more terrible than any other man has suffered. If we are going to understand Irenaeus we must see this clearly, otherwise we may conceive of Christ's victory as being purely a logical consequence of His divine nature, when in actual fact it was achieved only in the hardest conflict.

[85] It should perhaps be added that both are human factors, and it is not a matter of saying that one or other of them is divine. But from one point of view their interrelationship is analogous to the relationship between divine and human in Christ.

CHAPTER II

VICTORY

Conflict

CHRIST'S struggle is a struggle about man and for man. The conflict for man does not begin when Jesus becomes man. The first encounter in the struggle has long since been concluded by the time of Jesus's birth, and evil has triumphed. The world of men is defeated and in bondage. Christ's conflict with the enemies of humanity begins in a hopeless situation. Man's defeat is a fact.

The meaning of man's defeat, it will be recalled, is his subservience to two alien powers: *sin* has power over man, so that man does what is wrong, and *death* has power over man, so that life departs from him. Man is a slave to these two tyrants. Every means of overthrowing sin and death has been tried, and all human resources are now exhausted. But the primary factor in the power of the adversary is the strength of sin, for disobedience has cut man off from the source of life. The power of death is a fruit of the power of sin.[1] The only possibility of transforming defeat into victory and freedom for man is that the tyranny of sin must first be destroyed by man's resisting every temptation to do wrong—then death's hold over man can be broken.

Jesus Christ is man. He belongs to our race. As man He must confront both sin and death. In His temptation He takes sin upon Him, and on the Cross death itself finally enfolds Him. But neither of the two enemies of humanity can get this man into its power. Christ resists temptation and He rises from the dead. And when a man forces both evil and corruption to turn

[1] Cf. Bonwetsch, *Theologie des Irenäus*, p. 79 f.; and Klebba, *Anthropologie des hl. Irenaeus*, p. 53.

away from Him, as Jesus does, the purpose for man is realised, for man was ordained to live and to live in righteousness.

Christ has come into the world in order to fight a battle. He was born not only to reveal God and show man's nature in its purity, but also was sent as an armed man into enemy-occupied territory. His purpose was battle and His mission was victory, for only so could man be rescued and God's image revealed. Since the victory of our Lord was completed when death had been crushed, it is very often said that the Son came "to defeat death."[2] But such a definition in fact includes the whole of His conflict in all its aspects, from the beginning of His life, through His temptations and sufferings on the Cross, to the decisive victory of His Resurrection.[3] The Resurrection revealed that Jesus was the strong and invincible one who confronted Satan in the wilderness and along the whole of the way to the Cross. The conflict is immediate, though the victories do not appear until later. When the final mighty victory was disclosed at Easter, it was the climax of a succession of victories which was then revealed. Irenaeus strongly emphasises that the suffering and obedience of Jesus means the abolition of sin, the destruction of the domination of disobedience and the expulsion of evil from humanity. Christ is man, and He is obedient to God—by this act the Devil stands powerless before man, and for the first time since man's defeat at the dawn of the human race man holds his ground before the attack which is made on him.[4] The victory which breaks through in Christ's resurrection from the dead is essentially the same reality as the victory of Christ's obedience over temptation. To the Devil both mean the same thing: man, hitherto in bondage, is free, pulled from the clutches of his enemy, and restored to the Life of righteousness.

Irenaeus particularly emphasises that the struggle between Christ and Satan is a struggle which concerns *man*. In his exegesis of Mt. XII.29 Irenaeus examines the meaning of

[2] E.g. *Epid.* 6, and also 31, 33, and 37–9; cf. *Epid.* 78 and the last part of *A.h.* IV. lxiii. 3 (Stier. IV. xxxviii. 4).

[3] Cf. *Epid.* 34. This becomes especially clear in his extended exegesis of the Temptation narrative in *A.h.* v. xxi–xxiv (Stier. ibid.).

[4] *A.h.* III. xix. 5 (Stier. III. xviii. 5–6). See Scharl, *Orientalia*, 1940, pp. 412 ff., in which, however, Scharl's interpretation issues in a Bride-mysticism which is not typical of Irenaeus.

"goods" and "house." It is clear beforehand that he who enters into a strong man's house and spoils his goods after he has first bound the strong man is the Lord in His overpowering of the Devil. And the "goods" of the strong man which Christ snatches from him are we who have wrongfully and unnaturally been put into the house of evil. Jesus has power to spoil the house of the strong robber and release us.[5] The Devil is a usurper who has taken man into his possession and got him into the false position of bondage to evil. The divine Word, who is the Creator of all life, had therefore to take upon Himself the form of man, had to become a man, and break man's fetters from within, and defeat man's overlord. When he is free and when he is himself, i.e. in communion with God the Creator, man has also a richer life than his adversary, the fallen angel, for his enemy was never created or destined to become the image of God, even before his fall and in uncorrupted Creation, but man was.[6] Man's inhumanity is his depravity, and the fact that he is the robber's possession. His deliverance through the work of Christ restores his humanity to him, and in his deliverance Satan is now subject to man. In Christ man has power over evil. The Incarnate One says to men: "Behold, I have given you authority to tread upon serpents and scorpions, and over all the power of the enemy" (Lk. x.19).[7]

The conflict between the Son of man and His adversary, who

[5] *A.h.* III. viii. 2 (Stier. ibid.). Cf. III. xxxiii. 2 (Stier. III. xxiii. 3), IV. xxxviii. 1 (Stier. IV. xxiv. 1), IV. lxvi. 2 (Stier. IV. xl. 3), and V. i. 1 (Stier. ibid.), and most important of all V. xxi. 3 (Stier. ibid.).

[6] It was man's higher position which from the beginning aroused the "envy" of the angels, and this in turn brought sin.

[7] "Quemadmodum autem si quis apostata regionem aliquam hostiliter capiens, perturbet eos qui in ea sunt, ut Regis gloriam sibi vindicet apud ignorantes quod apostata et latro sit: sic etiam Diabolus, cum sit unus ex angelis his, qui super spiritum aeris praepositi sunt, quemadmodum Paulus Apostolus in ea quae est ad Ephesios manifestavit, invidens homini, apostata a divina factus est lege: invidia enim aliena est a Deo. Et quoniam per hominem traducta est apostasia ejus, et examinatio sententiae ejus, homo factus est, ad hoc magisque semetipsum contrarium constituit homini, invidens vitae ejus, et in sua potestate apostatica volens concludere eum. Omnium autem artifex Verbum Dei, per hominem vincens eum, et apostatam ostendens, e contrario subjecit eum homini: Ecce, dicens, do vobis potestatem calcandi super serpentes, et scorpiones, et super omnem virtutem inimici; ut quemadmodum dominatus est homini per apostasiam, sic iterum per hominem recurrentem ad Deum, evacuetur apostasia ejus," *A.h.* V. xxiv. 4 (Stier. ibid.). For the description of the angels' rebellion see also *Epid.* 16.

is a manslayer, a "murderer" from the beginning (Jn. VIII.44), has resulted in his utter defeat. The Giver of life takes man and gives him human life again. God has triumphed utterly, and His victory has been achieved through One who was indeed a man, who was tempted and put to death, who penetrated into enemy territory, and demolished every stronghold of the enemy.[8] But before the triumphant Christ has gone through all this His enemy has inflicted terrible sufferings on Him. There is something false in any intepretation of Irenaeus which by-passes the need and humility of Christ, and from the beginning simply adopts the standpoint of the victory which has been achieved, without taking into consideration the price of the conflict. Christ's victory over death and unrighteousness is indeed determined *a priori* in the counsel of God, and, according to the Irenaean concept of the sovereignty of God, which tends always to run into a concept of pre-existence, it already exists in God before it is achieved on earth in the actual human conflict—the victory already exists in God because what God wills *is*. We can thus understand those who in their interpretation of Irenaeus dismiss the lengthy struggle which Jesus had to endure, and disregard time as well, treating evil timelessly as meaningless and insignificant.[9] But their method of reading Irenaeus, though intelligible, does not square with what he actually says. To treat the work of God in Christ timelessly is to disregard the humanity of Jesus, and hardly anything is less typical of Irenaeus than this timelessness. It is in the *man* Jesus that God's victory is to be achieved, and His humanity implies a long-drawn-out, gradual conflict.

Irenaeus methodically adduces proofs of the humanity, humiliation, and weakness of Jesus. On the Cross He was broken as a man who has suffered is broken. The events of the Crucifixion were throughout within the will of God, but not in such a way that Christ's humanity was thereby annulled in His suffering and death; God rather used this humanity in order to

[8] *A.h.* III. xix. 5–6 (Stier. III. xviii. 6–7) speaks of the victory in powerful terms.

[9] There is a tendency to do this in D. B. Reynders in *Recherches de théologie ancienne et médiévale*, 1936, pp. 225–52, and in Escoula in *N.R.T.*, 1939, pp. 390–400; see p. 397, footnote. Among German Protestant Irenaeus scholars there is generally no such timelessness, but rather a progressive, even, historical, evolution which destroys the idea of a *conflict* between good and evil.

attain His purpose of opening the way for man to righteousness. Irenaeus's consideration of the suffering of our Lord is very closely connected with his exegesis of Isaiah LIII.[10] And here as elsewhere the point of his polemic is directed against Gnosticism which, with its basically docetic view, made the Saviour's human agony and forsakenness into a fiction, or at least found great difficulty in the idea that Christ had really suffered and known the agony of fear.[11] In studies of Irenaeus this stress on the human aspect of Christ's suffering has frequently escaped notice and it has been disputed whether such a feature of *qua homo* consideration of the death of Christ is to be found in the statements which Irenaeus makes about Christ's death and atonement. The explanation of this lack of critical discernment may well be that scholars have had a fixed idea in advance of how the subject-matter, which emphasises Christ's work as a man, should be arranged: in which case the emphasis would be on the substitutionary sacrifice which was offered to God, the idea of satisfaction, and the conception of the offering made by Jesus as man to God, which God is willing to regard as having been performed by the whole of mankind. It would be extremely difficult to find this idea in Irenaeus, who sees the significance of the humanity of Jesus as something completely different.[12]

As man Jesus Christ confronts the power which has defeated man. It is not in the first instance to God that Jesus addresses His work, but rather He faces the enemy of God, who is at the same time man's enemy, for by His creation man is God's. The humanity of Jesus therefore means that when Jesus in His work of salvation achieves His victory over God's enemy, man in the same act is restored and purified, since it is in man that the victory has been achieved. Only then has God triumphed, since it was man whom the enemy seized and destroyed. The destruction of Satan could have been effected apart from the humanity

[10] See *Epid.* 68–70.

[11] *A.h.* III. xix. 2–6 (Stier. III. xviii. 3–7). The doctrines of *recapitulatio* and of *imago* and *similitudo* are here connected.

[12] Cf. the characteristic exposition of the problem in Harnack, *History of Dogma*, VOL. II, pp. 291–3. Aulén's understanding of the subject as compared with Harnack's has meant an important alteration in the very framing of the problem. See *Den kristna försoningstanken*, p. 41 f.

of Jesus, but man whom God had created would not then have been redeemed but rather destroyed, and a wholly different, new, and pure creation would instead have come from God's hand. The humanity of Jesus means that original Creation is saved and revived.[13] And the restoration of original Creation to righteousness required Jesus's struggle as a man, the struggle which He waged in His human life in the face of bitter opposition from inhuman forces. He could not abandon His humanity without betraying both God His Father and His brother men. Only in humility and destitution could His work be accomplished. For this He underwent the ultimate human experience of death. If He had fled from death man would never have gained life, for death would then have remained undefeated in the world.

Jesus's likeness to fallen man, however, was seen not only in His death on the Cross, but as clearly was shown in His temptations in the wilderness. That which befell the Son of man when He was tempted by the Devil is exactly parallel to what happened to Adam when he was tempted. Both were tempted to eat and to satisfy the human desire for food. Irenaeus explicitly points out that Jesus's hunger in the wilderness is a proof of His true humanity.[14] Irenaeus later returns to the examination of the humanity, submissive to God and quite without power, in Jesus's answer to each of the temptations to which He was exposed—Jesus's victory lay in the fact that He was a man who was obedient, and obedient to the same God as Adam disobeyed when he fell, viz. the God of Creation and of the Law. He said first: "Man shall not live by bread alone"; then: "You shall not tempt the Lord your God"; and finally: "You shall worship the Lord your God, and Him only shall you serve" (Mt. IV.1–10).[15] Jesus's whole attitude is the opposite of Adam's.

[13] Christ's *humanity* is inadequately treated by Aulén, *op. cit.*, pp. 65–7. This is bound up with his relative lack of interest in Irenaeus's concept of Creation. The concept of recapitulation relates everything in Irenaeus to his belief about Creation. Cf. Rivière, *Dogme de la rédemption*, pp. 110–12. The victory is God's, though it is achieved by a pure man. See *A.h.* III. xxxii. 2 (Stier. III. xxiii. 1), IV. lii. 1 (Stier. IV. xxxiii. 4) and V. xxii. 1 (Stier. ibid.).

[14] ". . . postea esuriit, ut hominem eum verum et firmum intellegamus: proprium enim est hominis, jejunantem esurire," *A.h.* V. xxi. 2 (Stier. ibid.).

[15] "Elatio itaque sensus quae fuit in serpente, dissoluta est per eam quae fuit in homine humilitas . . . et soluta est ea quae fuerat in Adam praecepti Dei praevar-

Jesus is as a man without divine power, but even so He is obedient, i.e. is one with God. Adam listens to the word, "You shall be as gods," but he is disobedient, i.e. he is cut off from God. Adam reaches out after God-likeness and life, but falls and dies. Jesus descends to human destitution and death, but rises to life indestructible through His Resurrection.[16]

The words with which Jesus repulses and vanquishes Satan and exposes him are words from the Old Testament, from the Law (Deut. VIII.3, VI.16, 13).[17] The One who was tempted in the wilderness stands under the Law and is a man, obedient to God who created man and gave the Commandments. Both the defeat of man (in Adam) and his victory (in Jesus) take place in the Kingdom of the Creator. The former goes against the Creator's commandment and corrupts His Creation, the latter follows His commandment and purifies His Creation. Irenaeus's exegesis of the Temptation narrative fits into his theological outlook as a whole particularly well, and it is quite unjustified to remove this exegesis as a special detachable "source," as some scholars suggest should be done.[18] Since man has been overcome by temptation and since Christ has come in the Incarnation to save men, He not only renews man's creation in His birth and becoming man, but He has also tc reverse man's defeat and end his bondage. In the *recapitulatio* the conflict which Jesus waged as a man was as necessary a part as His birth or Incarnation. With commendable clarity Irenaeus holds together these two sides of his belief about Christ. Funda-

icatio, per praeceptum legis, quod servavit Filius hominis non transgredien, praeceptum Dei," *A.h.* v. xxi. 2. Cf. also Harnack, *History of Dogma*, VOL. IIS p. 290; Bonwetsch, *Theologie des Irenäus*, pp. 102–4; and Rivière, *Dogme de la rédemption*, pp. 106–8.

[16] The significance of the victory is developed in *A.h.* v. xxi. 3 (Stier. ibid.) in reference to Mt. XII. 29. Jesus's victory over the Devil has already initially been won in the wilderness when the Tempter is forced to retreat. In the Crucifixion too it is *obedience* which is triumphant and which removes the sting from death. Disobedience and death are related just as obedience and life are related. Sec *Epid.* 34. Cf. too Hering, *Biblischen Grundlagen*, pp. 29–34.

[17] The whole of the line of thought from *A.h.* v. xxi. 2 to v. xxiv. 4 (Stier. ibid.) is dominated by this fundamental thesis and its consequence—the unity of Creation and Incarnation.

[18] This, roughly, is Bousset's position, see *Schulbetrieb*, p. 279; the hypothesis is developed by Loofs, *Theophilus von Antiochien*, pp. 81, 96 ff. Cf. Cremers in *Bijdragen*, 1938, p. 37.

mentally they are both one, for the Incarnation continues in conflict. Through His birth, temptations, and suffering, Christ becomes a man among men.

Irenaeus treats the death of Jesus in the same way as His temptation in the wilderness. The Crucifixion is not principally a sacrifice offered to God, but is Jesus's entering into the darkness where man is held prisoner. As Jesus was tempted in order to destroy sin, so He was put to death in order to destroy death.[19] In both temptation and Crucifixion Christ breaks right through the opposition of His adversary without being held back by the snares in which Adam was caught—in fact, these bonds of the enemy are torn aside by Christ's power and are rendered ineffective as shackles to hold man in bondage. The Incarnate One *is* man—in and through His survival and freedom man survives and is free.[20] Man has been created to live and not to die, and he reaches this goal of his humanity in the Resurrection of Jesus. The resurrection life is not an unnatural addition to what is truly human, but is the uncorrupted life of Creation, and as such it breaks through into an unnatural world in which death holds dominion. Jesus's way forward to the victory of the life of Creation passed through the Crucifixion. Christ had to descend into human life as it was, and then—with man alive within Himself—break out of the barriers and shatter all that was pressing man's life out of him.

Irenaeus always thinks of life as a manifestation of God's creative power and of death as a manifestation of the Devil's

[19] Disobedience and death which hold sway in man form a connected whole. See e.g. *A.h.* v. xxiii. 1 (Stier. ibid.). The temptations in the wilderness and the death on the Cross are therefore different forms of a single mighty attack on Jesus, and ultimately Jesus's victory over His temptations in the wilderness is as injurious to His enemy as His obedient agony on the Cross and His resurrection from the grave. In both the same power, the same freedom, and the same pure and unharmed humanity, are manifested, for death is as unnatural and inhuman as sin. Jesus removes the power from both.

[20] "Propter hoc et Dominus semetipsum Filium Hominis confitetur, principalem hominem illum, ex quo ea quae secundum mulierem est plasmatio facta est, in semetipsum recapitulans: uti quemadmodum per hominem victum descendit in mortem genus nostrum, sic iterum per hominem victorem ascendamus in vitam. Et quemadmodum accepit palmam mors per hominem adversus nos, sic iterum nos adversus mortem per hominem accipiamus palmam," *A.h.* v. xxi. 1 (Stier. ibid.). It is *man*, recapitulated man, who is victorious in Christ's resurrection. On the idea of salvation as the nullifying of man's defeat, cf. *A.h.* v. xix. 1 (Stier. ibid.).

power of destruction. The death and life of Jesus, the Cross and the Resurrection together, are a battle between God and Satan in which at first evil seems to have succeeded, but immediately afterwards it is the Satanic power which falls in its own arrogant rapacity. Behind the life of Jesus—His whole life, both before the Cross and after the Resurrection—we must continually be thinking of the Creator, and behind death the active attack on the Creator. The battle surges to and fro. The death of Jesus cannot be isolated from His earthly life and Resurrection. Like the hunger and destitution in the wilderness, the Crucifixion was a moment when the Satanic powers rallied in their greatest force, but such tremendous concentrations of evil made possible the destruction of the power of evil. Christ has gone through it all undefeated, and man, who is protected by Christ and cannot be harmed, is now in Christ.[21] The more violent the attack of the enemy, the more crushing his defeat becomes. In the death of Jesus the strength of the Devil is spent, and when it comes to an end in the Resurrection, the whole of this alien domination is broken, and man lives directly from God as in Creation before sin had entered in.[22]

It has been a frequent allegation in works on Irenaeus that for him the Crucifixion has no essential significance for man's salvation.[23] The basis for such an assertion is a doctrine of the Atonement which came to be formulated at a later period, and which gave a significance to the death of Jesus that was completely independent of His Resurrection, and indeed which

[21] "Sic igitur Verbum Dei homo factus est, quemadmodum et Moyses ait: Deus, vera opera ejus. Si autem non factus caro parebat quasi caro, non erat verum opus ejus. Quod autem parebat, hoc et erat; Deus, hominis antiquam plasmationem in se recapitulans, ut occideret quidem peccatum, evacuaret autem mortem, et vivificaret hominem: et propter hoc vera opera ejus," *A.h.* III. xix. 6 (Stier. III. xviii. 7). The passage referred to in the Pentateuch is Deut. XXXII. 4.

[22] Cf. *A.h.* V. xxi. 3 (Stier. ibid.), the last section.

[23] See Seeberg, *Lehrbuch der Dogmengeschichte*, VOL. I, pp. 411–13; and also, surprisingly enough, Bonwetsch, *Theologie des Irenäus*, p. 113; Lietzmann, *Church Universal*, p. 214; Tiililä, *Das Strafleiden Christi*, p. 122, n. 2; a similar theory appeared earlier, in Bousset, *Kyrios Christos*, p. 418 f. Others too hold the same opinion. Stoll *Lehre des hl. Irenäus*, has greater understanding of the central place of the Crucifixion, pp. 69–72, where death, though not sufficiently clearly, is connected with the resurrection. Aulén, on the other hand, *Den kristna försoningstanken*, pp. 58–64, connects the two with good arguments; see in particular p. 60 f., note. Cf. Prümm in *Pisciculi*, p. 210 f.

might even be said to have rejected the Resurrection, for the doctrine of the Atonement has in fact gradually lost its Resurrection content. In Irenaeus the Crucifixion and the Resurrection are integrally related and bound up with Christ's victory over the Devil, just as the humanity of Jesus is bound up with His victory. God's victory over Satan is realised in the humanity of Jesus, and therefore in the Crucifixion. Only by entering into Adam's condition could Christ achieve His purpose, and in doing so He has defeated death by His Resurrection, which is the end of all Creation, and the means of fulfilling this end for all Creation. The eternally valid decision for the whole of humanity is made in the death of Jesus with its unbroken obedience which destroys sin and consequently also destroys death, and is thus already the basis of the Resurrection. At the Cross man's destiny is decided.[24] We shall perhaps more clearly understand Irenaeus's line of thought here if we note how he incorporates the statements in the Gospel about the tribulations, suffering, and death of Jesus into his central theological concept of recapitulation.

Recapitulatio

In this chapter our task will be to assemble statements about *recapitulatio* of a quite distinctive type, i.e. those which describe Christ as recapitulating the "warfare," thus turning Adam's defeat into victory, and re-enacting what happened to Adam, but with the opposite result and effect. We shall therefore deliberately limit ourselves to the group of statements about ἀνακεφαλαίωσις in which Christ's conflict and victory are simultaneously proclaimed.[25] The problem is how this aspect of

[24] Cf. Brunner, *The Mediator*, p. 259. In common with Stoll, however, Brunner shortens the perspective slightly, so that the resurrection is included in Christ's work of salvation as it was not in the early Christian Church. Pp. 561–90, in which the significance of the belief about the resurrection is developed, fall outside the interpretation of Irenaeus.

[25] We shall still, however, restrict ourselves to discussing Christ alone, and avoid the passages in Irenaeus which describe Christ's work for other men. We shall thus stop at Jesus's conflict during His own life, which is bound in time on one side by His birth, and on the other by His resurrection. We shall be dealing with the question of how men are brought through Christ into the struggle between flesh and Spirit and led to victory in Part III, "From Death to Life," which deals with the Church. In the Church also the incarnate Christ works as *recapitulator*, as in the Consummation at the last time.

recapitulation is related to the one which we took up first in connexion with our analysis of Christ's becoming man, recapitulation as the return of uncorrupted Creation. There is, as we shall see, a profound unity between *recapitulatio* as the recommencement of the first Creation and *recapitulatio* as the struggle against sin and death. If it were something entirely new which was revealed in the Incarnation, then that which was old and fallen might have remained as it was, impure and forgotten, and without any conflict having been waged to cleanse and renew it. But what is revealed in Christ's birth and becoming man is in fact the first primal Creation. The conflict was, therefore, inevitable, for evil had to be expelled. Creation in its purity returns at the moment when Christ's struggle is crowned with victory. His victory is the natural fulfilment of His becoming man. As long as the fight against evil was uncompleted, the first, original, good Creation had not wholly returned, but the secondary and intermediate factor which had been brought in by Satan and which was alien to Creation blocked the way to the purification of humanity. When the conflict is recapitulated and resumed, so is the creation of Adam. When the obstructive powers have been destroyed, life, i.e. human life as it was, for long in bondage, begins to develop and grow again.

The recapitulation of the enmity between the Serpent on the one hand and man, the creation of God, on the other, has, of course, its best scriptural support in Gen. III.15, the word of the Creator to the Serpent in the Garden of Eden after the Fall: "I will put enmity between you and the woman, and between your seed and her seed; he shall bruise your head, and you shall bruise his heel."[26] In Christ, the Son of the woman, the conflict is renewed, Christ is "bruised" in death, yet bruises the head of His enemy, and in the crushing of the Devil man is victorious, for the Lord is a man born of woman. Besides expounding *recapitulatio* as conflict or the abolishing of the Fall and man's defeat, Irenaeus frequently mentions the two women, Eve and

[26] *Καθὼς ἡ γραφή φησιν εἰρηκέναι τῷ ὄφει τὸν Θεόν· καὶ ἔχθραν θήσω ἀνὰ μέσον σου, καὶ ἀνὰ μέσον τῆς γυναικὸς, [και ἀνὰ μέσον τοῦ σπέρματος σου, καὶ ἀνὰ μέσον τοῦ σπέρματος αὐτῆς· αὐτός σου τηρήσει κεφαλὴν, καὶ σὺ τηρήσεις αὐτοῦ πτέρναν] καὶ τὴν ἔχθραν ταύτην ὁ Κύριος εἰς ἑαυτὸν ἀνεκεφαλαιώσατο, ἐκ γυναικὸς γενόμενος ἄνθρωπος, καὶ πατήσας αὐτοῦ τὴν κεφαλήν, A.h.* IV. lvi. 2 (Stier. IV. xl. 3).

Mary, the former as the means of bringing a curse into the world, and the latter of a blessing.[27] A woman brings about both defeat and victory. A woman misled man in Adam, and a woman gave birth to the man Jesus, who is the way to life for misled man. And just as both death and health have been given to the human race through a woman, so the acts of disobedience and obedience have take place on a tree: the condemnation which came from the tree in the Garden of Eden has been overcome by the good which streams from the tree at Golgotha. The exact correspondence between the defeat of Adam and the victory of Christ points to an inner connexion, and agreements in detail between the two prove that *recapitulatio* is here involved.[28]

There are several scholars who also hold that the actual conflict of Christ, and not merely the Incarnation by itself, is an important part of the Irenaean concept of ἀνακεφαλαίωσις, e.g., Stoll, Bousset, Aulén, Rivière, and Scharl, but Bonwetsch is by far the most detailed at this point.[29] As we have just suggested, it is very easy also to discover the systematic connexion between the recapitulation of Adam's creation and that of his conflict. Creation is not attained or restored in its whole unblemished purity until the conflict has been concluded and the poison expelled. But at the same time it is clear that there are certain problems, etymological ones in particular, which we

[27] See especially the long and extremely interesting passage on the tangled threads which Eve left behind and which Mary had to unravel in *A.h.* III. xxxii. 1 (Stier. III. xxii. 4). The basic idea is that Eve brought death into the world through disobedience, while Mary brought in life through obedience. Cf. Gen. III, 6 with Lk. 1.38: "Quemadmodum enim illa per angelicum sermonem seducta est, ut effugeret Deum praevaricata verbum ejus, ita et haec per angelicum sermonem evangelisata est, ut portaret Deum obediens ejus verbo. Et si ea inobediret Deo, sed et haec suasa est obedire Deo, uti virginis Evae virgo Maria fieret advocata. Et quemadmodum adstrictum est morti genus humanum per virginem, salvatur per virginem," *A.h.* v. xix. 1 (Stier, ibid.). On the text, however, see Lundström, *Studien*, p. 24 f.

[28] On obedience and disobedience on the tree, see *A.h.* v. xvi. 2 (Stier. v. xvi. 3), v. xvii. 3–4 (Stier. ibid.), and also v. xix. 1 (Stier. ibid.) and *Epid.* 34. Irenaeus traces the most minute parallels throughout between man's fall and salvation.

[29] See Stoll, *Lehre des hl. Irenäus*, p. 51 f.; Bousset, *Kyrios Christos*, p. 435 f.; Bonwetsch, *Theologie des Irenäus*, pp. 101–04 (cf. *Z.S.T.*, 1923, p. 644 f.); Aulén, *Den kristna försoningstanken*, pp. 59 f.; Rivière, *Dogme de la rédemption*, p. 106 f.; and Scharl, *Orientalia*, 1940, pp. 411–14. Hugo Koch expressly denies on the other hand that the meaning *Wiederherstellung* could be found in the Irenaean ἀνακεφαλαίωσις (see *Theol. Stud. u. Krit.*, 1925, p. 198). Koch does not think of sin as a real intrusion, and it has therefore no real significance in the metaphors of conflict.

are to note here. The term *recapitulare* seems to lose any uniform or definite meaning when in one sentence it is Adam who is said to be recapitulated, whereas elsewhere it is something evil or negative which is recapitulated, e.g. enmity or death.[30] In the latter case the old certainly also returns and is repeated or re-created, but in such a way that it is done away with and disappears, rather than that it should remain as it was and be confirmed. Opposition and death are obliterated when they are recapitulated in the Crucifixion, and man is given eternal life when he is recapitulated in the Incarnation.

The primary and fundamental factor is that Christ recapitulates man—Adam. Since Adam's life had in it both good and evil, recapitulation affected both, although in fact the good was brought to perfection in Christ and evil vanquished. "Since," Irenaeus says, "in Himself He recapitulated the whole human race from beginning to end, He also recapitulated its death."[31] When Adam's death is recapitulated it is transformed into life (the Resurrection of Jesus), and in just the same way man is recapitulated in order to become what he was created from the beginning to become.[32] In neither case does ἀνακεφαλαίωσις imply a mechanical reproduction of the first Creation. In the Irenaean understanding of *recapitulatio* there are, as we saw, two points at which the dynamic character of his whole conception is most obvious—first, in his concept of growth, and second, in his concept of conflict. Man grows and is to grow—this is the first point. But there is conflict between God and Satan about this growing being—on the one hand man as a growing being is enslaved and strangled, but on the other hand he is liberated and given new possibilities of life. This is the second point. In Christ we see both of these dynamic functions. In the first place, in Him man is stronger than in Adam; he is

[30] In *A.h.* v. xix. 1 (Stier. ibid.) Irenaeus speaks of the Lord as "*facientem* recapitulationem ejus quae in ligno fuit inobedientiae, per eam quae in ligno est obedientiam," by which he means that disobedience is *reversed* when it is recapitulated through *obedience* in the recurring situation of temptation. On the recapitulation of Adam's *death* in the death of Jesus, see *A.h.* v. xxiii. 2 (Stier. ibid.), where it comes out in the context that Christ's *recapitulatio* of the death of fallen man delivers man from death, i.e. it is *life*, re-creation. Cf. v. xiv. 1 (Stier. ibid.).

[31] "Recapitulans enim universum hominem in se ab initio usque ad finem, recapitulatus est et mortem ejus," *A.h.* v. xxiii. 2 (Stier. ibid.).

[32] Cf. *A.h.* III. xxx (Stier. III. xxi. 10).

full grown and developed. When Christ recapitulates Creation, i.e. perfect Creation, things are not wholly as they were in the beginning, but rather Creation is strengthened, secured, and made more powerful. In the second place, and for this very reason, the whole conflict about man has a completely different orientation from before. When enmity, evil enmity, is recapitulated, it is not wholly the same as it was in Adam, but obedience and life emerge triumphantly from precisely those situations which in Adam's case led to disobedience and death.[33]

It cannot be denied that the word *recapitulare* is used in such widely different connexions that the exact meaning of the word is almost in danger of escaping us. But we can also accentuate the problem unnecessarily and make the question hopelessly difficult by working with certain assumptions which are alien to what Irenaeus himself says. If we conceive of man as being static and unmoved, perfectly developed and good, complete in every respect at the beginning of Creation, but having suffered some sort of loss at the Fall, then man's recapitulation in the Incarnation means that the same perfect substance is again present in Creation. It then becomes intolerably difficult that Irenaeus can go on to speak of a recapitulation of an activity, and even of an evil activity such as enmity, or, indeed, disobedience and death. In actual fact Irenaeus is continually thinking in terms of action and function. Man in Creation is in the process of development—he is a growing child with a destiny towards which he is moving. Man's recapitulation is renewed growth. The function of Creation reappears. There is nothing inherently new involved when we afterwards hear Irenaeus speaking of a recapitulation of a happening or an event in his statements about man's conflict. On the contrary, this is a natural development, quite characteristic of Irenaeus. Adam's life is ended, but the circumstances of his life return. The pattern of all human life is at its deepest point a unity, and when Christ is man the same pattern reappears in His life. But

[33] On the line of thought as a whole, cf. *A.h.* v. xxi. 1–3 (Stier. ibid.), where the narrative of Jesus's temptation in the wilderness is expounded as we have described in the immediately preceding section, and where every single point is elucidated from the recapitulation of Adam. See the following passage up to v. xxiv. 4 (Stier ibid.).

the fully-developed growth, power, and purity of Christ preclude the recurrence of any evil results from the repeated situations in the life which He lived, and in His case whatever He did issued in victory and life. Adam is precisely thus recapitulated and renewed, *with no element of hostility or inhumanity in his renewal.*[34]

We see now from our discussion above that Christ's perfection and power as man are dependent on the fact that God is in Him. In the Incarnation something happens that has never before happened in Creation—God becomes man. Humanity does not on that account cease to be human, but evil turns away from the man in whom God dwells bodily. Since Christ is God, He is true man, free and without sin, One who has grown to the goal which God set before His child in Creation as his, i.e. man's, destiny. In Christ, the Creator is in a man. Jesus's strength in His temptations, and in His humanity and forsakenness on the Cross, is *God's* strength. The victory which ensues from Jesus's conflict is therefore God's victory over the Devil, the victory of the Creator over the Destroyer of God's work of Creation.[35] The Father accomplishes His first decree for Creation in the life which Jesus lived. Uncorrupted human life ends in *resurrection*—lordship over death—by the same inner necessity which brought Adam's perverted life to end in death—the destruction of the power of life. The conflict which Jesus had to undergo for His life to be fully human and the reverse of Adam's embraced the Resurrection also, and not merely the period up to His death. His victory over death is Adam's restoration, and *recapitulatio* as conflict is concluded only when

[34] Cf. *A.h.* v. xiv. 2–3 (Stier. ibid.): "Habuit ergo et ipse carnem et sanguinem, non alteram quandam, sed illam principalem Patris plasmationem in se recapitulans, exquirens id quod perierat . . . justa caro reconciliavit eam carnem, quae in peccato detinebatur, et in amicitiam adduxit Deo. Si quis igitur secundum hoc alteram dicit Domini carnem a nostra carne, quoniam illa quidem non peccavit, neque inventus est dolus in anima ejus, nos autem peccatores, recte dicit. Si autem alteram substantiam carnis Domino affingit, jam non constabit illi reconciliationis sermo. Reconciliatur enim illud quod fuit aliquando in amicitia. Si autem ex altera substantia carnem attulit Dominus, jam non illud reconciliatum est Deo, quod per transgressionem factum fuerat inimicum." See also Hitchcock, *Irenaeus of Lugdunum*, p. 179 f.

[35] *Epid.* xxxvii and *A.h.* III. xix. 6 (Stier. III. xviii. 7). This thesis is basic to Irenaeus's theology. Cf. Rivière, *Dogme de la rédemption*, p. 106 f., and *A.h.* III. xxi. I (Stier. ibid.).

this last period has been reached.[36] The triumph of the Resurrection over man's enemy, death, is a revelation of pure humanity which has been achieved through God's becoming man.[37]

Since Irenaeus understands the salvation bestowed by Christ as a return to the natural condition of human life, and life without Christ as something unnatural, he is unable to speak of the Devil as having any right to man. For Irenaeus this would be like saying that a thief has a right to something which he has stolen by misrepresentation. Later theology often states that Satan has a right to man, and does so in order to stress that man is evil and demonic, that he is voluntarily obedient to the voice of God's enemy, and that consequently he is guilty before God. In Irenaeus there is not the same strong emphasis on man's guilt. Irenaeus does not deny this guilt, but in fact, as we saw earlier, explicitly underlines it. It is not, however, this truth about man which Irenaeus repeats continually.[38] His primary assertion is rather this, that it is the Creator who acts in Christ, and that man returns to his own true nature when he is delivered by Christ from his evil and unnatural will. The Devil has power over man, but he does not have a right to man.[39] Salvation in Irenaeus is also characterised as forgiveness of sins, the removal of man's guilt, but above all Christ offers man freedom from the power of sin and death.[40] In Christ's work of salvation natural human life is victorious.

[36] *A.h.* v. xxi. 1 (Stier. ibid.), *Epid.* 31 and 33. Christ is Adam. Cf. *A.h.* iv. xxxviii. 1 (Stier. iv. xxiv. 1): "... esse autem hujus Filium Verbum ejus, per quem constituit omnia, et hunc in novissimo tempore hominem in hominibus factum, reformasse quidem humanum genus, destruxisse autem et vicisse inimicum hominis, et donasse suo plasmati adversus reluctantem victoriam."

[37] Cf. Bonwetsch, *Theologie des Irenäus*, pp. 96 f., 108 f.

[38] See Aulén, *Den kristna försongingstanken*, p. 56 f.

[39] See *A.h.* iii. xxxii. 2 (Stier. iii. xxiii. 1), where the emphasis on the victory of life over death is very strongly pronounced, and v. ii. 1 (Stier. ibid.) with its express assertion of *Christ's* right to man: "... non aliena in dolo diripiens, sed sua propia juste et benigne assumens: quantum attinet quidem ad apostasiam, juste suo sanguine redimens nos ab ea; quantum autem ad nos, qui redemti sumus, benigne." In the passage which follows the concept of *grace* is clearly expressed.

[40] On the question of the relation between forgiveness of sins and the healing of man see Irenaeus's exposition of Mt. ix. 2–8, the story of the man who was sick of the palsy, in *A.h.* v. xvii. 1–3 (Stier. ibid.), and especially v. xvii. 3. The one who forgives sins in Christ is the God of Creation and the Law, against whom man committed his transgression and before whom he stands guilty. The healing miracles witness that the Creator is in Christ. Sin is therefore really forgiven when Christ has forgiven

The problem of who has a "right" to man is related to a further question which is concerned with the view we take of the death of Jesus. The idea that the Devil was justified in taking possession of man and has thus the right to possess man means in consequence that the death of Jesus is regarded as payment made to the Devil and in this sense as a "ransom." Scholars have debated whether such a line of thought is to be found in Irenaeus, and it is generally agreed that there is no such line to be found.[41] It is quite true that at times Irenaeus clearly states that man voluntarily followed the Tempter and was therefore personally responsible for the evil which he did, and became Satan's possession from within without any mechanical compulsion. Man is not simply something good which a wicked thief has stolen, but is evil, and unable to escape from his guilt. But at the moment of temptation the Tempter lied—and this destroys any assertion of right on his side.[42] Satan's nature is lying and deceit in all his dealing. However guilty man may be—and it was clear to Adam that his temptation was to disobedience—this does not mean that the Devil has any right against God. The Liar and Murderer has only power, but no right. Man has to be torn from the Devil's grasp in conflict. Christ gives His life as a ransom for man, not as a payment which is received by God's enemy. The metaphors of conflict are here substituted for juridical ones. A man who joins battle in order to deliver his friend does not give his life as a payment to the enemy, though he does give it as a "ransom" for the other—victory is won through conflict and death, and by victory the captive is delivered.[43]

it. "Bene igitur Verbum ejus ad hominem dicit: Remittuntur tibi peccata; idem ille, in quem peccaveramus in initio, remissionem peccatorum in fine donans" (v. xvii. 1).

[41] See Hitchcock, *Irenaeus of Lugdunum*, p. 168, and Rivière, *Dogme de la rédemption*, pp. 110–26.

[42] See *A.h.* v. xxiii. 1 and v. xxi. 3 (Stier. ibid.). In the former passage Irenaeus expounds Gen. II. 16–17 and III. 4–5. "Sed quoniam Deus verax est, mendax autem serpens, de effectu ostensum est, morte subsecuta eos, qui manducaverant."

[43] The statement which is usually cited as the basis of the view that Irenaeus has a doctrine of Jesus's death as a payment made to Satan is *A.h.* v. i. 1–2 (Stier. v. i. 1). Irenaeus speaks here of ransoming or redemption, but not of the Devil as recipient. The whole passage contradicts such an interpretation, for Adam's defeat is not described as a persuasion but rather as the Devil's robbery by violence of what belongs to God. Statements such as these in Irenaeus are as little designed to eradicate the idea of man's guilt as to stress any idea of the Devil's *right*.

But our Lord, in distinction from His opponent, wages His conflict righteously, *juste*. In the whole of His struggle against the stronger power Jesus speaks only the truth, and is obedient at every moment to the Father. Behind Irenaeus's somewhat naïve discussion of the Devil's lying there is an important theological concept. In His own person Christ effects a unity of obedience, creative power, and truth. He can be truthful, because His conflict is allied to life itself and has the Creator behind it. To oppose God is to oppose the One who created and still creates all things, i.e. it is opposition to reality—a fight such as that waged by God's enemy can be fought only by lies. It *is* a lie.[44] The whole of Irenaeus's teaching is centred on the idea of the Creator as the Lord of reality. To obey the God who creates is life; to disobey Him is death. When Adam renounces God's commandment in the Garden of Eden, Satan entices him away from his own true life by a lie. When Jesus abides by God's commandment in the wilderness, the lie loses its force, and man's true life, which has for long been suppressed, emerges victorious.[45] Adam is hostile to God and thus loses his own humanity—for man comes from God, the creative source of life. Jesus is obedient to God, and thus realises uncorrupted humanity through suffering and death.

All this is implied in what Irenaeus says about Christ's warfare as a warfare which is waged *juste*.[46] He, whose only weapons are truth and obedience, has foregone the possibility of employing wrong in His struggle, but by so doing has victory already within His grasp. For to do wrong means defeat, and it was wrongdoing which constituted Adam's defeat. Any success which has been wrongfully achieved is merely apparent, for death is hidden deep within it. Any reverse which good encounters is temporary, for Life, the resurrection from the dead, has only this outward covering of pain. Christ's power does not lie merely in His goodness, but His goodness is related to the

[44] Cf. *A.h.* v. xxi. 2 (Stier. ibid.) and v. xxiv. 3 (Stier. ibid.).

[45] Irenaeus lays stress on the fact that it is with the word of the Law (i.e. of the Creator) that Jesus in His temptation defeats the Devil. See especially v. xxi. 2. Cf. v. xvi. 2 (Stier. v. xvi. 3).

[46] The section from *A.h.* v. xxi. 1 to v. xxiv. 4 (Stier. ibid.) forms a systematic unity of great importance. The term *juste* means more than Rivière, *Dogme de la rédemption*, p. 99 f., and also Aulén, *Den kristna försoningstanken*, pp. 54 ff., suggest.

fact that He is the only man who has had unbroken contact with reality and the source of life. One instance of this contact, or unity, with the Creator is Christ's resurrection from the dead. In his submissive obedience Jesus is an ordinary man, but a man in union with God. In the same way Jesus turns to other men with no extra qualities than ordinary men possess to convince them, instruct them, and speak the truth to them. Moreover, His manner of bestowing life does not do away with what is human, but on the contrary preserves humanity, freedom, responsibility, and faith.[47] Any other way, i.e. any more miraculous way, would have led not to the redemption but to the rejection of humanity. But Christ came into the world to save man, which means to make man human. The "righteousness" of His conflict is to be seen in His attempt to convince in freedom. The unrighteous one cannot tolerate freedom, but has to imprison his victim.

Recapitulatio as conflict and victory opens out into *recapitulatio* as the restoration of Creation. The unity of these two aspects of *recapitulatio* is seen most clearly when it is said that it is through Christ's struggle that the *imago* and *similitudo* of God are restored from their deprivation. By his surrender to Satan man had lost his own nature. He was created in the image and likeness of God, but by his disobedience his growth towards this goal ceased and became transformed into its complete opposite. In the Incarnation the Lord destroys man's enemy, and frees man for new growth. By this, man's creation is made new again and completed through the Son who in His conflict restores man to the *imago* and *similitudo* of God.[48] Christ combats man's perdi-

[47] See *A.h.* v. i. 1 (Stier. ibid.). Cf. *A.h.* IV. lxiv. 1 (Stier. IV. xxxix. 1).

[48] "Non autem Dominus antiquam illam et primam adversus serpentem inimicitiam in semetipso recapitulatus fuisset, adimplens promissionem Demiurgi, et perficiens praeceptum ejus, si ab alio venisset patre. Sed quoniam unus et idem est, qui ab initio plasmavit nos, et in fine Filium suum misit, praeceptum ejus perfecit Dominus, factus ex muliere, et destruens adversarium nostrum, et perficiens hominem secundum imaginem et similitudinem Dei. Et propter hoc non aliunde eum destruxit, nisi ex dictionibus legis, et Patris praecepto adjutore usus ad destructionem et traductionem apostatae angeli," *A.h.* v. xxi. 2 (Stier. ibid.). "Ostendimus enim, quia non tunc coepit Filius Dei, exsistens semper apud Patrem; sed quando incarnatus est, et homo factus, longam hominum expositionem in seipso recapitulavit, in compendio nobis salutem praestans, ut quod perdideramus in Adam, id est, secundum imaginem et similitudinem esse Dei, hoc in Christo Jesu reciperemus," *A.h.* III. xix. 1 (Stier. III. xviii. 1).

tion, and when He has resisted His temptation and vanquished death, the one man in Creation who is uncorrupted stands forth as the *imago* of God on the third day. The image of God will be realised in all who are drawn into the dominion of Christ,[49] and this ingrafting into the Body of Christ is achieved through the Church. Before, however, we go beyond the limits of our analysis of the conception of the Church in Irenaeus, it may be appropriate to attempt first of all to define the meaning of Christ's lordship.[50]

The Lord

The dominion of Christ can be seen from two different points of view. Firstly, Christ has shown Himself to be Lord over His enemies. His victory includes His lordship over the opponent against whom he previously fought and who is now defeated. Secondly, as a result of His victory, Christ has obtained control over those who were formerly in the power of the enemy, i.e. men. Satan has been driven from the throne which he wrongfully occupied. The tyrant's subjects return to their natural owner, and Christ gains control in the world. These two aspects of Christ's position as Lord can be related to one another. The key to the whole of Christ's dominion is His conquest of evil and death. When evil has been eliminated and death put to flight, the property of the vanquished belongs to the victor. Christ in His triumph takes possession of His spoils, i.e. men, not only because His is the stronger power, but in the strictest sense "righteously," since He is the rightful owner, and indeed the one in whom man was made, while the Serpent lured into his power those whom God had created.[51]

[49] Christ snatches men from the grasp of the enemy and conveys them into the dominion of the Creator where they belong. He comes to His own, and men return to God's purpose for them when they become Christ's possession. He redeems them "by His blood," therefore through the Crucifixion "restaurans suo plasmati quod dictum est in principio, factum esse hominem secundum imaginem et similitudinem Dei," *A.h.* v. ii. 1 (Stier. ibid.). Irenaeus passes immediately from this to the Eucharistic cup and our participation in it.

[50] Christ rules as Lord, and men belong to His dominion. It is thus beginning to be completely impossible now to limit our discussion to Christ alone. In our exposition of victory we are compelled to pass to the Church which came into being as a result of Christ's victory.

[51] On the connexion between Creation, Christ's dominion, and the Last Judgement, see *Epid.* 48: "Now hereby he proclaimed that He came into being before

Within the rule of Christ, however, there are not only the Devil who has been defeated, and man who has been freed, but also the whole of nature and the external universe. The world in its totality was created through the Word, and in its totality was destroyed through the power of evil within it. For this reason Christ's conquest of the enemy of Creation, His Resurrection, and His dominion which is based on His Resurrection, must necessarily have consequences for the whole universe. Irenaeus devotes the whole of the conclusion of the *Adversus haereses* to a very detailed account of the eschatological consummation at the end of time, and in his analysis of these two questions he represents nature and the physical world as subject to Christ's sway, and sharing in the restoration of Creation.[52] Later on we shall have occasion to touch on this early Christian survival in the theology of Irenaeus. In regard to the time in which Irenaeus himself lived, there is no comparable idea of Christ's rule over the external universe. His power is still connected in the first instance with His Word, which is proclaimed by men and for men, and which gathers men around Christ as Lord. Christ's dominion has thus a history and a future: it is a present fact in history, and will ultimately pass over into a new phase of development. Our particular interest is in the present manifestation of His lordship and His power which is focused on men.

As we have just indicated, Christ's power over men stems from His power over evil and death. When men come to Christ they come to the One who has defeated their tormentor. They see the image of themselves in Him, not an image of what they are in their degradation, but rather they see their own destiny —true manhood. Man is free in Christ; he does not reach out for freedom, but actually possesses it. Christ, through His

all, and that He rules over the Gentiles and judges all mankind and the kings who now hate Him and persecute His name; for these are His enemies." Christ's dominion over the nations is yet more strongly emphasised in *Epid.* 49. His dominion over them is given concrete form in the preaching of His Word. On the obedience of the evil powers to the risen Lord, see *Epid.* 96, at the end: "And there is *none other name* of the Lord *given under heaven whereby men are saved*, save that of God, which is Jesus Christ the Son of God, to whom also the demons are subject and evil Spirits and all apostate energies." (Cf. Acts IV. 12.) See also *Epid.* 97. In *A.h.* III. xii. 2 (Stier. ibid.) Irenaeus quotes Peter's long speech in Acts II with its summary in Acts II.36.

52 The section includes *A.h.* V. xxv–xxxvi (Stier. ibid.), viz. 12 chapters.

freedom, in being unimpeded, is Lord. Men, on the other hand, are conscious that they are fettered. A tyrant may be so completely defeated on the battlefield that his enemy has complete power over him, and yet there may be a vast number of combatants who are unaffected by the victory which they are still awaiting. The victory with all its fruits has not yet reached them. The victor and the victory have still to come. The day will come when everything that belongs to the enemy shall be rooted out. Christ's resurrection from the dead is the victory which has been won on the battlefield. His handing over of the Kingdom to the Father (1 Cor. xv.24–8) is the great triumphal day when all that remains of the scattered forces of the enemy shall be swept away.[53] Between these two events there is a period of time which is marked by a characteristic dualism—Christ's lordship is at the same time absolute and in process of continuing conflict. The victory is won. Neither His temptation in the wilderness nor His Crucifixion can be repeated. Christ is risen, and His throne is established. His destitution in the wilderness and His agony on the Cross precede the moment of His victory and His Resurrection. But there are many who have not yet shared in His victory. Some of these, we must suppose, will be numbered among the saved but others among the damned on the great Day of Judgement. But in the present time, i.e. in the intervening period, Christ's dominion pushes out to embrace men.

It is from this point that we shall be able to see the Church in its proper perspective. The Church is to be classed under the larger concept of Christ's dominion. It is of primary significance that it is human beings who are incorporated into the Church, and only them. And they are governed not by other men, but by Christ Himself. They belong to Him. The expansion of the Church takes place here on earth through Christ's word being apprehended and heard in the world. Those who are brought into the Church and who receive all that Christ has attained are evil, sinful men, the bondslaves of Satan, who are delivered from their captivity. They are snatched from the hand of the enemy, and experience instead the dominion of Christ which is joy and freedom. The period during which the Church increases among men is bounded in one direction by the Resurrection of Christ,

[53] These verses from 1 Cor. xv are a corner-stone of Irenaeus's eschatology.

the moment of victory, and in the other by Christ's Second Advent, and the Final Judgement and Last Day.[54] As we have just said, Christ's dominion stretches out among men during this period, and the Church is the expression of this extension. For a modern static view of the Church which conceives of the Church as a conflux of so many members, encircled by so many more who are not "within" the Church, the idea of progression is not of the *esse* of the Church—even though it may be held that mission numerically increases the first group as it diminishes the second. For Irenaeus the Church *is* mission, and this does not mean simply that one sociological group is supported at the expense of another, or that there is merely a territorial extension, but that the progress of the Church is a movement from the point of victory to the Last Day, from Easter to the Parousia, and this is a movement in time and not only in space. Christ's dominion thrusts itself forward as the Church expands, and its goal is the mighty act of the last age, not simply an eventual identity between the inhabitants of the earth and the membership of the Church. It is for this reason that progress belongs to the concept of the Church—the Church is Christ's dominion in its present functioning, and a dominion which extends into the future.[55]

As pure man, unfettered by the Destroyer of humanity, Christ is Lord over man's enemies. His pure humanity witnesses to His lordship and power. But Jesus's life is a life of undestroyed

[54] For Irenaeus Easter and Pentecost are inseparably connected. We shall return to all the aspects of Irenaeus's thought which we have here touched upon. Cf. the general direction taken by Cullmann in dealing with *regnum Christi* and the Church in early Christian belief, *Königsherrschaft Christi*, pp. 13–40. On Irenaeus's part there is, as usual, a profound relationship between Creation and the Incarnation, Creation and the Church. Man has been created in the *imago* and *similitudo* of God. Christ is the *imago* and *similitudo* of God. The Church consists of *men*, and in this way is *Christ's Body*. Creation continues in the Church. The goal is the resurrection, i.e. eternal life for the "body."

[55] Even although the members of the Christian Church are relatively few in number compared with the unbaptised, this does not affect faith in Christ's absolute power, for it is not the sum total which counts but the *function*, the continuing expansion through preaching to new multitudes. This function is directly connected with the *future*—the cosmic perspective. Christ's dominion is irresistible and progressive. Separation and distress are part of the emergence of His dominion. In the extreme distance is to be seen not the vast, uninterrupted quest for members of the Church, but the Last Judgement, which means the manifestation of Christ's total dominion in the world.

humanity only because God dwells in Him, and has power to drive man's enemies out of this man, Jesus. Jesus has become pure man, i.e. He has become victor, by reason of His divinity. His victory over the Devil is God's victory achieved through man.[56] God is Creator, and cannot become united with man without creating him further. Man is created, and as such is receptive; he cannot be made one with the Creator without being subjected to the creative power of God, i.e. without "growing." On the ground of His divinity the man Jesus is more than Adam, just as the man is more than the "child."[57] Jesus is the strong man, the fully grown man. His victory over temptation is a testimony to His full growth and strength. Growth and victory belong together.

The accession of power which Jesus represents is to be seen in very many different ways. The New Testament is in every respect richer than the Old. Some examples of this are worth mentioning. In face of the attempt of the Gnostics to argue that the Demiurge of the Old Testament was a god who exacted punishment and was revengeful and without grace, while the God of Jesus on the other hand was gentle and good, and did not exact punishment on men, Irenaeus insists that it was the same God who was active in both Covenants, and that both severity and mercy receive clear expression in Israel's history, but that both of these qualities are increased and come to their height in Christ. Jesus is more severe than any other, yet more gentle than any other. His judgement is eternal and not temporal, and it relates to thoughts and words and not simply to deeds.[58] His love knows no bounds, and He invites the poor, the

[56] Jesus Christ is "God's name" (*Epid.* 96, end). On God's victory in Jesus see *A.h.* v. xxii. 1 and v. xxiv. 4 (Stier. ibid.).

[57] Cf. also Böhringer, *Kirche Christi*, VOL. II, pp. 543–6. It would seem, however, that Böhringer in this passage is working with an artificial contrast between Logos and the Spirit (e.g. p. 546). He unfortunately disregards the Irenaean concept of the Church, which he considers to be "Catholic," but his best work appears in his treatment of Christology with its combination of divinity and humanity.

[58] "Quemadmodum enim in novo Testamento ea quae est ad Deum fides hominum aucta est, additamentum accipiens Filium Dei, ut et homo fieret particeps Dei; ita et diligentia conversationis adaucta est, cum non solum a malis operibus abstinere jubemur, sed etiam ab ipsis malis cogitationibus, et otiosis dictionibus, et sermonibus vacuis, et verbis scurrilibus: sic et poena eorum qui non credunt Verbo Dei, et contemnunt ejus adventum, et convertuntur retrorsum, adampliata est; non solum temporalis, sed et aeterna facta," *A.h.* IV. xliv. 2 (Stier. IV. xxviii. 2).

sick, the sinful, and the wicked, to come to Himself. In particular Irenaeus develops this "increase" of grace and judgement in his exegesis of the parable of the man who had no wedding garments (Mt. XXII. 1–14).[59] In various connexions Irenaeus reiterates that in God love and wrath, mercy and righteousness, have become one.[60] Christ's divinity is also demonstrated in the fact that at the one time He judges and forgives.[61] Irenaeus frequently expresses this by saying that Christ's grace and judgement are in a sense divided between His first and second advents, so that accordingly God's grace comes to men through the earthly life of Jesus, and God's judgement in this same Jesus comes to men through the Parousia at the end of time.[62] Christ's twofold coming gives the concept of His dominion a peculiar inner tension which we shall now deal with in closer detail.

This tension is related to the two ages.[63] A new age has begun in Christ; His Resurrection has opened the way to the Kingdom in which He is King. His Kingdom appears in power through the resurrection of the dead. But those who now have part in the Son are at the same time living in the old age in which man's enemies, though slain in the Resurrection of Christ, have not wholly been destroyed. Sin and death have been vanquished by Christ, but are still sufficiently powerful to ensnare men, who can exist only in communion with Christ. Christ's dominion reaches out to men and will shortly come upon them, but when it does come to them and encompass them completely, the end of the world will also have come, and the old aeon will disappear.[64] To live in the Church is to live in expectation. Christ's

The whole exposition in IV. xliv and xlv (Stier. IV. xxviii and xxix) is centred on the problem which we have mentioned.

[59] *A.h.* IV. lviii. 4–7 (Stier. IV. xxxvi. 4–6).

[60] See, for example, *Epid.* 60. Cf. Irenaeus's interpretation of Jn. XIX. 11 in *A.h.* IV. xxxi. 2 (Stier. IV. xviii. 3).

[61] *A.h.* V. xvii. 1–3 (Stier. ibid.). Cf. also *Epid.* 60. Christ embraces in Himself God's work, and every revelation is thus far a revelation of Christ—He is Lord of both "Testaments."

[62] The subject is dealt with most fully in *A.h.* IV. l. (Stier. IV. xxxiii. 1). Cf. IV. lviii. 4 (Stier. IV. xxxvi. 4).

[63] Cf. Nygren, *Commentary on Romans*, p. 16 f.

[64] The final transition with its gradual deletion of the old is described in *A.h.* V. xxxvi (Stier. ibid.). Cf. Loofs, *Theophilus von Antiochien*, p. 279 f. on Aphraates. The time limits of Christ's *regnum* are not absolutely fixed in any direction, either in regard to its beginning or its end.

dominion is at once revealed yet hidden.[65] His suffering and the Cross are, so to speak, a contradiction of His power, and yet even when He is crucified He actually *has* His kingdom, although it is hidden behind the veil in which it must appear for as long as the conflict lasts.[66] His death looks as though it were a defeat, but is in fact His mighty descent into the kingdom of the dead in order that His Word should reach the godly believers of the old Covenant and all the dead.[67] Under the surface of death He thus extends His dominion and gives men life in place of death. The whole of the state between the Crucifixion and the Parousia is wrapped in mystery.

We need constantly to remember that what Irenaeus and other writers of the early Church have to say about Christ's dominion over all men and the whole world belongs to a period of martyrdom. Those who declared that Christ is Lord and subordinate to none had seen many members of Christ's Body put to death, and had themselves to face the possibility of having their own lives on earth terminated in violent suffering. And yet they were convinced of Christ's eternal power over all men and all creatures. Christ had also been put to death by temporal powers on earth. His life was a life of conflict with

[65] Cf. *Epid.* 62. In *A.h.* II. xliii. 1 (Stier. II. xxviii. 7) it is put thus: "Nos autem adhuc in terra conversantes, nondum assidentes throno ejus."

[66] In the last part of *Epid.* 56 Irenaeus stresses that when He submits to the ignominy of the Crucifixion the government is upon His shoulders (Is. IX.6). See here the striking passage in *A.h.* V. xviii. 2 (Stier. IV. xviii. 3). Those who are not able to see through the veil cannot believe in Christ as King—the only lords they see are those sovereigns who are reigning on earth for the time being. Cf. *Epid.* 95.

[67] The connexion between the *descensus* and Christ's dominion is to be seen in *A.h.* IV. xxxiv. 2 (Stier. IV. xx. 2), IV. xxxvi. 1 (Stier. IV. xxii. 1), which are well explained in Loewenich, *Johannes-Verständnis*, p. 135, and also to a certain degree in IV. xlii. 4 (Stier. IV. xxvii. 2) and *Epid.* 78. See, however, C. Schmidt, *Gespräche Jesu mit seinen Jungern*, pp. 492–8, and Cullmann, *Königsherrschaft Christi*, p. 6, n. 4, and p. 47. It is quite common for Irenaeus's doctrine of the *descensus* to be regarded as being emptied of its early Christian content. *Epid.* 83 is an infrequently quoted argument against the alleged transference of Christ's victory into the future—the evil powers have already suffered defeat. A more inclusive and active view of Christ's descent is to be found in Lindroth's article, "Descendit ad inferna," in *S.T.K.*, 1932, pp. 132–5. In several passages Irenaeus quotes an apocryphal prophecy from Isaiah or Jeremiah which he makes the basis of his doctrine of the *descensus*. On this point see C. Schmidt, *Gespräche Jesu mit seinen Jungern*, pp. 467–73, where he uses the prophecy to show an early Christian falsification of the book of Jeremiah. The same apocryphal quotation appears in Justin in the *Dialogue*, lxii (*Die ältesten Apologeten*, ed. E. J. Goodspeed, Göttingen 1915, p. 182).

death, at times apparently powerless in face of death, but under the surface irresistible, and finally breaking through everything in its way without hindrance.[68] The tension which exists in the period between Jesus's crucifixion and His resurrection extends to the whole period between the Incarnation and the Last Judgement. Christ's life on earth is marked throughout by love and grace. At His first advent and in His presence in the Church He gives gifts to men without ceasing. But the sun will not rise on good and evil for ever. One day the Judgement will be pronounced,[69] and all earthly powers will then collapse, and only Christ's dominion will endure.[70] The Church awaits that day in its martyrdom.

Christ is thus Lord, but His government is mediated to men in the preaching of the Word and points to the future when the Kingdom will appear in power. His dominion is present here and now as an appeal to men, but the Lord who now appeals to men and stands at the door and knocks is the same Lord who has the Last Judgement in His hand, and who at the appointed hour will break down all resistance. The alternation between appeal and power, which characterises Christ's dominion, is clearly reflected in Irenaeus's doctrine of the freedom of man. Man is free and responsible.[71] He may receive Christ's Word in faith, or reject it in unbelief. But in neither case does his freedom contradict Christ's lordship. Freedom is a reflection of Christ's government in its present form, a government exercised through the preaching of the Word.[72] Free man is implicated in

[68] Cf. *A.h.* v. xxviii. 3–xxix. 1 (Stier. v. xxviii. 4–xxix. 1).

[69] *Epid.* 44, 48, and 85.

[70] ". . . quoniam duos adventus ejus omnes annuntiaverunt prophetae: unum quidem, in quo homo in plaga factus est . . . secundum autem, in quo super nubes veniet, superducens diem quae est sicut clibanus ardens," *A.h.* IV. l (Stier. IV. xxxiii. 1). Cf. Mal. IV. 1. In this analysis of Christ's double advent Irenaeus also cites the prophecy about the Lord's descent to the dead which has just been mentioned. The *descensus* belongs to Christ's first coming, and signifies salvation for those who have been imprisoned by death.

[71] *A.h.* IV. lix–lxi (Stier. IV. xxxvii. 1–7).

[72] *Epid.* 55: "Moreover He is also our Counsellor, giving advice; not compelling as God, even though He is *Mighty God,* (as) He says." This is said of Christ and is an exegesis of Is. IX.6, the passage about the "Wonderful Counseller." Christ's *speaking* and "counselling" is contrasted with power and compulsion. *Ταῦτα γὰρ πάντα τὸ αὐτεξούσιον ἐπιδείκνυσι τοῦ ἀνθρώπου, καὶ τὸ συμβουλευτικὸν τοῦ Θεοῦ, . . . ἀποτρέποντος μὲν τοῦ ἀπειθεῖν αὐτῷ, ἀλλὰ μὴ βιαζομένου,* *A.h.* IV. lx. 1 (Stier. IV. xxxvii. 3); see also the following section. In the Latin texts "con-

preaching, in the *kerygma*, as subject, as recipient: were it not for man, vacillating between faith and unbelief, the *kerygma* would not be the *kerygma*. If, however, free man is taken away and Christ's government is prevented from extending into freedom among men, the eschatological direction of Christ's government is also displaced, and the final outcome becomes transferred to the present. In Irenaeus the whole movement is towards the resurrection and Last Judgement.[73] There is no one alive, and there never will be any, who is free to resist Christ for all time to come, for no one has freedom independently of Christ, who has power to judge men with a final, annihilating judgement. Our present freedom is grounded on the fact that Christ has not yet begun the Final Judgement, and for the present He addresses us in His *kerygma*, which is the means of His appeal to us.

The Gnostics, with their theories about the classification of men into those who are naturally "pneumatic" and those who are "sarkic" or "hylic," were much less concerned than Irenaeus to emphasise human freedom. But it is characteristic that their doctrine of the classes of men in point of fact detracts from the power of God. The "pneumatic" are saved, but the "sarkic" are lost. God is a passive spectator as some men ascend to heaven while others descend to hell—He is unable to break the power of the different substances, and man is predestined from within his own inescapable nature. Irenaeus's doctrine of man is in direct opposition to the Gnostic theory of men who are imprisoned in their various groups. Man's freedom for Irenaeus is, therefore, an expression of God's power. Divine sovereignty and human freedom are not in opposition to one another, but belong together and are mutually dependent. Man's freedom is a sign of Christ's dominion: *all* men can be raised from the condition in which they are, and the Gospel, which is now spreading apace throughout the world, is proclaimed to all. Those who deny men's freedom "allege that the

silium" is regularly used in these passages. The aspect of appealing is strongly accentuated.

[73] Revelation to all men is linked with the Last Judgement. Before the Judgement the Gospel is heard, and men receive it in faith, or reject it in unbelief. See *A.h.* IV. xi. 3–5 (Stier. IV. vi. 4–7). In the Judgement man has to answer for the way in which he has used his freedom. Cf. *A.h.* IV. vii. (Stier. IV. iv. 3).

Lord is powerless" and helpless in dealing with human nature.[74] Christ's dominion is extending more widely now, and cannot be limited. The Day of Judgement will soon be at hand.

We shall fail to understand the Irenaean concept of the Church if we do not keep this universal perspective in mind. The Church is not a group, but a manifestation of Christ's progressive dominion. Its redemptive function continues, and it is meaningless to start dealing with rejected groups of men.[75] This whole question is the concern of the Lord, and not our concern, and it relates to the future and not to the present. What is done in the Church counteracts the Fall.[76] Countless numbers outside the Church have not yet heard the message of Christ's victory, but they are encompassed in hope by the Church.[77] No one at all is to be regarded as lost.[78] God reveals Himself to whom He will, and all men have freedom, i.e. Christ's dominion may be firmly established in the hearts of all men.[79] Irenaeus's view of the Church is marked by an

[74] "Qui autem his contraria dicunt, ipsi impotentem introducunt Dominum, scilicet quasi non potuerit perficere hoc quod voluerit: aut rursum ignorantem natura choicos, ut ipsi dicunt, et eos qui non possunt accipere ejus incorruptelam," *A.h.* IV. lxi. 1 (Stier. IV. xxxvii. 6). Were there no freedom of the will, the *Church* would not be reaching out to men on the one hand and to the Last Judgement on the other, but there would then be the clearly defined group of the pneumatics, who would already have secured perfection. In such a case Christ's dominion would in fact be denied, for it is grounded on freedom and unlimited possibility for men.

[75] Not even the Gnostics are lost without hope of salvation. See *A.h.* III. xlii. 2 (Stier. III. xxv. 7) and the preface to V (Stier. ibid.).

[76] The preaching of the Gospel proclaims to men that an inheritance has fallen to them. The next phase, the actual appearance of the inheritance, is soon to come. The *kerygma* of the Church relates to the future. "Propter hoc autem et Christus mortuus est, uti testamentum Evangelii apertum, et universo mundo lectum, primum quidem liberos faceret servos suos; post deinde haeredes eos constitueret eorum quae essent ejus, haereditate possidente spiritu," *A.h.* V. ix. 4 (Stier. ibid.). The latter passage refers to the resurrection of the flesh.

[77] Cf. W. Schmidt, *Die Kirche bei Irenäus*, p. 172 f.

[78] Irenaeus stubbornly maintains that *Adam* is saved against all doctrines which exclude the first man from salvation. Man as such is sought by God in His Son. No one is excluded. The Gospel is absolutely universal. See *A.h.* III. xxiii–xxxvi (Stier. III. xxiii. 2–7), especially the end section.

[79] The thought in the background is always that Christ's dominion is a *present* dominion through the *kerygma* which is addressed to men. Preaching presupposes freedom. But on the Day of Judgement this dominion will become visible. It will then no longer be preached, since the time of Christ's appeal to men is ended, and resistance will no longer be conceivable.

exceptional breadth and openness.[80] Christ's dominion embraces the whole of humanity, and His Church represents in the present time this dominion in process of expansion. It will eventually extend to all humanity, and meantime awaits the future judgement of the Lord. Irenaeus's whole view of Christ and His Church is simple and evangelical. Christ's dominion is in the present age a dominion of grace into which sinners are brought undeservedly. None will therefore have any excuse when the Judgement comes.

As soon as we speak of the Lord, as we have just done, we can no longer think of Christ alone, but must widen our picture of Christ. I propose to pass on now to a direct analysis of man under Christ's dominion, and the completely new situation in which man is set as a result of Christ's victory. In Part I we dealt with man and his movement through Creation and defeat, from life to death. We then left our treatment of man, and in Part II attempted to define the meaning of Christ's becoming man and His victory. The present chapter which has concentrated on Christ is now complete. Christ's lordship means the victory of life over death. The place of men's captivity has been opened by Christ the victor. We must now return to man and follow his progress from death to life. As death came through man's defeat by the Devil, so life comes through Christ's victory. All that we shall be saying in the following section is already implied in the fact that Christ is Lord. Not only the Church, but also the Consummation, is a consequence of His lordship.[81] From His Resurrection up to the

[80] Cf. the characteristics of Irenaeus as given by Jules Lebreton in *Histoire de l'église, depuis les origines jusqu' à nos jours*, 1935, VOL. II, *De la fin du 2e siècle à la paix constantinienne*, Saint-Dizier 1935, p. 64 f., Eng. trans. *History of the Primitive Church*, London 1942, VOL. III, p. 562 f.; and T. Zahn (art. on "Irenäus von Lyon") in *Realencyklopädie für protestantische Theologie und Kirche*, 3rd edn. Leipzig 1901, VOL. IX, p. 411.

[81] See *A.h.* III. xvii. 6 (Stier. III. xvi. 6). The Church is part of the long chain of events constituted by *recapitulatio*. We cannot really say what the Church is if we are not able to use temporal categories and say *when* the Church is, *where in a succession of events* Christ is active in the Church as *recapitulator*—i.e. between Easter and the Parousia. His dominion then passes over into its next phase, the Consummation, through which *recapitulatio* is completed. Cf. *A.h.* III. xvii. 7–8 (Stier. III. xvi. 7–8) and V. xviii. 2 (Stier. V. xviii. 3). Time is constitutive. See Escoula in *N.R.T.*, 1939, p. 399, n. 11: "La 'récapitulation' est essentiellement l' achèvement, la réalisation dans le temps du plan éternel de Dieu." Cullmann's general appraisal of Irenaeus in *Christ and Time*, p. 56 f., is of very great importance.

Last Day Christ is active in both in restoring the primal and pure Creation. The Consummation is the restoration of the wholeness of Creation. But let us follow the process of healing from the beginning, and see first how the Lord takes hold of fallen man in His Church in order to renew him and restore the *imago* and *similitudo* from its depravation.

PART III

FROM DEATH TO LIFE

CHAPTER I

THE CHURCH

Imago and Similitudo

We have come now to the situation in which Irenaeus proclaimed his message, and the situation in which he lived was that of the Church. Christ's life on earth lies behind the present time. The Son of God has lived, died, and risen in God's fallen Creation. Irenaeus was not contemporaneous with the life of Jesus, but he was contemporaneous with the Church. In his youth he had heard the Gospel about Christ's finished work, and was now himself a preacher of the same Gospel. Day by day he derived sustenance from the Church. Christ is present in the Church *now*. At the same time the Church includes men, and the *kerygma*, baptism, and the Eucharist exist for men. When the Gospel comes to a man, or when he is baptised, or when the bread and the wine are handed to him, the encounter between Christ and man takes place. If we investigate the relationship between man and the Incarnation according to Irenaeus, we shall soon notice that all his lines of thought point to the Church. The Church is the actual meeting-place in the present time of man and the Incarnation. All the realities which we have touched upon above—Creation, sin, and Christ—meet in this simple fact, that in the Church we hear Christ's word spoken to us.[1] Every man is God's pure

[1] All the ideas which we have developed in the previous chapters will help to clarify the present Part III, but our discussion has in a way been in the abstract. *Creation* and *defeat* are both present now in sinful man. *Christ*, whom we have considered up to this point apart from other men, has in actual fact been given for the salvation of the world, and in the Church He now gives all that He has to sinful man. All that we have said in the preceding Parts is now taken up into the encounter between Christ and man in the Church. In the first place, this chapter on the Church deals with *the present*, and we are concerned with the present throughout. As soon as we have passed to the following chapter on the Consummation we shall once more be out of the present, and shall then be discussing the future.

creation who has been defeated by the Devil, and at this very moment stands before Christ who is God's creating Word, and therefore intact in His humanity and Lord over man's tormentor. We shall notice the distinctive aspects of the encounter between Christ and man better if we re-examine here the double concept of *imago* and *similitudo*.

We have seen above that Christ is the *imago* and *similitudo* of God, and that man has been created in the *imago* and *similitudo* of God. There is an absolute distance between Christ and man, inasmuch as Christ creates and man is created, and Christ gives and man receives. The distinction is not dependent on sin, but is already based on the eternal decree of God, and cannot in consequence ever be abolished at any future period. In the present, however, Christ and man encounter one another in the Church.[2] But the relationship between the two is still that of Christ as the one who creates and man as the one who receives. Man is created in the Church, i.e. he "grows," for when God creates, His work of Creation is expressed in man's natural growth towards his own destiny. Man's growth had ceased when he became imprisoned in his evil will. But now his free growth is resumed. We have already seen in the part of the present inquiry which deals with Christ that the Creator who is present in Christ brings humanity to perfection. Our present task is to try to see how the Creator who works in Christ brings life to sinful men within the Church. Our attention was centred above on the full growth of Jesus's own human nature in comparison with the child Adam. Here in the Church Christ now encounters other men, fallen and defeated men. Two things must be done to them by means of Christ's power: the enemy's hold over them must be broken amidst conflict, and they must be given nourishment in order to be able to grow. Both these things are done in the Church. As usual, conflict and growth are related.

But as Christ's dominion is in process of moving towards the Last Day, so everything that the Church gives is also, seen from below, viz. from the point of view of the individual, a pledge of glory that awaits him in the future. Man lives in the conflict

[2] Man and the Incarnation may both be defined in terms of *imago* and *similitudo*. The same formula recurs in the concept of the Church, for in the Church man and the Incarnation meet.

now, and the conflict will not cease or end in conclusive victory until the Consummation.[3] And man lives in the process of growth now, and his growth shall continue through his death and resurrection and reach its destiny in Creation only in eternity.[4] Both man's conflict and his growth are possible only in the Church which is the Body of Christ. He can become man again only by being ingrafted into the pure and whole man by the Gospel, baptism, and the Eucharist. The ruthless powers outside the Church bind man to themselves and will not deliver him from death. There is at work in the Church now the only one who has achieved the purpose for human life while remaining pure. Within the protection of Christ's Church the child in man is released, and his life is conformed to its destiny in Creation.[5] But the free life of man which is thus reborn remains until the day of the resurrection a life of conflict and growth and yearning for perfection. What is offered to man in the Church is a beginning, a first-fruits, and, indeed, a promise. The Gospel is a letter about an inheritance which is to come. We may, perhaps, best describe it by saying that even when we have described Irenaeus's conception of the Church in full, we are left with the impression that we have still left something unsaid, like a speaker who stops in the middle of a sentence. Everything calls for a continuation. And yet Christ, the Head of the Church, is absolutely perfect. But *men* are continually growing, and are moving towards the universal government of the perfect man. And as men struggle against sin, they grow.[6]

[3] Jesus was tempted in the wilderness and on the Cross by His enemy who attacked Him from without. He had no sin in Himself. Man, on the other hand, has been defeated. He has evil within himself, and can fight only on the basis of Christ's already won victory. Man's conflict goes right through his own being, and is a conflict between flesh and Spirit (Gal. v.17), i.e. between Satan and God (Christ). See *A.h.* v. 10–11 (Stier. ibid.).

[4] Christ was the first to rise without death being able to hold Him, and His rising is connected with His absolute victory over evil. There was no sin in Him. Man, on the other hand, remains involved in the struggle between flesh and Spirit. He cannot rise from the dead until Christ's dominion has fully come to men in the last time and conferred on them absolute victory. Cf. *A.h.* v. ix. 4 (Stier. ibid.) and v. viii. 1 (Stier. ibid.).

[5] *Epid.* 46 and *A.h.* III. xxxviii. 1 (Stier. III. xxiv. 1).

[6] Man is in death's power when He encounters Christ in the Word. Through Christ he is taken *from death to life*. But "life" means eternal life, the indestructable life of the resurrection. Before the eschatological consummation man is constantly "on the way."

When Christ encounters man through His Gospel, it is evil, sinful man whom He meets. We must emphasise this point here, because there is something new involved. When we were considering Christ by Himself, we had occasion to pause to consider the attack made upon Christ by the Tempter, but not to deal with sin, for Christ held His own. But now Christ gives Himself to other men, and within humanity the righteous Christ counters His enemy Satan—within man, that is, who is incorporated into the Church.[7] Christ meets with opposition when He comes to His own. Some in unbelief reject the Gospel and do not welcome the Spirit at all. Man's defeat in the Fall meant that man became alienated from the Word who created him, and man's alienation is seen when the Word is incarnate and in Jesus Christ seeks to reach mankind. Some, however, do believe. But even in them it is the unnatural which dominates. They have been born in captivity, and they do not understand what it is to be man, or what freedom from evil will means.[8] God's image and likeness is no longer the goal towards which they are striving; they are distorted and arrested in their natural growth. And they themselves are responsible for their perversity of will. Christ now consequently stands before them without sin. In no other does God reach down to them, for everything else that is human is enslaved and severed from God. Only in Christ is righteousness to be found.[9]

The basic factor in the Church is the *Gospel*, and in the Gospel forgiveness of sins is given. It is of the essence of the Gospel that it is directed to men, and in particular to men who are guilty and sinful. The man who was sick of the palsy was paralysed, and to that extent bound by death, for sickness and old age are expressions of the power of death, but he receives

[7] Bonwetsch, *Theologie des Irenäus*, p. 80 f. Irenaeus, however, speaks more about the condition which comes about through sin than about sin and disobedience itself.

[8] Irenaeus sees original sin for the most part from the point of view that men have been born in captivity, born in a place of imprisonment. They have never experienced freedom. See *A.h.* III. xxxiii. 1 (Stier. III. xxiii. 2). Cf. the description of deliverance through Christ which corresponds to this, *A.h.* V. xxi. 3 (Stier. ibid.).

[9] The doctrine of Christ's descent into hell is of significance in this connexion. The dead have no deliverance until Christ comes among them. And yet the patriarchs of the old Covenant, for example, already have faith in Christ by their trust in the promises. It is not in such a faith, but in *Christ*, that salvation is found.

forgiveness of sins (Mt. IX.2), since Christ attacks death at its root, which is sin. When Jesus speaks the work of the forgiveness of sins, it is God the Creator, the Lord of the Law, who forgives man his offences. There is no other who has the power and the right to forgive.[10] The Gospel gives the Spirit to man.[11] Inasmuch as Adam, or man, became a transgressor in the whole of his body, the Gospel clothes itself in the form of baptism, and embraces man, purifying and regenerating him.[12] In *faith* man opens himself to the Spirit, who thus becomes Lord in him and takes up the struggle against sin in him, a struggle which finally ends in the unending dominion of the Spirit in the resurrection.[13] Christ is passing on to men in the Church the fruit of His victory which He accomplished in His earthly life—the completion of this work is still to come in the future.[14] Christ and the Spirit, who were the Creator's "hands," will again at the last time have control over a pure and sinless Creation, but at present Christ and the Spirit are *in the Church*, the Church which is eagerly awaiting the future.[15] These immense powers which govern the world are concealed at present in the small, persecuted Church.

E. Scharl and M. Werner point out that the Pauline expression "new creation" is not used by Irenaeus.[16] Precisely the opposite expression is sometimes used in the writings of Ire-

[10] The text about the man sick of the palsy is expounded clearly and in detail in *A.h.* v. xvii. 1–3 (Stier. ibid.). M. Werner, *Enstehung des christlichen Dogmas*, p. 414, wrongly holds that Irenaeus interprets religion in terms of "works."

[11] *A.h.* v. viii. 1 and v. ix (Stier. ibid.). The government of the spirit is now beginning and will be brought to perfection in the resurrection. In the forgiveness of sins there is expressed the power which can rouse the dead. Cf. the expression "Spiritus remissionis peccatorum, per quem vivificamur," *A.h.* IV. xlviii. 2 (Stier. IV. xxxi. 2); Stoll, *Lehre des hl. Irenäus*, p. 54 f., comments on this expression.

[12] Cf. *A.h.* v. xv. 3 (Stier. ibid.), in which the washing in Siloam is compared with Tit. III. 5. See Cullmann, *Urchristentum und Gottesdienst*, Basel 1944, pp. 60 and 75, n. 75, Eng. trans., *Early Christian Worship*, London 1953, pp. 75 and 102, n. 1. The analysis in Bonwetsch, *Theologie des Irenäus*, pp. 113, 143, is too schematic.

[13] *A.h.* v. ix. 1–2 (Stier. v. ix. 2). Cf. the future perspective in *A.h.* v. xii. 5 (Stier. v. xii. 6).

[14] Cf. *A.h.* IV. lvi. 1 (Stier. IV. xxxiv. 2): "Omnia enim ipse adimplevit veniens, et adhuc implet in Ecclesia usque ad consummationem a Lege praedictum novum Testamentum." Such an expression has extensive validity and defines the relationship between the Incarnation, the Church, and the Consummation.

[15] Cf. P. Gächter in *Z.K.T.*, 1934, p. 526 f. See also *Epid.* 41.

[16] Scharl, *Orientalia*, 1940, p. 397, n. 2, and Werner, *Enstehung des christlichen Dogmas*, p. 289.

naeus, as when, for instance, he says in the *Epideixis* that Christ came in order to seek the lost sheep, i.e. man, and that therefore there was no completely new Creation—in that case what had been lost would not have been found again, but a substitute for what was lost would instead have been created anew.[17] Christ assumes Adam's form, and it is Adam, defeated man, who is re-established in the new Covenant. We are conscious that Irenaeus fights shy of such passages as II Cor. v.17 and Gal. vi.15, and hardly ever quotes them. But it is not true that the idea of the new creation of man is completely absent from Irenaeus's thought. That which is done through Christ is directly parallel to Adam's first Creation and is called a *secunda plasmatio*.[18] In the same way the work of the Spirit may be described by saying that it was outpoured "in order to re-create man unto God."[19] Irenaeus attempts for several reasons to describe man's refashioning in the Incarnation otherwise than by defining it as "new creation." Throughout the period in which he lived there was in early Christendom a marked preference for the expression "new birth."[20] Irenaeus, with his doctrine of man as a child, chose rather to adopt those expressions which were concerned with "birth" and "growth."[21] Man is received into the Church as a child of God. For Irenaeus the ideas of adoption and new birth are very closely related.[22] The same fact is expressed by both, viz. that the child is ready to grow towards his appointed destiny, nourished within the Body of Christ, which is the Church.[23]

[17] *Epid.* 33. Note the polemical situation which gave a completely new and un-Pauline significance to the term "new creation": Irenaeus rejects any separation of Creation from the work of Christ as the act of a different God. Cf. *Epid.* 31.

[18] *A.h.* v. xxiii. 2 (Stier. ibid.). Cf. Heinrich Schumacher, *Kraft der Urkirche*, Freiburg-im-Breisgau 1934, p. 77 f., and *A.h.* III. xix. 2 (Stier. III. xviii. 2).

[19] *Epid.* 6.

[20] Harnack, *Die Terminologie der Wiedergeburt und verwandter Erlebnisse in der ältesten Kirche*, Leipzig 1918, pp. 106–8.

[21] Cf. Prümm in *Scholastik*, 1938, p. 221 f.

[22] See the short notice in Harnack, *Die Terminologie der Weidergeburt*, p. 103. Cf. *A.h.* IV. lxvii–lxviii 1 (Stier. IV. xli. 2–3).

[23] It is implied in the concept of *recapitulatio* that this new child of God is the same as the *infans*, *νήπιος*, of Creation. Cf. what Irenaeus says about the preservation of Adam's "plasmatio" in the time of Noah, *A.h.* IV. lviii. 4 (Stier. IV. xxxvi. 4). Irenaeus means that the connexion back to the first man is never severed, as it is in Gnosticism.

It is quite clear from this that what happens to man through the Spirit or through Christ in the Church is a continuation of his creation as man. He becomes man when he receives the Spirit.[24] He returns to his original nature, but at the same time he presses forward, for it is the nature of the child to grow, and man was created as "child."[25] In the very restoration of the first Creation there is an advance towards something greater than the first Creation, for the first Creation was marked by the fact that it was in the process of growth. For this reason some of Irenaeus's remarks can be interpreted to mean that the Spirit does not primarily belong to man, while elsewhere he can be interpreted as making the Spirit purely human. Endless discussion has arisen in Irenaean exegesis from this dualism. There are some, for instance, who maintain that Irenaeus has a dichotomous understanding of man, according to which man consists merely of body and soul, while the Spirit is something divine and superhuman, and others again who insist that Irenaeus has in fact a trichotomous understanding of man, according to which man, as man, consists of body, soul, and Spirit. If such a contrast is maintained between two interpretations which are both static, we shall make nothing at all of Irenaeus's subject-matter.[26] The Spirit is something which

[24] "Neque enim plasmatio carnis ipsa secundum se homo perfectus est; sed corpus hominis, et pars hominis. Neque enim et anima ipsa secundum se homo; sed anima hominis, et pars hominis. Neque spiritus homo: spiritus enim, et non homo vocatur. Commixtio autem et unitio horum omnium perfectum hominem efficit," *A.h.* v. vi. 1 (Stier. ibid.). After this Irenaeus quotes 1 Thess. v. 23. In *A.h.* v. ix. 1 (Stier. v. ix. 2) he puts it this way: "Quotquot autem timent Deum, et credunt in adventum Filii ejus, et per fidem constituunt in cordibus suis Spiritum Dei, hi tales juste homines dicentur, et mundi et spiritales et viventes Deo, quia habent Spiritum Patris, qui emundat hominem, et sublevat in vitam Dei." Man is destined to be *God's* man, to have communion with God. See Bonwetsch, *Theologie des Irenäus*, pp. 71–3.

[25] In *A.h.* v. x. 1–2 (Stier. ibid.) the conflict between flesh and Spirit in man is identified with the conflict between the Devil and God. The one who receives the Word is snatched out of the grasp of the man-slayer, and thus redeems his humanity. Of those who live under the protection of God it may be said that they "in pristinam veniunt hominis naturam, eam quae secundum imaginem et similitudinem facta est Dei" *A.h.* v. x. 2 (Stier. v. x. 1). Their regained health finds expression in the fact of their growth and bearing fruit.

[26] There are glaring difficulties, e.g. in Klebba, *Anthropologie des hl. Irenaeus*, pp. 164–6, where Irenaeus is forced into a rigidly dichotomous anthropology. Klebba's main thesis is that the Spirit is something *supernatural*. For this reason he has therefore to make a sharp distinction between *imago* and *similitudo*. In general,

grows together with man, and in proportion as it does, man becomes what he was destined to become, viz. man.[27] This goal has not yet been reached within the Church, but the Spirit strives against the flesh. Sin, the inhuman element, still remains.[28] But one day, in the resurrection, the Spirit will wholly penetrate the flesh, drive out sin, and make man *man*.[29]

What function does the Spirit have in man in the present? There are many possible answers to this question, but one of them is of particular interest to us, i.e. that the Spirit forms man in the image of God. The Spirit thrusts itself upon man, and fashions him.[30] The same process, which from one point of view is called the formation by the Spirit of true humanity—for to conform to the *imago* and *similitudo* of God is in fact to become man, to be created to perfection—can also be described as ingrafting into Christ. The Saviour is at work as Christ, as the "anointed," when He gives His own the Spirit and gathers together His Church. Christ is the *imago* and *similitudo* of God: to be in Him is to be at home in humanity's true being.[31]

the trichotomous view comes nearer to the essential Irenaeus, provided only that we can combine it with the idea of growth—man in Creation is destined for the Spirit of Christ, which is the same as saying that he is destined to become man.

[27] Böhringer, *Kirche Christi*, VOL. II, pp. 466–70, deals well with the question here. The best solution of the problem is in Hunger, *Scholastik*, 1942, p. 169 f. Strangely enough, Hunger believes himself to be in agreement with Klebba; see p. 171, n. 35. On the Spirit as gradually "accustoming" itself to dwelling in mankind, cf. *A.h.* IV. xxv. 2 (Stier. IV. xiv. 2) and III. xviii. 1 (Stier. III. xvii. 1).

[28] On man as being in the midst of the struggle between flesh and Spirit, see the whole section *A.h.* v. ix. 1–v. xii. 5 (Stier. v. ix. 1–v. xii. 6). *When the Spirit subdues sin in us, we are formed after the* imago *and* similitudo *of God*. This takes place in the present while man lives in the Church. Conflict makes man grow.

[29] The Spirit which takes possession of man and enters into him is the same Spirit which makes Christ *Christ*, i.e. "anointed," for it is *Himself* whom Christ gives to man in the Church. Cf. Wieten, *Irenaeus' geschrift*, p. 187.

[30] "And *in us all* is the Spirit, who cries *Abba Father*, and fashions man into the likeness of God," *Epid.* 5. Cf. Scharl, *Orientalia*, 1940, p. 389.

[31] Cf. *Epid.* 97: "He *appeared* . . . mingling and mixing the Spirit of God the Father with the creature formed by God, that man might be after the image and likeness of God." Thus man's creation is accomplished: "Ubi autem Spiritus Patris, ibi homo vivens, sanguis rationalis ad ultionem a Deo custoditus, caro a Spiritu possessa oblita quidem sui, qualitatem autem Spiritus assumens, conformis facta Verbo Dei. Et propterea ait: Sicut portavimus imaginem ejus qui de terra est, portemus et imaginem ejus qui de caelo est," (1 Cor. xv. 49), *A.h.* v. ix. 2 (Stier. v. ix. 3). See also the discussion of the Spirit as "figurans" in *A.h.* v. ix. 1 (Stier. ibid.); and also "figuratio" in IV. xiv (Stier. IV. vii. 4). Cf. Bonwetsch, *Theologie des Irenäus*, p. 114 f.

Human life in its purity wells up in the Christian congregation, which drinks from Christ as from the source of Creation. But those who have been ingrafted into Christ must still taste the tyranny of sin and death, which still persists, in their suffering and struggling on the earth. This agony, however, which at times culminates in martyrdom, does not lead them away from the Lord, but on the contrary brings them nearer to Him, since Jesus Himself was crucified. When members of the Christian congregation are thrown to the wild beasts, or burned at the stake, *then*, says Irenaeus, "man is made in accordance with the image and likeness of God," since the "hands of God," the Spirit and the Son, which created man at the beginning, now carry their work of Creation forward to the day of the resurrection in the martyred Church.[32] By this man is impressed into the crucified Christ who alone is Lord, and alone possesses power of resurrection.

Man and the Church belong together. When man is formed after the pattern of the Son it means that the Church, where man is, and in which he is formed, is set forth as the Body of Christ. In the clearest possible way Irenaeus brings together statements about man's coming to maturity and the destined union of the Church with Christ, for the two are organically interrelated.[33] In the fashioning of man which takes place in the Church, God's creating of man is continued in the present. The

[32] "Et propter hoc in omni tempore, plasmatus initio homo per manus Dei, id est, Filii et Spiritus, fit secundum imaginem et similitudinem Dei, paleis quidem abjectis, quae sunt apostasia; frumento autem in horreum assumto, quod est hi qui ad Deum fide fructificant. Et propterea tribulatio necessaria est his qui salvantur, ut quodammodo contriti, et attenuati, et conspersi per patientiam Verbo Dei, et igniti, apti sint ad convivium Regis," *A.h.* v. xxviii. 3 (Stier. v. xxviii. 4); Irenaeus then cites the well-known words of Ignatius on Rom. IV (*Die apostolischen Väter*, ed. Bihlmeyer, p. 98). The Latin text quoted above is correctly amended by Lundström, *Studien*, p. 50. Cf. the passage which follows in *A.h.* v. xxix. 1 (Stier. ibid.), and IV. liv (Stier. IV. xxxiii. 9); and also IV. lxiii. 2–3 (Stier. IV. xxxviii. 3–4). In the latter passage man is said to attain to the *imago* and *similitudo* by passing through death.

[33] E.g. *A.h.* IV. lxi. 2 (Stier. IV. xxxvii. 7) ". . . praefiniente Deo omnia ad *hominis perfectionem*, et ad aedificationem, et manifestationem dispositionum; uti et bonitas ostendatur, et justitia perficiatur, et *Ecclesia ad figuram imaginis Filii ejus coaptetur*, et tandem aliquando *maturus fiat homo*, in tantis maturescens ad videndum et capiendum." On the Gnostic combination of ἄνθρωπος and ἐκκλησία, or *homo* and *ecclesia*, see *A.h.* I. i. 18 (Stier. I. viii. 5), I. vi. 2 (Stier. I. xii. 3) and several other passages in the first book.

hands of the Creator, the Son and the Spirit, began their work far back in the beginning, and will soon have achieved their purpose in the resurrection, but for the present they are engaged in their work of fashioning man. Faith and good-will keep man's heart submissive, so that the Creator can work him like good clay. Unbelief and ingratitude make the clay dry and hard in God's hand, so that it can no longer be moulded; and man crumbles away.[34] The period of faith and of the Church is the period of man's fashioning. Death, it is true, consumes Creation, and the outward man perishes, but God uses the evil power of death in order to destroy in man what from God's point of view ought to be destroyed, viz. sin. When death has served God's purpose and helped to make man like Christ, God's crucified image, then death itself, the last enemy, will also be defeated.[35] For when man dies, Christ's body follows its head, Christ, through the darkness to the light, through the Cross to the resurrection.[36] The sufferings are not those of destruction, but of birth.

It would be quite unlike Irenaeus to make a contrast between spiritual and material, or a distinction between Spirit and body. Man's growth develops into "the spiritual body," the resurrection body, in which the long-drawn-out conflict waged during his life on earth between sin and the Spirit, between the

[34] "Praesta ei autem cor tuum molle et tractabile, et custodi figuram qua te figuravit artifex, habens in temetipso humorem, ne induratus amittas vestigia digitorum ejus . . . Si vero statim obduratus respuas artem ejus, et ingratus exsistas in eum, quoniam homo factus es, ingratus Deo factus, simul et artem ejus et vitam amisisti. Facere enim proprium est benignitatis Dei: fieri autem proprium est hominis naturae. Si igitur tradideris ei quod est tuum, id est, fidem in eum et subjectionem, recipies ejus artem, et eris perfectum opus Dei. Si autem non credideris ei, et fugeris manus ejus, erit causa imperfectionis in te qui non obedisti, sed non in illo qui vocavit," *A.h.* IV. lxiv. 2 (Stier. IV. xxxix. 2–3). On the text see Lundström, *Studien*, p. 130. Cf. IV. xxi. 2 (Stier. IV. xi. 2) and Seeberg, *Lehrbuch der Dogmengeschichte*, VOL. I, p. 410.

[35] Cf. *A.h.* III. xxi. (Stier. III. xx. 1–2) and III. xxxv. 2–xxxvi (Stier. III. xxiii. 6–7), with its reference with the Pauline statement, "The last enemy that shall be destroyed is death" (1 Cor. xv. 26)). As usual, time in Irenaeus has constitutive significance.

[36] See *A.h.* IV. lvi. 4 (Stier. IV. xxxiv. 4) and III. xx. 3 (Stier. III. xix. 3), besides the passages on martyrdom just quoted. The categorical statement in Bousset, *Kyrios Christos*, p. 419, that the Pauline "Mitsterben und Mitauferstehen mit Christus" is entirely absent from Irenaeus's way of thinking has no strong basis. We shall be discussing again the relationship between Christ and His Body, the Church, in the next section.

flesh and the Spirit, is brought to an end through the victory of the Spirit. The Spirit then has dominion over human kind, as the resurrection of Christ is the Spirit's dominion over Jesus's humanity, and is for that reason a bodily resurrection. As soon as we make the distinction between natural and supernatural the basis of our thinking, human and divine will be sharply divided, and the somewhat naive transitions from body to Spirit, which are characteristic of Irenaeus, will be lost. We can see a typical illustration of such a misrepresentation of Irenaeus in the dogmatic historians who refuse to see *imago* and *similitudo* as constituting a unity, and instead attempt to give the term *imago* one meaning and *similitudo* another.[37] Irenaeus speaks of "imago et similitudo" in an overwhelming number of expressions as constituting a unity. Were there not a scholastic tradition of medieval origin which separated *imago* and *similitudo* into two distinct concepts, no theologian today would have thought of separating these two terms in Irenaeus. But there is now this later tradition, and there are certain scholars who have accordingly been asking what attitude Irenaeus took to the doctrinal tradition which they were discussing. Their own quesion, however, is entirely anachronistic. Naturally, too, they then find indications of support from Irenaeus for this scheme of natural-supernatural, but the history of the humanistic sciences will show that in such cases a positive answer can almost always be produced in reply to the question which is unrelated to the subject-matter.

With a view to safeguarding the whole man, body, soul, and Spirit, Irenaeus once in fact quite clearly separates *imago* from

[37] To start with *A.h.* v. vi. 1 (Stier. ibid.), a passage which we intend to deal with further directly, and make a distinction between *imago* and *similitudo* is quite common in writings on Irenaeus. See e.g. Wendt, *Christliche Lehre*, p. 22; Klebba, *Anthropologie des hl. Irenaeus*, pp. 22 ff. (note the author's difficulties on pp. 174–6); Dufourcq, *Saint Irénée*, p. 163 f.; Stoll, *Lehre des hl. Irenäus*, p. 6 f.; Beuzart, *Essai sur la théologie d'Irénée*, p. 66 f.; and to a certain extent also Seeberg, *Lehrbuch der Dogmengeschichte*, VOL. I, pp. 396 f., 431 f.; and Bonwetsch, *Theologie des Irenäus*, p. 74; also Gächter in *Z.K.T.*, 1934, p. 528; Prümm in *Scholastik*, 1938, pp. 213–15; Brunner, *Man in Revolt*, pp. 91, 532 f.; and Niebuhr, *Nature and Destiny of Man*, VOL. I. p. 286. There is a more penetrating analysis by Koch in *Theol. Stud. u. Krit.*, 1925, pp. 186 ff., where, however, the term "supernatural" is used in a confusing way; and, despite his division of the sources, in Loofs, *Theophilus von Antiochien*, p. 59 f., especially n. 3 (cf. p. 303 f.), and also by Hunger in *Scholastik*, 1942, pp. 169–72.

similitudo.[38] He proceeds from the proposition that man is created "secundum imaginem et similitudinem Dei." After this he proceeds to take issue with the Gnostics who denied the salvation of the body. It is in this polemical situation that Irenaeus makes the distinction which he does, and we ought to notice that his opponents, whom he wanted to refute, made the same distinction between *imago* and *similitudo* as signifying at times body and at times Spirit. Irenaeus takes a weapon out of their own armoury by saying that if we let only the body be saved, then one has the *imago* without the *similitudo*, and if we let only the Spirit be saved, then one has the *similitudo* without the *imago*—but in neither case are we speaking about the whole and completed man.[39] For man is wholly man only where body, soul, and Spirit are united and grow together after the *imago* and *similitudo* of God, which happens in the faith of the believer in God and his righteousness towards his neighbour.[40] The strange thing is that this passage, in which a distinction is made between *imago* and *similitudo*, is one of the clearest demonstrations of any in Irenaeus that the Spirit is not a supernatural addition to the purely human, but is on the contrary humanity's own completion.[41] And the Spirit is such a completion in man precisely

[38] *A.h.* v. vi. 1 (Stier. ibid.). To this should be added v. xvi. 1 (Stier. v. xvi. 2). These are the only passages in which *imago* and *similitudo* are separated. Otherwise both terms are almost monotonously held together to form a single concept.

[39] "Cum autem spiritus hic commixtus animae unitur plasmati, propter effusionem Spiritus spiritalis et perfectus homo factus est: et hic est qui secundum imaginem et similitudinem factus est Dei. Si autem defuerit animae Spiritus, animalis est vere, qui est talis, et carnalis derelictus imperfectus erit: imaginem quidem habens in plasmate, similitudinem vero non assumens per Spiritum. Sicut autem hic imperfectus est, sic iterum si quis tollat imaginem, et spernat plasma, jam non hominem intelligere potest, sed aut partem aliquam hominis, quemadmodum praediximus, vel aliud aliquid praeter hominem," *A.h.* v. vi. 1 (Stieren has the better punctuation; cf. Robinson in *J.T.S.*, 1931, p. 382, whom we follow above in his correction of Harvey's text).

[40] *A.h.* v. vi. 1, at the end. The discussion of the Spirit, faith, and righteousness are intended as an exegesis of the content of *imago* and *similitudo*.

[41] With regard to *A.h.* v. xvi. 1 (Stier. v. xvi. 2), it is worth noting that the expression "imaginem ostendit" is paralleled by "ostendit similitudinem" in iv. lii. 1 (Stier. iv. xxxiii. 4). Cf. the use of "similitudo" in *A.h.* iv. lx. 2 (Stier. iv. xxxvii. 4) and v. xxi. 1 (Stier. ibid.), and of "similis Deo" in iv. vii (Stier. iv. iv. 3) on free will; also "similes sibi" in iv. lxiii. 3 (Stier. iv. xxxviii. 4). An objective examination of the subject-matter makes the interpretation of the scholastic distinction between *imago* and *similitudo* impossible. On the other hand, we must frankly admit that in these two passages Irenaeus does actually separate *imago* and *similitudo* in such a

because it is God, i.e. creating, forming, and fashioning. The Spirit will complete its work of forming man in the resurrection and the life eternal, when the body will be permeated by the Spirit, i.e. by Life.[42] The resurrection is thus the end of man's creation, something that is to come, seen from the point of view of the Church militant, and not something that is past. The Church is in the midst of this dynamic process which is to bring the true man into being, or, which is the same thing, to let Christ be formed in men.

The Body of Christ

It is of the nature of Christ that He has a Church, and gathers men around Himself. Had He lived for Himself otherwise, He would not have been Christ. For Irenaeus, as Bousset says, the Church is as self-evident as the air which he breathes.[43] Speaking generally, one can note widespread agreement on this point during the last century in writings on Irenaeus, though there too, as almost universally, scholars have regarded the Irenaean concept of the Church as "Catholicising." As a consequence, Protestant writers have refrained from going deeply into the study of Irenaeus, and Roman Catholic writers have to a certain degree read later ideas of the Church into him.[44] Neither of these consequences has been of benefit. Whatever contemporary confession Irenaeus might resemble in his view of the

way that for the scholar who is confessionally bound, and not historically interested, what he says must lend support to the later Roman Catholic way of thinking. Loofs, *Theophilus von Antiochien*, p. 211 f., without good grounds, regards the distinction between the two terms which emerged in a particular polemical situation as a sign that Irenaeus borrowed from a literary source which can be isolated.

[42] *A.h.* IV. viii (Stier. IV. v. 1), which is quoted by Prümm, *Christentum als Neuheitserlebnis*, p. 236, n. 5, as the *only* instance in Irenaeus of the idea of the "supernatural," deals with man's "growth" and not with the "supernatural." See Prümm in *Scholastik*, 1938, p. 212, top of page, and 347, foot of page, or better still in *Pisciculi*, p. 199 f., nn. 27 and 28, and also p. 217, n. 100.

[43] Bousset, *Kyrios Christos*, p. 423.

[44] On the Protestant side, see Albrecht Ritschl, *Die Entstehung der altkatholischen Kirche*, 2nd edn. Bonn 1857, pp. 312 ff.; R. A. Lipsius, "Die Zeit des Irenäus von Lyon und die Entstehung der altkatholischen Kirche," in *Historische Zeitschrift*, 1872, pp. 241 ff.; and also Böhringer, *Kirche Christi*, VOL. II, pp. 419 ff.; and Beuzart, *Essai sur la théologie d'Irénée*, p. 131; and on the Roman Catholic side, the extremely influential Pierre Batiffol, *L'Église naissante et le catholicisme*, 6th edn. Paris 1913, pp. 195–276, in which Irenaeus is represented as the very gateway to "Catholicism."

Church, we must make an objective attempt to understand what he means by *ecclesia*. There is hardly any better starting-point for an analysis of what he means than his concept of the Church as the "Body of Christ."[45]

The idea which modern thought finds difficult to grasp of the Church as being a body for Christ, something in which He lives, and which lives in Him, is connected by Irenaeus in many ways with other more easily grasped theological concepts. The idea that Christ rose in a spiritual body, in which His believers now grow as time moves on towards the Parousia, is not the only connecting line between Christology and Ecclesiology.[46] The line of thought acquires a slightly different shade of meaning in the light of Paul's words about husband and wife in Eph. v—men love their wives as their own bodies (v.23, 28). Christ is the husband of the Church, the Church is the Bride of Christ, and as such the Body of Christ.[47] The idea of the Body of Christ lies in the background wherever Irenaeus uses metaphors or names referring to a woman of the Church, which he very frequently does, with profound theological significance. Never, in fact, did Irenaeus so directly or powerfully promote the early Christian concept of grace as in his description of the Church as the elect and beloved Bride.

For it was an unworthy woman whom Christ chose as His Bride. As Hosea took a harlot as his wife, Christ takes the Church from the godless world which is sunk in sin. The Church's holiness consists simply and solely in its communion with Christ. Paul holds that an unbelieving wife is sanctified by her husband (1 Cor. vii.14), and in the same way the Church is sanctified. It is taken by pure grace without any qualifications of its own from the heathen people, as Moses chose an Ethiopian woman to marry. It is to this "marriage of the Word" with the multitudes who are ignorant of God that Christ alludes when

[45] Cf. W. Schmidt, *Die Kirche bei Irenäus*, p. 91 f.

[46] Cf. Cullmann, *Königsherrschaft Christi*, pp. 29 ff.; and, on the "growing body" according to the Pauline view, Ernst Percy, *Der Leib Christi*, Lund and Leipzig 1942, p. 53 f.

[47] See ii Clem. xiv. 2, in which the womanliness and *soma*-character of the Church in relation to Christ are logically connected: *οὐκ οἴομαι δὲ ὑμᾶς ἀγνοεῖν, ὅτι ἐκκλησία ζῶσα σῶμά ἐστιν Χριστοῦ· λέγει γὰρ ἡ γραφή· Ἐποίησεν ὁ θεὸς τὸν ἄνθρωπον ἄρσεν καὶ θῆλυ· τὸ ἄρσεν ἐστὶν ὁ Χριστός, τὸ θῆλυ ἡ ἐκκλησία.* Cf. Joseph C. Plumpe, *Mater Ecclesia*, Washington 1943, p. 6 f.

He says to the Pharisees: "The tax collectors and the harlots go into the kingdom of God before you" (Mt. xxi.31).[48] In order to win His Church Christ endured death and suffering: His Bride was won through His faithfulness and patience.[49] The Church is Rachel, for whose sake Christ bears His burden. There is an intense consciousness of election, an assurance of having been undeservedly drawn out of the world of death, running through these and similar statements by Irenaeus—he thinks directly of himself as being in the number of redeemed publicans and harlots. The only holiness of the Church resides in the fact that she is loved by Christ.[50]

As the Bride of Christ the Church is both the Body of Christ and the mother of the redeemed. The mother metaphor is wholly in line with Irenaeus's statements about the Church as the Bride chosen from heathendom, the woman impure in herself, but yet loved. The food and drink which are offered to men in the Church is the incarnate Christ Himself, or the Spirit.[51] From these the child derives power to grow and become stronger. The view of the believer as a child is, of course, connected with the discussion of the Church as a mother and with the idea of new birth. "Growth" too, therefore, becomes an expression of man's connexion with the Church, for the child grows through receiving life from its mother. From this basic point of view it is of very little importance whether Irenaeus employs concepts which relate to new birth or to adoption, for

[48] See the passage *A.h.* IV. xxxiv. 12 (Stier. IV. xx. 12) which is fundamental to Irenaeus's conception of the Church. On the two Covenants and the two peoples, cf. *A.h.* IV. xxxv. 2 (Stier. IV. xxi. 2) and IV. xlviii–xlix (Stier. IV. xxxi–xxxii).

[49] "Omnia autem ille faciebat propter illam juniorem, bonos oculos habentem, Rachel; quae praefigurebat Ecclesiam, propter quam sustinuit Christus," *A.h.* IV. xxxv. 3 (Stier. IV. xxi. 3).

[50] Cf. Nygren's general appraisal of the Irenaean theology, in *Agape and Eros*, pp. 392–412.

[51] See in particular *A.h.* III. xxxviii. 1 (Stier. III. xxiv. 1). On this point cf. Plumpe, *Mater ecclesia*, pp. 41–4; and R. Knopf, *Ausgewählte Märtyrerakten*, ed. G. Krüger, Tübingen 1929, e.g. p. 28, the Epistle from Lyons and Vienna on the persecution there in the year 177. Apart from this we do not know much about the two Churches during Irenaeus's time. See, however, C. Martin, "Saint Irénée et son correspondant, le diacre Démètre de Vienne," in *Revue d'histoire ecclésiastique*, 1942, pp. 143–52. On the juxtaposition of mother and Church in Irenaeus see also *Epid.* 94 and *A.h.* IV. lxii. 1 (Stier. IV. xxxviii. 1) and V. xiv. 4 (Stier ibid.): the body of the Church grows through the power which God has supplied to the world in the Incarnation.

in either case he arrives at the idea of child and growth, at one time by way of baptism as the laver of regeneration, at another time by way of baptism as the act of adoption, the reception of Japheth into the house of Shem with full right of inheritance.[52] The dead man receives life, the bond-slave is made free. If any man has been ingrafted into Christ, his new situation is characterised by his having a future and a hope. All that Irenaeus has to say on this point is marked by a double cause of rejoicing, first, that we have been plucked out of the doomed heathen world, and second, that it is possible even now in the Church to foresee what is to be.

We should particularly notice the fact that baptism, as we have just said, is often defined in Irenaeus as an act of adoption by which a stranger or outsider is constituted the heir of all the gifts of God. The same fundamental view is expressed in the concept of adoption as in the metaphor of marriage to a foreign or impure woman.[53] The accent lies on the foreignness and unworthiness of the adopted one, i.e. on the inscrutable mercy of the God who elects. For Irenaeus, the Church, the *ecclesia*, is the Church of the Gentiles. It comes into existence when old Israel with its law of bondage withers away and the Apostles are driven by the Spirit from Jerusalem—Jerusalem which was ripe for destruction and downfall, and which after Easter and Pentecost had no longer any function to fulfil. The external, geographical aspect of the Church, viz. the fact that it is filled with children from people outside the land of Israel, with

[52] *Epid.* 41 f., 96, and *A.h.* v. xv. 3 (Stier. ibid.). By baptism we are adopted into the Church, and through baptism the Spirit is given. See *Epid.* 3 for a summary of baptism. Cf. Hitchcock, *Irenaeus of Lugdunum*, pp. 264–9. Gen. IX.27 is fulfilled in adoption.

[53] On the combination of Spirit, Church, and adoption, cf. *A.h.* III. vi. 1 (Stier. ibid.), ". . . de Patre, et Filio, et de his qui adoptionem perceperunt, dicit: hi autem sunt Ecclesia," IV. pref. iii (Stier. IV pref. iv, towards the end), and also v. xii. 2 (Stier. ibid.), v. xviii. 1 (Stier. v. xviii. 2), which is of particular interest owing to the identification occurring there of *adoptio* and *generatio*, and v. xxxii. 2 (Stier. ibid.), with its reference to the word of John the Baptist, "God is able of these stones to raise up children unto Abraham" (Lk. III. 8). The Church consists of such "stones" which have been raised to life, and which do not spring from Abraham, but yet are Abraham's children. There is, finally, the great affirmation of Irenaeus which should be put in here: "Ubi enim Ecclesia, ibi et Spiritus Dei; et ubi Spiritus Dei, illic Ecclesia," III. xxxviii. 1 (Stier. III. xxiv. 1). Adoption is, therefore, eternal life. See Bonwetsch, *Theologie des Irenäus*, p. 141.

foreigners, strangers, and adopted people, and the internal and essential aspect, viz. the fact that the Church is built on the Gospel, while old Israel was based on the Law, are not contradictory, but simply two different aspects of the same reality. The movement outwards from Jerusalem to the waiting, captive people is the concrete form which the Gospel must take.[54] The vital form of the Church cannot be different from the vital form of mission—as we saw earlier, it is of the essence of the Church to move forward into the world of men.

Those who have been adopted have all the possessions of the children, and are accordingly the seed of Abraham, the new peculiar people, Israel of the new "Testament."[55] But there is a great difference between the old Israel and the new. In the old Covenant the eschatological perspective narrowed down to a point; in the beginning God worked with his "hands," the Son and the Spirit, in Creation as a whole in order later to concentrate the work of the Spirit and the Word on a single people, and finally incarnate them in a single man, Christ. But now in the new Israel the perspective widens out; behind the Church stands the Incarnate One who is continually extending His government through the *kerygma*, and is embracing humanity in the advancing Church in order ultimately in the resurrection to establish the same unbounded domain as existed at the beginning of Creation, when God will act in power with the world as a whole, and the Spirit will irresistibly occupy the bodies of men.[56] The dynamic which will transform everything

[54] See here *Epid.* 21, a quite typical passage in which the Church signifies preaching to the Gentiles, and 93: *A.h.* III. xviii. 2 (Stier. III. xvii. 3), in which Jg. VI.36–40 is graphically expounded, IV. xxxv. 3 (Stier. IV. xxi. 3) and V. xxxiv. 1, 3 (Stier. ibid.). Cf. Bonwetsch, "Der Schriftbeweis für die Kirche aus den Heiden als das wahre Israel bis auf Hippolyt," in *Theologische Studien Th. Zahn dargebracht*, Leipzig 1908, pp. 12–14. On the fall of Jerusalem at the time when the Church was spreading from there as being in accordance with the will of God, see especially *A.h.* IV. v (Stier. IV. iv. 1) and IV. lviii. 2 (Stier. IV. xxxvi. 2). When freedom comes, bondage is at an end.

[55] *A.h.* IV. xv (Stier. IV. viii. 1) and several other passages; also IV. xxiv. 3 (Stier. IV. xiii. 4).

[56] The universal aspect is strong in Irenaeus's view of the Church. He has no constricting sectarianism. The eschatological foundation of universalism will, however, be lost if one begins to operate with later, institutional conceptions of "catholicity," etc., by which universalism is, as it were, thought into the categories of the earlier period. The adjective καθολικός is nowhere found in Irenaeus as an attribute of the Church. It does not make for clarity to speak, as is frequently done,

in the last age is now within the Church, for the Church is in fact Christ and the Spirit at work in the world, accomplishing their work in the hearts and common life of men.[57] Those who possess Christ and the Spirit are sinners, and therefore need to grow and to struggle, but Christ and the Spirit are in them, and therefore they *can* grow and struggle. In this kind of life there is direct communion with God the Creator Himself. There is freedom for man from the outpouring of the Spirit at Pentecost, i.e. the possibility of being man.[58] By participating in the Body of Christ true humanity is fashioned after the *imago* and *similitudo* of God.[59]

In Irenaeus the word *sacramentum* means "secret," and is never used to denote baptism or the Eucharist,[60] nor do we find in Irenaeus any one definition by which the external factors which constitute the Church may be described. The distinctive marks of the Church, however, are the true proclamation of the Word, which is based on Scripture and is the responsibility of the Ministry which has been handed down, and baptism and the Eucharist.[61] The theological conflict in which Irenaeus was involved concerned the content of the Christian proclamation,

of "catholicity" in the Irenaean concept of the Church. See e.g. Ladislas Spikowski, *La Doctrine de l'Église dans saint Irénée*, Strasbourg 1926, pp. 105 ff.; W. Schmidt, *Die Kirche bei Irenäus*, pp. 88 ff.

[57] *A.h.* III. xxxviii. 1 (Stier. III. xxiv. 1), v. viii. 1 (Stier. ibid.); and Lindroth in *S.T.K.*, 1939, pp. 35 ff.

[58] Cf. *A.h.* III. xii. 2 (Stier. ibid.), III. xii. 17 (Stier. III. xii. 14), and III. xviii. 1 (Stier. III. xvii. 1).

[59] Cf. *A.h.* III. xviii. 2 (Stier. III. xvii. 3): ". . . commendante Domino Spiritui sancto suum hominem, qui inciderat in latrones, cui ipse misertus est, et ligavit vulnera ejus, dans duo denaria regalia, ut per Spiritum imaginem et inscriptionem Patris et Filii accipientes, fructificemus creditum nobis denarium, multiplicatum Domino annumerantes." The passage is influenced by Lk. x. 35 and Mt. xxv. 15–30. The combination here of *Spiritus* and *imago* without *similitudo* is a matter of some concern to Klebba, *Anthropologie des hl. Irenaeus*, p. 184.

[60] *A.h.* II. xlvii. 1 (Stier. II. xxx. 7), at the end. Cf. Beuzart, *Essai sur la théologie d'Irénée*, p. 162; and Hitchcock, *Irenaeus of Lugdunum*, p. 264. On the general question see also Lietzmann, *Church Universal*, p. 211 f.

[61] The question has been raised whether, at least in embryo, a practice of penance might not be found in Irenaeus, but the material appears to be too insubstantial for a clear answer to be given. For discussion on the question see Hugo Koch, "Die Sundenvergebung bei Irenäus" in *Z.NT.W.*, 1908, pp. 35–46; Bonwetsch, *Theologie des Irenäus*, p. 131 f.; W. Schmidt, *Die Kirche bei Irenäus*, pp. 129–36 and K. Müller and von Campenhausen, *Kirchengeschichte*, 3rd edn. Tübingen 1941, VOL. I, PT. I, pp. 255–7.

and it might be said that the whole of his struggle against Gnosticism was centred upon the question of the proper exegesis of the Bible. We shall understand what Irenaeus has to say about Ministry and *successio*, as we shall see directly, from a study of doctrine rather than of the proper administration of baptism and Eucharist. Any controversy that there is is not about baptism and the Eucharist by themselves, and for this reason both are less frequently mentioned in the polemical *Adversus haereses* than we might expect from the Irenaean concept of the Church; in the *Epideixis*, on the other hand, baptism occupies a central position, which is bound up with the special character of this writing.[62] Since we have just touched upon Irenaeus's doctrine of baptism, our immediate task will be to discuss the two great statements on the Eucharist which are found in the *Adversus haereses*.

In the Eucharist man receives the body of Christ and the Christian community is thereby built up as the body of Christ. The main emphasis in Irenaeus is laid on man's participation in Christ, and his nourishment by the bread and the wine, and not on the offering. This does not mean that the idea of sacrifice in connexion with the Eucharist is to be thrust aside. On the contrary, it is of dominant importance. But when Irenaeus speaks about sacrifice, he never says that Christ is offered, but always that the pure gifts of Creation, bread and wine, are offered.[63] The offering is made to God who made everything

[62] On *A.h.* see Bousset, *Kyrios Christos*, p. 423, n. 1, and also Felix L. Cirlot, *The Early Eucharist*, London 1939, pp. 86 f., 119. With regard to baptism in *Epid.*, see the lively debate which followed in the years immediately following the discovery of the document, e.g. Wieten, *Irenaeus' geschrift*, pp. 150 ff.; S. A. Becker, *Ο ΚΑΝΩΝ ΤΗΣ ΑΛΗΘΕΙΑΣ*, Copenhagen 1910, pp. 109 ff.; and Nussbaumer, *Das Ursymbolum*, pp. 111 ff.; cf. the inquiry in van den Eynde, *Normes de l'enseignement*, pp. 281 ff. Allusions to baptism and Eucharist often occur in Irenaeus without explanation. Typical of such passages are *A.h.* III. xi. 9 (Stier. III. xi. 5), and IV. xxxvi. 1 (Stier. IV. xxii. 1); see the excellent exegesis of these passages in Loewenich, *Johannes-Verständnis*, pp. 133–5.

[63] *A.h.* IV. xxix. 5–IV. xxxi. 5 (Stier. IV. xvii. 5–xviii. 6): the Eucharist is represented as the pure offering of the new Covenant which replaces the now abolished sacrificial system of the Old Testament. Protestant writers sometimes show a tendency to underestimate the significance of the concept of sacrifice, just as Roman Catholic writers tend to read later ideas of the sacrifice of the Mass into the text of Irenaeus. J. W. F. Höfling, *Die Lehre der ältesten Kirche vom Opfer*, Erlangen 1851, pp. 71–107, is very much influenced in his argument by his opposition to the offering of the Mass; Höfling bases his position, furthermore (pp. 98 ff.), on the

that is good, but at the same time it benefits the brethren, i.e. the other members of the congregation, since all, even the poor, taste the bounties which are offered.[64] When Irenaeus sees in the bread and wine Christ Himself, the emphasis passes immediately from the offering to the communion. We receive Christ in bread and wine, and thereby our own bodies participate in the body and blood of Christ. And those who are in Christ and have Christ within themselves have the hope of eternal life.[65] To deny the resurrection of the flesh is to deny that the cup is the communion of the blood of Christ, and the bread the communion of the body of Christ.[66] As the vine, rooted in the earth, bears its fruit in its season, and the grain of corn, sown in the earth, bursting into growth, springs up and increases by the Spirit of God which embraces all creation, and the bread and wine which have thus sprung out of the earth have the Word of God spoken over them and become the Eucharist, i.e. the body and blood of Christ, so also our bodies, which have been nourished by similar food, will, without perishing, be able to be buried in the earth and there be resolved into their elements, in order finally to rise again in their due time when the Word of God resurrects them. God directs life through a series of "deaths," which all reveal within themselves the seed of the renewal of life.[67] And this is what is done when God's strength "is made perfect in weakness."

so-called Pfaff fragments which were later shown by Harnack to be forgeries (*Die Pfaff'schen Irenäusfragmente*, Leipzig 1900, pp. 32 ff.). As strongly influenced by his desire to find the sacrifice of the Mass in Irenaus is Franz Wieland in *Der vorirenäische Opferbegriff*, Munich 1909, p. 148 f. Cf. Seeberg, *Lehrbuch der Dogmengeschichte*, VOL. I, pp. 457–61, and Cirlot, *The Early Eucharist*, p. 223.

[64] *A.h.* IV. xxxi. 5. The offering does not propitiate God, *A.h.* IV. xxxi. 2 (Stier. IV. xviii. 3).

[65] *A.h.* IV. xxxi. 4 (Stier. IV. xviii. 5). On the text see Harnack, *Die Pfaff'schen Irenäusfragmente*, p. 56; and Seeberg, *Lehrbuch der Dogmengeschicht*, VOL. I. p. 459, nn. 1 and 2. On the subject cf. Simonin in *Rev. des sciences*, 1934, pp. 290 ff., and also Hitchcock in *C.Q.R.*, 1939–40, pp. 221–3, although his Anglicanism predominates a little too clearly.

[66] See *A.h.* V. ii. 1–3 (Stier. V. ii. 2–3). On baptism and the body see the similar statement in III. xviii. 1 (Stier. III. xvii. 2), and Bonwetsch, *Theologie des Irenäus*, p. 128.

[67] *Καὶ ὅνπερ τρόπον τὸ ξύλον τῆς ἀμπέλου κλιθὲν εἰς τὴν γῆν τῷ ἰδίῳ καιρῷ ἐκαρποφόρησε, καὶ ὁ κόκκος τοῦ σίτου πεσὼν εἰς τὴν γῆν καὶ διαλυθεὶς, πολλοστὸς ἐγέρθη διὰ τοῦ Πνεύματος τοῦ Θεοῦ, τοῦ συνέχοντος τὰ πάντα· ἔπειτα δὲ διὰ τῆς σοφίας τοῦ Θεοῦ εἰς χρῆσιν ἐλθόντα ἀνθρώπων, καὶ προσλαμβανόμενα τὸν*

To say that the Church is the Body of Christ also means that it holds together and does not become divided by the fact that one member is different from another member of the Body. The advantage which comes from separation from other Christians is always less than the loss which the wider fellowship suffers as a result of this separation.[68] Fellowship within the Church cannot be continued merely on the basis of submission to some central authority, e.g. the Church of Rome, notwithstanding the fact that Rome is the largest and most important of all communions, but fellowship must rather rest on love and freedom, provided that the foundation of belief is not destroyed. It was for this reason that Irenaeus took the side of Asia Minor in the Easter controversy and sought to overturn the coercive measures of the Bishop of Rome, in spite of the fact that he regarded Rome as right and Asia Minor wrong in the question at issue.[69] We have fellowship in the Church, the Body of Christ, even with those who in some respects are different in their practice from ourselves. The Gnostics, on the other hand, denied the central point of the Scriptural message, viz. Christ's work of salvation, and so destroyed the very content of the faith.[70] There could,

λόγον τοῦ Θεοῦ, εὐχαριστία γίνεται, ὅπερ ἐστὶ σῶμα καὶ αἷμα τοῦ Χριστοῦ· οὕτως καὶ τὰ ἡμέτερα σώματα ἐξ αὐτῆς τρεφόμενα, καὶ τεθέντα εἰς τὴν γῆν, καὶ διαλυθέντα ἐν αὐτῇ, ἀναστήσεται ἐν τῷ ἰδίῳ καιρῷ, τοῦ λόγου τοῦ Θεοῦ τὴν ἔγερσιν αὐτοῖς χαριζομένου εἰς δόξαν Θεοῦ καὶ πατρός, A.h. v. ii. 3. The idea of sacrifice is not dealt with in *this* context.

[68] *A.h.* IV. liii. 1 (Stier. IV. xxxiii. 7).

[69] See Eusebius, *The Ecclesiastical History*, tr. Kirsopp Lake, London 1926, v. xxiv. 9–17. Cf. Seeberg, *Lehrbuch der Dogmengeschichte*, VOL. I, pp. 389–91; and Gustave Bardy, *La Théologie de l'église*, Paris 1945, pp. 210–15. The difficult and probably corrupt text of *A.h.* III. iii. 1 (Stier. III. iii. 2) on the "potentior principalitas" of Rome has evoked widespread discussion. Each in its own way typical are F. X. Roiron, "Sur l'interprétation d'un passage de saint Irénée," in *Recherches de science religieuse*, 1917, pp. 36–51; and Koch, "Irenäus über den Vorzug der römischen Kirche," in *Theol. Stud. u. Krit.*, 1920–21, pp. 54–72. Outlines of the various interpretations appear in Bonwetsch, *Theologie des Irenäus*, pp. 120–3, long note, and W. Schmidt, *Die Kirche bei Irenäus*, pp. 78–87; see also van den Eynde, *Normes de l'enseignement*, pp. 171–9, with its fresh interpretation of "principalitas" (= ἀρχαιότης); and Friedrich Heiler, *Altkirchliche Autonomie und päpstlicher Zentralismus*, Munich 1941, p. 191 f.; and finally Bardy, *op. cit.*, pp. 204–10, and Wilfred Knox, "Irenaeus, Adversus haereses 3 : 3 : 2," in *J.T.S.*, 1946, pp. 180–4. All are agreed that the meaning of the passage is somewhat obscure. But Irenaeus's position on the Easter controversy is quite clear.

[70] The meaning of the term "regula" in Irenaeus is also a matter of acute controversy. We may simply note here that every attempt to discover a precise, technical reality behind the term has broken down. The "rule of truth" or "rule

therefore, be no fellowship with the Gnostics, who rather had to be opposed if truth were to be recovered, and thereby their own salvation achieved.

A sign of the unity of the Church is the Ministry which has been handed on without a break ever since the Apostles. Irenaeus had laid some stress on the unbroken *successio episcoporum*. This article of doctrine was not based on any conception which Irenaeus held of a special grace of Ministry, channelled through succession—in the context Irenaeus is not dealing with either the validity or the efficacy of the Sacraments—but here as elsewhere Irenaeus is concerned with the content of the *kerygma*, and at this point is mainly engaged in refuting the Gnostic teaching. His starting-point was the claim of the Gnostics to possess a secret oral tradition—the Church should, of course, the Gnostics held, preserve the Apostolic writings, but the deepest, esoteric secret is not to be found in their writings, but has been entrusted by the Apostles to certain chosen individuals in oral and occult form. The Gnostics now possess this secret truth, while the Church on the other hand has never obtained it. Irenaeus says: Let us assume that the Apostles had a secret, unwritten tradition. But would they then have given congregations to some, and the secret, saving truth to others? It is quite clear that they did not, and they must have entrusted the congregations to those representatives who had been commissioned with the administration of the oral tradition. But—and this is the vital point—we know the names of the bishops who had the care of the local congregations since the days of the Apostles, and none of them were Gnostics. Their preaching was the same as ours is today. If there is an oral tradition, then it must exist within the Church. By this fact alone any argument about an esoteric Christian truth outside the Church is des-

of faith" is the preaching of the Apostolic truth in its entirety. See Becker, *Ο ΚΑΝΩΝ ΤΗΣ ΑΛΗΘΕΙΑΣ* pp. 253 ff.; Seeberg, *Lehrbuch der Dogmengeschichte*, VOL. I, p. 376 f.; Bonwetsch, *Theologie des Irenäus*, pp. 45–7; and van den Eynde, *Normes de l'enseignement*, pp. 286 ff., 291. We do not have time here to discuss the profuse apocryphal literature which for long had engaged the attention of Irenaeus. With regard to studies of the Apostolate there is an account of the history of these studies in J. de Ghellinck, *Patristique et moyen âge*, VOL. I, *Les Recherches sur l'histoire du symbole des apôtres*, Gembloux 1946. On the "regula veritatis" see also the passages cited by Sanders, *Fourth Gospel*, pp. 69, 72. There are several closely connected statements in *A.h.* See e.g. III. xv. I (Stier. ibid.) on Luke.

troyed. Irenaeus's concept of *successio* gets its meaning in the light of his controversy with the Gnostics.[71]

The Irenaean concepts of Church and Ministry are very closely connected with his general theological attitude.[72] This is true in particular of his concept of the Body of Christ, which to a certain extent dominates the whole of his thinking. His discussion of those who belong to Christ as being those who live in the Spirit is very closely related to his view of man as having been created in the *imago* and *similitudo* of God, and of Christ as being the *imago* and *similitudo* of God. Man is restored from his ruin when he is born into the Body of Christ. The natural, undestroyed life of Creation returns to the earth when the righteousness of the pure man, which took form in Jesus Christ, extends to others and re-fashions them. The Church is the way by which the risen Lord moves out into the world of men, who thereby regain their freedom. And the way outwards to men is at the same time the way forwards to the Parousia. As the Church has to expand spatially, it has also a time in which it has to grow—to grow up to Him who is the head, namely, Christ.[73] Man's death and resurrection are on the line which leads from

[71] "Etenim si recondita mysteria scissent Apostoli, quae seorsim et latenter ab reliquis perfectos docebant, his vel maxime traderent ea quibus etiam ipsas ecclesias committebant," *A.h.* III. iii. I (Stier. ibid.). After this there comes an examination of "successio." Cf. IV. xl. 2–xlii. I (Stier. IV. xxvi. 2–5) and IV. liii. 2 (Stier. IV. xxxiii. 8). See here especially Bonwetsch, *Theologie des Irenäus*, pp. 116–18, and also Karl Müller, "Kleine Beiträge zur alten Kirchengeschichte," in *Z.NT.W.*, 1924, pp. 216–22. Roman Catholic authors regularly take up the question which is not found in Irenaeus of whether the Ministry stands over Scripture or Scripture over the Ministry; see e.g. Hoh, *Lehre des hl. Irenäus*, pp. 96–8, and Reynders, "Paradosis," in *Recherches de théologie ancienne et médiévale*, 1933, pp. 174–7; and even more clearly in another essay by Reynders "La polémique de saint Irénée," in the same journal, 1935, p. 17. Irenaeus never posed the question whether a proper exegesis of Scripture could come into conflict with the tradition of the Church; the only interpretation of the Bible which went against tradition known to him was the demonstrably wrong interpretation of the Gnostics which he was refuting exegetically. Reynders's observations on the dualism in the concepts of succession and tradition are incontestable; cf. Johannes Munck, "Billedet af Kætterne hos Irenaeus," in *Teologisk Tidsskrift*, Copenhagen 1936, pp. 207–9. See, finally, *A.h.* v. xx. 1–2 (Stier. ibid.), where Scripture and Church are held together.

[72] Loofs, *Theophilus von Antiochien*, p. 342, holds that the section on "regula," "successio," etc., originate from "Irenaeus selbst," as distinct from the other more valuable—and borrowed—material.

[73] Christ *has* risen and *will* return. Between these two events the Church's double process of growth continues.

the present to the future, which is marked by perfection. Man's enemy does not triumph in man's suffering and outward ruin. Rather, the Church takes its form as the Body of Christ to the full in adversity and distress, when it follows its head, Christ, into His Kingdom.[74]

The Consummation has not yet been reached. At present Christ is not the Judge of the world, but He is Head of the Church, "caput Ecclesiae."[75] In His position as *caput* of His Body we have the distinctive feature of the present stage of development of the work of recapitulation. Recapitulation has not come to an end with the Church or in the Church, but has entered a new phase since Christ has become "head" of a body of growing and struggling men. We must now try to describe this new phase more closely.

Recapitulatio

It will be recalled from our earlier investigations into the concept of recapitulation that it is only the Incarnate, the One who was made flesh, who recapitulates. In the birth of Jesus Adam is recapitulated, and Christ continues the work which began at His baptism through His struggle during His life on earth, and through His dying and rising again. And He does all this as the Incarnate, i.e. as man. *Recapitulatio* is effected *now* in the Church, for Christ is active now, after His resurrection but before the Last Judgement, in the Church—He lives now as man among those who hear His Word. The *Ecclesia* is those who have

[74] The righteous must suffer (Is. LVII.1): "Haec autem in Abel quidem praemeditabantur, a prophetis vero praeconabantur, in Domino autem perficiebantur, et in nobis autem idipsum est, *consequente corpore suum caput*, *A.h.* IV. lvi. 4 (Stier. IV. xxxiv. 4); on the death of Abel as a prophecy see also *Epid.* 17. As the body follows the head in death, so also it follows it in the resurrection: ". . . ut quemadmodum caput resurrexit a mortuis, sic et reliquum corpus omnis hominis qui invenitur in vita, impleto tempore condemnationis ejus, quae erat propter inobedientiam, resurgat, per compagines et conjunctiones coalescens et confirmatum augmento Dei (Eph. IV. 15 f.), unoquoque membrorum habente propriam et aptam in corpore positionem. Multae enim mansiones apud Patrem, quoniam et multa membra in corpore," *A.h.* III. xx. 3 (Stier. III. xix. 3). Cf. IV. liv (Stier. IV. xxxiii. 9), IV. lxi. 2 (Stier. IV. xxxvii. 7), and V. xxviii. 3–xxix. 1 (Stier. V. xxviii 4–xxix. 1).

[75] *A.h.* III. xvii. 6 (Stier. III. xvi. 6). Irenaeus's tendency to use the metaphor of the Church as a woman or a mother is connected with his concept of Christ as the Head of the Church. Cf. Eph. V.23.

gathered around Christ. Christ's work in itself is finished and complete, but it has not yet extended to every part of human life.[76] This process of extension continues while time moves on to the ultimate dissolution and transformation of every part of Creation.

Since it is *men* who constitute the Church, which is Christ's Body, Christ is active as Head of the Church among "His own," in the Creation which is destined for Him. God prevailed over humanity by allowing His Son to be born at Bethlehem and live in the world, and God still prevails over humanity by permitting His Son to gather men around Himself and to govern them on earth. But Christ's human nature was good and pure. Now, however, He dwells among others who are wicked and impure, and the struggle which He waged in His temptations and on the Cross is now continued among those who belong to Him—a conflict between Spirit and flesh which stimulates and arouses the members of His Body and makes believers live in continual combat. The ethical life of the Christian believer is a part of the mighty, invisible conflict between God and Satan. God repels His enemy from his attack on men when a man obeys God's commandment and the fruits of the Spirit increase among men in their common life together.[77] When the destroyer of human life is thus expelled, as man's life is being renewed, from the area in which his hold has been secure, man emerges in his pure, original form. All that he does is now a manifestation of his Christ-likeness and therefore of the *imago* and *similitudo Dei* in which man was created from the beginning.[78] The new fellowship in the Church is an expression of recapitulation.

[76] The idea of restoration is typical of Irenaeus, and in his concentration on the future he perhaps parts from the New Testament with its stronger emphasis on what the Christian already has and is. Cf. Ernst Percy, *Die Probleme der Kolosser- und Epheserbriefe*, Lund 1946, p. 296 f. The individual is certainly involved in the work of recapitulation, but the goal for the individual has not yet been reached. *Recapitulatio* is a long, temporal process which is still going on.

[77] *A.h.* v. x. 2 (Stier. v. x. 1), where the parable of the wheat and the tares (Mt. xiii. 25–30) is introduced into the discussion of the contrast between flesh and Spirit. Cf. v. ix. 2 (Stier. ibid.).

[78] ". . . in pristinam veniunt hominis naturam, eam quae secundum imaginem et similitudinem facta est Dei. Sed quemadmodum oleaster insertus [Stieren: inserta], substantiam quidem ligni non amittit, qualitatem autem fructus immutat, et aliud percipit vocabulum, jam non oleaster, sed fructifica [Stieren: fructifera]

It is one of Irenaeus's main propositions that the fruit of the Spirit—love, joy, peace, longsuffering, and goodness (see Gal. v.22 f.)—increases *in the same body* which previously, in unbelief, engendered unkindness, dissension, wrath, and other "carnal" evil. This antithesis of evil and good cuts right through man. The Devil as well as God can make use of man for his purposes. The fruit of the Spirit increases in the outward life of fellowship. Irenaeus sees the resurrection from the dead as being in line with the Spirit's ethical government of man, in the Spirit's government of the body, and in good works done by man, which can be achieved only by the use of men's hands and bodily strength.[79] The resurrection is the absolute dominance of the body by the Spirit, and is connected with the complete victory over Satan in the last times. But Satan has not yet been so completely destroyed that he has been rendered inoperative. His supremacy has been broken, but remnants of his power still remain. For this reason individuals are involved in the present time in the struggle between flesh and Spirit despite Christ's finished victory—and the fight is in their own bodies. Victory in this ethical struggle is a foretaste of the resurrection; it is also a gift of the present, risen Lord. And the life of the resurrection is the restored and uncontaminated life of Creation.[80]

Victory in the conflict is vouchsafed to man because his strength is derived from Christ, the Head of the Church. The work of recapitulation is conveyed to men through the connexion which Christ, who is "Head" of His own Body, has with those who are struggling against evil, and His gift to them of

oliva exsistens, et dicitur: sic et homo per fidem insertus, et assumens Spiritum Dei, substantiam quidem carnis non amittit, qualitatem autem fructus operum immutat," *A.h.* v. x. 2 (Stier. v. x. 1–2). (On the text see Lundström, *Studien*, p. 29.) It is clear from this that the possession of the Spirit cannot be wholly denied to the first man—not to have Spirit is sin. Cf. v. xi. 2 (Stier. ibid.).

[79] "In quibus igitur periebamus membris, operantes ea quae sunt corruptelae, in iisdem ipsis vivificamur, operantes ea quae sunt Spiritus. *Ὡς γὰρ φθορᾶς ἐπιδεκτικὴ ἡ σάρξ, οὕτως καὶ ἀφθαρσίας· καὶ ὡς θανάτου, οὕτως καὶ ζωῆς*, *A.h.* v. xii. 1 (Stier. v. xi. 2–xii. 1): after this comes Irenaeus's doctrine of the resurrection of the flesh.

[80] Cf. *A.h.* v. xii. 3–5 (Stier. v. xii. 3–6). The faithful are already victorious and their victory issues in the resurrection, which is the obliteration of the power of man's enemies, sin and death. By this, Creation is liberated and the final goal of recapitulation achieved. To possess the Spirit is to have that for which man was created—Life.

new power. Christ's position as the *caput* of His Church represents the present stage of development of *recapitulatio*.[81] It is quite clear that the noun *ἀνακεφαλαίωσις* in Irenaeus contains an allusion also to *κεφαλή*, or head.[82] We also notice in the Latin text the close connexion between Christ's work as *recapitulator* and as *caput*. The fall of man from the purity of Creation had the effect of subjecting mankind to an unnatural lord. Man lost his connexion with the Word in which he had been created. Sin is the anomaly which came into being when man lost his source of power, his rightful Head, and his master. In Christ mankind recovers its true Head. And the beginning of the new humanity is the Church, which now lives in a continual, vital relationship to Christ, the only man whom sin and the Fall have never harmed. In the Church all peoples and tongues are included: by adoption they will be incorporated into the ongoing dominion of Christ, until at length the whole of the human race appears before the judgement seat of Christ on the last day. The Church has an endless future. It is the "congregation of the first born."[83]

The content of the term *recapitulatio* is both rich and diverse. There is, for instance, the idea of a restoration of the original in the word, a purificatory movement pointing backwards to the first Creation. This restoration is accomplished in Jesus's struggle against the Devil in a conflict which repeats the history of Adam, but with the opposite outcome. The idea of a repetition is thus part of the conception of recapitulation, but in a modified form—modified, that is, by the idea of victory. But since man was a growing being before he became enslaved, and

[81] "Super omnia quidem Pater, et ipse est caput Christi: per omnia autem Verbum, et ipse est caput Ecclesiae: in omnibus autem nobis Spiritus, et ipse est aqua viva, quam praestat Dominus in se recte credentibus, et diligentibus se," *A.h.* v. xviii. 1 (Stier. v. xviii. 2); significantly, the conclusion of this chapter passes immediately to the Last Judgement. Cf. v. xx. 2 (Stier. ibid.): "Haec igitur in semetipsum recapitulatus est, adunans hominem spiritui, et spiritum collocans in homine, ipse caput spiritus factus est, et spiritum dans esse hominis caput." Cf. here Scharl, *Orientalia*, 1940, pp. 404–7, where *recapitulatio* = Be-hauptung.

[82] This is the case *in Irenaeus*. This is not to say that his derivation from *κεφαλή* is etymologically correct. There is strong evidence that the origin of the word is *κεφάλαιον*. But Irenaeus links his concept of *ἀνακεφαλαίωσις* with his concept of the Church and Christ as *κεφαλή*. Loofs, *Theophilus von Antiochien*, p. 368, has a different opinion.

[83] *Epid.* 94.

since he is not restored until he has begun again to progress towards his destiny, man's restoration in itself is more than a mere reversion to his original position.[84] The word *recapitulatio* also contains the idea of perfection or consummation, for recapitulation means that man's growth is resumed and renewed. That man grows, however, is merely a different aspect of the fact that God creates. Growth is always receptive in character, something derived from the source of life. Man's resumed growth is for this reason identical with the life which streams from Christ, the Head, to all believers. And Christ is the Creator's own creative Word, the "hand" by which God gives life to man. It is the pure Creation which is revealed in all its vigour in the fellowship which prevails in the Christian congregation. *Recapitulatio* is thus also the assembling of men under Christ as Head, the recapitulation or resumption of the contact with the source of life and therewith the renewal of life in men's public and private lives.[85] All this points forward to the final Consummation, when Christ will become King in visible form. Within the Church, however, Creation begins to grow pure. In the resurrection the primal state will be wholly freed from the power of destruction.[86]

[84] Bonwetsch, *Theologie des Irenäus*, pp. 89–101; also Percy, *Die Probleme der Kolosser- und Epheserbriefe*, p. 296. Percy, however, seems to limit very closely the function of the idea of recapitulation in the Irenaean theology. Koch, in accordance with his basic theory, which is, however, coloured by his evolutionism, resolutely denies that ἀνακεφαλαίωσις can mean "restoration" (*Theol. Stud. u. Krit.*, 1925, p. 198). Seeberg, *Lehrbuch der Dogmengeschichte*, VOL. I, p. 407, seems to be averse to saying that the term may also mean "repetition." But it is undeniable that the word in question contains all these meanings—restoration, repetition, (but with the opposite effect, i.e. victory in the circumstances which in Adam's case ended in defeat), a summary under a "head," or perfection. The dynamic features of *conflict* and *growth* make it possible to bring these different meanings into a single concept.

[85] Cf. Seeberg, *op. cit.*, pp. 408 ff. Contact with Christ is contact with the source of Creation. The Sacraments are taken from ordinary, external Creation—water, bread, and wine—and for this very reason are the means by which God and Christ reach men who are living in Creation.

[86] Irenaeus says of Christ, "Omnia enim ipse adimplevit veniens, *et adhuc implet in Ecclesia usque ad consummationem* a Lege praedictum novum Testamentum," A.*h.* IV. lvi. 1 (Stier. IV. xxxiv. 2). Our last chapter will deal with "consummatio," the Consummation. Cf. III. xvii. 6 (Stier. III. xvi. 6): ". . . ipse est Jesus Christus Dominus noster, qui et passus est pro nobis, et surrexit propter nos, et rursus venturus est in gloria Patris, ad resuscitandam universam carnem, et ad ostensionem salutis, et regulam justi judicii ostendere omnibus qui sub ipso facti sunt. Unus

The power of the risen Lord as *caput* is not something which belongs only to Himself; but Christ gives all that He has to His Body, i.e. His members in the congregation. The individual thus receives life and health directly from Christ. The struggle, waged by the Spirit against the flesh in the individual, is the very contest maintained by God and by Christ against the primordial enemy, Satan. God's progressive revelation within time of His riches has this temporal character, not because God needs time for itself, but because man needs time, created as he is in order to "grow."[87] When he receives the Spirit, which is given in baptism, the Gospel, and faith, and which constitutes the Church, he receives that which he is to grow up to; he receives, that is, perfect human nature which struggles within him against the destructive, Satanic element of the "flesh," which is at variance with man. He must in faith cling firmly to Christ the Head who proffers the Spirit to men, and in faith must cleave to the Man, the Incarnate Christ, who lives within the Church.[88] If the Spirit becomes *caput* in man's inner being, then man can be victorious in the struggle which he is waging. The life of the individual with its fruits of the Spirit is consequently ordained by Christ as the Head of the Church.[89]

igitur Deus Pater, quemadmodum ostendimus, et unus Christus Jesus Dominus noster, veniens per universam dispositionem, et omnia in semetipsum recapitulans. In omnibus autem est et homo plasmatio Dei: et hominem ergo in semetipsum recapitulans est, invisibilis visibilis factus, et incomprehensibilis factus comprehensibilis, et impassibilis passibilis, et Verbum homo, universa in semetipsum recapitulans: uti sicut in supercoelestibus et spiritalibus et invisibilibus princeps est Verbum Dei; sic et in visibilibus, et corporalibus principatum habeat, in semetipsum primatum assumens, et apponens semetipsum caput Ecclesiae, universa attrahat ad semetipsum apto in tempore." (On this text, however, see Lundström, *Studien*, p. 87.) After this Irenaeus shows the significance of *time*—every stage in the work of salvation occurs "at its proper moment," III. xvii. 7 (Stier. III. xvi. 7). With regard to "tempus," cf. v. xxxi. 2 (Stier. ibid.).

[87] *A.h.* IV. xix. 2 (Stier. IV. ix. 3) and IV. xxxiv. 7 (Stier. IV. xx. 7). Cf. Escoula in *N.R.T.*, 1939, p. 562.

[88] "Memor igitur, dilectissime, quoniam carne Domini nostri redemtus es, et sanguine ejus redhibitus, et tenens caput, ex quo universum corpus Ecclesiae compaginatum augescit, hoc est, carnalem adventum Filii Die, et Deum confitens, et hominem ejus firmiter excipiens," *A.h.* v. xiv. 4 (Stier. ibid.).

[89] Cf. *A.h.* v. xx. 2 (Stier. ibid.). See also v. vi. 1 (Stier. ibid.), concluding section, v. ix. 1–3 (Stier. ibid.), and especially v. viii. 1–2 (Stier. v. viii. 2–3) on the inhumanity of the unspiritual man. Man comes into being under Christ as Head. In the Church the primal, uncorrupted Creation is manifested. Cf. Barnabas VI. 11–19.

To illustrate what we have just said, it might be best to look at the distinctive character of Irenaeus's ethical thought. His description of Christian conduct is marked by a strong tendency towards simplicity. He quite deliberately refrains from detailed instructions, and his whole understanding of Christian conduct may be summarised in the formula of "faith and love."[90] Faith is union with Christ, communion with the eternal and inexhaustible source from which power comes streaming to man. Love is the sum total of every act of obedience to the will of God in human life. He who loves his fellow man does not break any commandment of the Law, for the Law is summed up in love to one's neighbour.[91] Love therefore signifies a unique freedom. He who does not love is a slave, subject to God's law of bondage. Since God is perceptible in every part of Creation, man is aware of his captivity in lovelessness, however he may seek to escape from it—bondage to the Law is identical with bondage to Satan, and the fact that man does not fulfil his own nature. He cannot become free until he is what in himself he is destined and created to be.[92] When death's hold within him is loosened and his unnatural state is terminated, the constraint of the Law from without ceases simultaneously, for the precise function of the Law is to conform man to the will of God, to make man like God, i.e. to impel him towards the *imago* and *similitudo* of God. And the image and likeness of God are achieved in

[90] See Bonwetsch, in *Z.S.T.*, 1923–4, p. 647. Irenaeus frequently develops this idea in reference to the double law of love, e.g. in *Epid.* 95. He can even speak of the "unity of faith and love" or of "love to God and one's neighbour," maintaining that love in this double form issues from faith. See *Epid.* 87. At the end of *A.h.* v. vi. 1 (Stier. ibid.) Irenaeus centres everything round "faith in God" and "righteousness to one's neighbour." Cf. the division into "faith and Commandments" in *Epid.* 2 f.

[91] In *A.h.* IV. xxxviii. 1 (Stier. IV. xxiv. 1) all that God has forbidden is centred on one thing—that which is injurious to one's neighbour.

[92] Freedom and love are one. Irenaeus interprets Lk. VI.29 and Mt. V.41 to mean that he who voluntarily yields his rights is *free*. He goes further than necessary on the way *in front of* his unsparing brother instead of going behind him as a slave at exactly the appointed distance; see the notable exegesis in *A.h.* IV. xxiv. 2 (Stier. IV. xiii. 3). Such a man who is both free and yet servant is like God who makes His sun to rise on the evil and on the good (note the expression, "*configurans* temetipsum Patri"—in the ethical transformation man is changed into the *imago* of God). In *A.h.* IV. liii. 2 Irenaeus says that love is to be found in the Body of Christ, i.e. the Church. It is for this reason, according to *Epid.* 89, that the period of the Law and of ancient Israel has come to an end through the Spirit, faith, and the Church.

man through the life which comes from Christ, who is the image of God and the head of the Church, in that faith begets love.[93] Love is the expression of the true and free man's life.

Irenaeus holds that the "natural laws" are the heart of all morality and that the righteousness which receives expression in this law is primordial and was in existence before Moses. The law of bondage has "come between." In the Church the natural laws revive without the regulations of bondage. But Christ has not only resuscitated the natural laws, which are grounded in Creation, He has also extended and enlarged them, e.g. by insisting on a right mind and enjoining love for one's enemies.[94] Christ's law is the old law, and yet it is also new. We can recognise here the concept with which we are now quite familiar of "growth"—in the Incarnation we see mature and full-grown nature. Those who have lived true human life, e.g. the patriarchs of the Old Testament who believed in the promise, have always lived in love towards their neighbour, but in Christ love breaks all bounds, expanding and growing without any hindrance. Another instance of the concept of growth is the very dualism implied in the antithesis between freedom and law. The Christian is free from the Law because he freely achieves the purpose of the Law. But the Spirit which gives men freedom is still in conflict with the flesh, and the works of the Spirit are therefore still accomplished in the struggling of the Christian man as acts of obedience to the law of Christ.[95] In the

[93] The freedom which existed before the Law of bondage was given returns in the new Covenant. Cf. *A.h.* IV.xxvii. 3 (Stier. IV. xvi. 3). Irenaeus reiterates the whole of the criticism of sacrifice which had been made by the Old Testament prophecy. Ethics consists of the simple Biblical realities—righteousness, mercy, and fear of God (see *A.h.* IV. xxix. 1–5 (Stier. IV. xvii. 1–4). With reference to Irenaeus's interpretation of the Sabbath commandment see IV. xvi–xvii (Stier. IV. viii. 2–3) and *Epid.* 96. Throughout the dominant idea is of love and freedom. Cf. Stoll, *Lehre des hl. Irenäus*, pp. 87–9, Harnack, *History of Dogma*, VOL. II, p. 310, and Seeberg, *Lehrbuch der Dogmengeschichte*, VOL. I, p. 433.

[94] ". . . neque solventis Legem, sed adimplentis et extendentis et dilatantis," *A.h.* IV. xxiv. 1 (Stier. IV. xiii. 1); ". . . superextendi vero decreta libertatis, et augeri subjectionem quae est ad regem," *A.h.* IV. xxiv. 2 (Stier. IV. xiii. 2); see the passage which follows. The sentences must be related to the main proposition that the new Covenant is freedom, whereas the old was bondage. In the chapter quoted here we come upon Irenaeus's definition of who one's *brother* is: "Man's brother is man," IV. xxiv. 3 (Stier. IV. xiii. 4).

[95] The problem of the indicative and imperative in Paul is analogous. Percy, *Die Probleme de Kolosser- und Epheserbriefe*, puts the problem into the same context as

resurrection life conflict is transformed into victory, and freedom is universal. Growth continues in the Church, but it has not fully reached its goal there.

The ethical life produces a growing likeness to Christ or imitation of Christ. Men's works do not constitute any basis for likeness to Christ, for the foundation for this likeness is laid in baptism, which is a baptism into a growing together with Christ. Nor do men's works bring the likeness to Christ which is established at baptism to perfection, for man is baptised into union with the death and Resurrection of Christ, and not simply to imitate His ideal life on earth; consequently man's likeness to Christ is not perfected until he himself has undergone death and resurrection as "the body follows the head." But integral to the likeness which begins in baptism and is fulfilled in eternity is also man's life of faith and works—man's growth is achieved now in "love, mercy, and gratitude."[96] And when this likeness to Christ increases, the believer becomes man. It is nature which defeats the unnatural, and not something "supernatural" which comes into existence. The purity of Creation can be dimly discerned beneath the covering with which the Destroyer conceals the true nature of humanity. Man is destined to become the *imago* and *similitudo* of God, and Christ, the Head of the Church, accomplishes this destiny. The Church is therefore like a well-spring in Creation; abiding in the Church there is a Giver who pours out gifts to the world through the Church.[97] What the old Covenant with its Law was never able

his discussion on "growth," see p. 301 f. and cf. p. 120 f. See also Nygren, *Commentary on Romans*, pp. 331–49. The freedom which is to come is also freedom from conflict. The freedom of faith is freedom from bondage, but is freedom in conflict.

[96] See the passage in *A.h.* III. xxi. 2 (Stier. III. xx. 2) which is difficult to translate in detail, but which is quite clear in its main point: ". . . et manens in dilectione ejus, et subjectione, et gratiarum actione, majorem ab eo gloriam percipiet provectus, accipiens dum consimilis fiat ejus qui pro eo mortuus est; quoniam et ipse in similitudine carnis peccati factus est, uti condemnaret peccatum, et jam quasi condemnatum projiceret illud extra carnem; provocaret autem in similitudinem suam hominem, imitatorem eum assignans Deo." Cf. the expression "configurans temetipsum Patri" with its clear ethical significance, *A.h.* IV. xxiv. 2 (Stier. IV. xiii. 3).

[97] On the Church as giving gifts to men, see *A.h.* II. xlviii. 3–xlix. 3 (Stier. II. xxxi. 3–xxxii. 4); cf. my article in *S.T.K.*, 1940, p. 143 f. Christ brings nature to man who is sunk in an unnatural condition. See in this connexion *A.h.* V. i. 1 (Stier. ibid.); cf. Wendt, *Christliche Lehre*, p. 25, and Rivière, *Dogme de la rédemption*, pp. 110–12. When Paul in Col. III. 10 speaks of "the new man" as "the image of Him that created him," Irenaeus sees here a definition of the work of Christ by

to do, the Spirit achieves in the new Covenant, viz. the rebirth of the lost, primal innocence.

Freedom from the Law is thus simply a consequence of the innocence of Creation. In this stubborn contravention of the will of God man becomes subject to the Law, and in refusing to allow himself to be created in the likeness of God, he discovers that God's will has become Law, an imperious power. The ultimate end of the Law is that man shall be like God in his works (cf. Lev. XIX.2 and Mt. V.48), i.e. he is to be love. Since man's destiny is the *imago* and *similitudo Dei*, the function of the law is accordingly to make man human, but man labours under the Law to attain his destiny without actually achieving it. His bondage to the Law comes to an end when Christ becomes man and consequently fulfils the Law. Fellowship in the Church means freedom, because it is the mighty fact of Christ's living as man in a body of men, who thereby have love towards one another and peace with the God who creates and destines man. The Law has lost its power to enslave. The uninterrupted contact with the source of Creation in Christ means freedom and peace. The discrepancy between man's destiny and his actual status is overcome when faith takes hold of Christ, who is man, and who gives all His righteousness to others who receive Him in His Church. From the ethical standpoint everything turns on the fact that man comes into fellowship with his fellow man. The object of ethics is one's brother, and not isolation from ordinary life, or asceticism.[98] It is typical of Irenaeus, for in-

which primordial man in Creation is renewed and recapitulated: "Et in eo quod dicit, secundum imaginem conditoris [Paul, κατ' εἰκόνα τοῦ κτίσαντος αὐτόν], recapitulationem manifestavit ejusdem hominis, qui in initio secundum imaginem factus est Dei," *A.h.* v. xii. 4 (Stier. ibid.).

[98] Cf. *Epid.* 95 f.: "For we have received the Lord of the Law, the Son of God; and by faith in Him we learn to love God with all our heart, and our neighbour as ourselves. Now the love of God is far from all sin, and to love the neighbour worketh no ill to the neighbour. Wherefore also we need not the law as a tutor." In the passage which follows there is as strong an expression of freedom from the Law as in *A.h.* IV. xxiv. 2 (Stier. IV. xiii. 3). Cf. also *Epid.* 61. When the Law looses its hold, it has been *fulfilled* in Christ. In regard to related lines of thought in Paul see Bring in *S.T.K.*, 1945, pp. 40 f., 50 ff.—Irenaeus rejected the Gnostic sects who repudiated sexual intercourse and marriage on the basis of Gen. I. 27–8, i.e. in basing his argument on the fact that God is Creator; see in this connexion *A.h.* I. xxvi. 1 (Stier. I. xxviii. 1). Cf. II. xlix. 1 (Stier. II. xxxii. 2); and Bonwetsch, *Theologie des Irenäus*, pp. 144–6. The later monastic stress on celibacy as the ethical goal of the Incarnation is quite foreign to Irenaeus. When he assumes that the

stance, that he directly countered those who preached celibacy as an ideal. In this point, as in others, we can discern the Biblical aspect of his ethics.

In the Church of Christ man becomes a new being, a child of God with a future destiny. But this progression is characteristic of the Church as a whole. For the Church is Israel, and it moves forwards towards its destination like Israel in the desert. The whole of this passing age is the spiritual Egypt from which the Church takes its flight. In front lies the Promised Land, but for the present it struggles, hopes, and believes. The act of God's adoption of the stranger with full right of inheritance, His election of His new chosen people, is, from another point of view, the "departure of the Church from the Gentiles."[99] Behind the Church there are Golgotha and Easter, as Israel had behind it the Red Sea with its violent death and mighty act of deliverance. The eyes of the pilgrims are now turned towards the Promised Land. Before the Church reaches its destination it has to undergo the tribulations and persecution of the last age. But if it endures to the end, it will ultimately be seen to have progressed from death to life without ceasing.

supposed source IQA had ascetical character, Loofs, *Theophilus von Antiochien*, pp. 238, 256, 287, is unable to discover any proof for his theory in Irenaeus without basing his hypothesis on extra-Irenaean sources.

[99] "Universa enim quae ex Aegypto profectio fiebat populi, a Deo typus et imago fuit profectionis Ecclesiae, quae erat futura ex gentibus," *A.h.* IV. xlvii (Stier. IV. xxx. 4). "Then he set forth in types beforehand that which was to be; now in very truth he has brought us out from the cruel service of the Gentiles," *Epid.* 46. "Quemadmodum enim illi per Aegyptiorum, sic et nos per Judaeorum caecitatem accepimus salutem," *A.h.* IV. xliv. 3 (Stier. IV. xxviii. 3). Cf. V. xxxiv. 3 (Stier. ibid.).

CHAPTER II

THE CONSUMMATION

The Kingdom of the Son

ISRAEL ended its desert wanderings in the land of Canaan. The Church in the same way will go into the Kingdom of the Son. It will not, however, thereby cease to be the Church. The Church will remain the centre of the mighty renewal of the whole of nature and Creation which "*regnum*" implies.[1] This *regnum* will be the first phase of eschatology; it will be a kingdom here on earth, on the first but renewed earth, before the Last Judgement. After that, new heavens and a new earth will be created, and with this the final, indescribable phase of eschatology will begin. This, however, is something beyond our present knowledge. The Kingdom of the Son precedes in time the ultimate transformation; in its earthly character it is oriented towards the period before the Consummation, and is thereby an object of logical enquiry. But the Kingdom of the Son has not come, and does not belong to the present. The present period is marked by the Church's conflict and patient expectation and by the non-appearance of Christ. But in the Kingdom of the Son Christ will reign as visible King, and the faithful will rule with Him over this world. As soon as we begin

[1] "Et propterea cum in fine repente hinc Ecclesia assumetur: Erit, inquit, tribulatio qualis non est facta ab initio, neque fiet. Novissimus enim agon hic justorum, in quo vincentes coronantur incorruptela," *A.h.* v. xxix. 1 (Stier. ibid.) (see Mt. xxiv.21). The promise to Abraham in Gen. xv.18 that he would possess the land, the earth, the "terra," is fulfilled in the Church, the seed of Abraham: "Si ergo huic promisit Deus haereditatem terrae, non accepit autem in omni suo incolatu, oportet eum accipere cum semine suo, hoc est, qui timent Deum et credunt in eum, in resurrectione justorum. Semen autem ejus Ecclesia per Dominum adoptionem quae est ad Deum accipiens, sicut dicebat Johannes Baptista: Quoniam potens est Deus de lapidibus suscitare filios Abrahae," *A.h.* v. xxxii. 2 (Stier. ibid.) (see Lk. iii.8). Cf. v. xxxiv. 1 (Stier. ibid.).

to speak of the Kingdom of the Son we have to speak of the future rather than of the present.[2]

We shall understand the eschatology of Irenaeus if we hold together two New Testament passages. The first is Rev. xx. 1–xxi.4 which speaks of "the first resurrection," which is the resurrection of the blessed and holy to reign with Christ a thousand years on the earth, and which then speaks of a resurrection of all who are dead after the thousand years' reign, a resurrection to the judgement and division of the whole of mankind, after which there will finally come the destruction of heaven and earth. The second passage is 1 Cor. xv.24–8 which speaks first of a Kingdom of the Son which awaits the time when all evil and every enemy shall have been decisively defeated, and then of a state after this reign of the Son when the Son will have delivered up the Kingdom to the Father, and all opposition will have been put down.[3] Irenaeus connects these two passages in the Bible. He speaks, exactly as the Book of the Revelation does, of two different resurrections: first, the resurrection of the just who have eternal life in themselves, and then the resurrection of all men according to their works. Irenaeus describes the state between the first resurrection and the second as "the Kingdom of the Son."[4] This means that the

[2] See *A.h.* v. xxiv. 2 (Stier. ibid.): "Et ne ad *hoc tempus* putetur dicta repromissio' dictum est prophetae: Et tu veni, et sta in sorte tua *in consummatione dierum*" (Dan. xii. 13). *A.h.* v. xxx. 2–3 (Stier. ibid.) is more detailed. Our previous chapter on the Church dealt with the present. The present chapter on the Consummation will deal with the future.

[3] Cf. Werner, *Entstehung des christlichen Dogmas*, p. 139 f., especially n. 131, where chiliasm is represented as a Pauline phenomenon rather than a Jewish-Christian one. There is a completely different opinion in Hoh, *Lehre des hl. Irenäus*, p. 149. Cullmann, *Christ and Time*, p. 142, has a positive and fair criticism of Irenaeus on this point.

[4] *A.h.* v. 36 (Stier. v. xxxvi. 3) Irenaeus draws together some eschatalogical passages from the New Testament, e.g., Jesus's words about drinking "of this fruit of the vine" (Mt. xxvi.29) and Paul's statement about Creation's bondage of corruption and future liberty (Rom. viii. 21). The passages referred to speak at the one time of both the future Kingdom and this present world. He goes on to say: "Et in omnibus iis et per omnia idem Deus Pater ostenditur, qui plasmavit hominem, et haereditatem terrae promisit patribus, qui eduxit illam *in resurrectione justorum*, et promissiones adimplet *in Filii sui regnum*." After the Kingdom of the Son comes the complete, unearthly transformation of the eschatological period— "No eye has seen, nor ear heard, nor the heart of man conceived, what God has prepared" (1 Cor. ii.9). In v. xxxv. 2 (Stier. ibid.) we find the same interpretation of *postea*: "*Post* enim *Regni* tempora, Vidi, iniquit, thronum album magnum..."

"Kingdom of the Son," like the thousand years' reign in the Apocalypse, has a beginning and an end. In the same way as the Church has been given a certain time in God's design for the world for its extension through preaching, the Kingdom of the Son has its appointed time. Afterwards the Kingdom is delivered to the Father, and the present world ceases to be the scene of redemptive activity.

When Christ delivers up the Kingdom to the Father, God becomes "all in all" (1 Cor. xv.28). It has sometimes been held by certain theologians that when this takes place the Son's position in the Trinity as Son will cease.[5] But this is surely an incorrect assumption. The Son has been begotten of the Father from all eternity, and like the Spirit, will remain what He is for all eternity. The Trinity existed before the Creation of this world and will remain as Trinity after its destruction. But the work which the Son began as the Incarnate One will come to an end when the Son "delivers up the Kingdom." And as we have seen, the work of the Incarnate One is precisely recapitulation. The work of the Son of God as *man* was complete when he restored man to his perfect health and drove all evil out of existence. As long as man's restoration is incomplete, the work of recapitulation will continue—Christ gives and man "grows." It is an essential feature of our picture of the Kingdom of the Son that man continues to grow in the Kingdom, and to receive, and to progress towards his destination.[6] The Son will not cease to be man until He has succeeded

after which Irenaeus quotes Rev. xx.11 f. After the Kingdom of the Son there comes the "*generalis resurrectio*" and the "judicium." 1 Cor. xv. 25–8 is cited in *A.h.* v. xxxvi (Stier. v. xxxvi. 2). On the two resurrections see also J. A. Robinson in *J.T.S.*, 1931, p. 393.

[5] Harnack, *History of Dogma*, VOL. II, p. 266 f., note. See also T. Zahn, *Marcellus von Ancyra*, Gotha 1867, p. 243 on Irenaeus and p. 185 on Marcellus.

[6] ". . . in qua regnabunt justi in terra, crescentes ex visione Domini, et per ipsum assuescent capere gloriam Dei Patris, et cum sanctis angelis conversationem et communionem, et unitatem spiritalium in regno capient," *A.h.* v. xxxv. 1 (Stier. ibid.). "Et sicut vere resurgit, sic et vere praemeditabitur incorruptelam, et augebitur, et vigebit in regni temporibus, ut fiat capax gloriae Patris," v. xxxv. 2 (Stier. ibid.). When man has grown up to his destination, the new heaven and the new earth which are described in Rev. xxi will follow. Cremers makes the point in *Bijdragen*, 1938, p. 60, that the vision of God is only gradually acquired in the "regnum" by man's accustoming and training himself to see Him, but Cremers is wrong in saying that such a thought is irreconcilable with Irenaean theology in

in making man *man*. Then Creation will be pure again, and the Son will deliver up the Kingdom to the Father. But then, too, the period of the first earth will have come to an end, and the new heaven and the new earth will appear.[7] The Incarnation is inseparably connected with this world.[8]

The Kingdom of the Son is the last phase in the restoration of Creation. It was through man who lived on earth that sin got power to destroy the earth. Since it is man in particular over whom the enemy of God has gained control, the restoration of man must occupy a central place in the purification of Creation. But since the righteous have risen from the dead and together with Christ "inherit the earth" in the Kingdom of the Son, as it is said in Mt. v.5 that the "meek" will inherit the earth, nature itself becomes different and "healthier" than it was before, since the renewal of Creation extends to the animate and inanimate world.[9] In his description of the "periods of the Kingdom" Irenaeus's account of the new abundance in nature occupies a large place.[10] But in the centre of the regenerated, external Creation there is Christ, the One who was made man, working with man. By his doctrine of a visible *regnum* of Christ on earth before the Judgement, Irenaeus integrally connects life on earth and the resurrection. The present age passes gradually into the resurrection, until finally the earthly framework disappears and the eschatological age merges into the ineffable. Irenaeus is continually directing his interest to the first phase of the eschatological age, viz. the Kingdom of the

other respects. The same process in actual fact continues in the Kingdom of the Son as has already existed for man in the Church. See Hugo Koch in *Theol. Stud. u. Krit.*, 1925, p. 199 f., note, and Prümm in *Scholastik*, 1938, p. 218 f.

[7] *A.h.* v. xxxvi.

[8] Christ will return to earth in the same flesh in which He lived on earth. See *A.h.* III. xvii. 8 (Stier. III. xvi. 8) and *Epid.* 38 f.

[9] For Irenaeus, Jesus's promise in the Sermon on the Mount is a pronouncement of very great significance. See *A.h.* III. xxxi. 1 (Stier. III. xxii. 1), v. ix. 3 (Stier. v. ix. 4), and v. xxxii. 2 (Stier. ibid.).

[10] See *A.h.* v. xxxiii. 3 (Stier. ibid.). These parts of *A.h.* seem to be primitive and undeveloped, and we can easily understand why attempts have been made to dispute the literary genuineness of such passages. Irenaeus himself, however, it seems, regarded the present condition of nature as a consequence of God's having "cursed the ground" because of man's sin so that man has to get his bread in the "sweat of his face" (Gen. III. 17–19). When man is restored and the curse is lifted, nature is transformed.

Son. Those who have part in the first resurrection belong to Christ and already possess all things. The word "resurrection" can, therefore, for Irenaeus, contain the whole of salvation. It is not necessary to wait for the final phase and the Judgement to obtain eternal life. Eternal life is already available in rising from the dead in the "resurrection of the just."

This comprehensive view of the renewal of nature in the *regnum* is in complete harmony with what is central to the theology of Irenaeus. When man becomes man and reaches his destination, God's decree for Creation is fulfilled. And it is an integral part of this original decree that man is to "rule" all other living creatures on the earth. There is a passage in Genesis which speaks of God creating man in His image and putting the earth under him, and of man having "dominion" over every living thing (Gen. I.26–8).[11] The failure of nature to serve man spontaneously and to the limit of its powers is to be explained by the fact that man is evil and is failing to achieve his destiny, and is not fulfilling his role of living in accordance with the *imago* and *similitudo* of God. God has "cursed the ground" because of rebellious man (Gen. III.17–19), and therefore Creation groans and travails and "waits for the revealing of the sons of God" (Rom. VIII.19–22). And the "son" of God is precisely the new man in Christ, man who has returned to what the Creator intended him to be. In the Church he grows towards the *imago* and *similitudo* of God; and in the Kingdom of the Son he has reached the resurrection from the dead. And when he has thus attained to his original destiny, God's decree for Creation is fulfilled in all its extent—the curse on the ground is ended, and the groaning of Creation is changed into freedom, when Christ and those who are His own rule over the earth.[12]

[11] Cf. Wilhelm Caspari, "Imago divina," in *Reinhold-Seeberg-Festschrift*, ed. W. Koep, Leipzig 1929, VOL. I, p. 208.

[12] ". . . mysterium justorum resurrectionis et regni, quod est principium incorruptelae, per quod regnum qui digni fuerint paulatim assuescunt capere Deum: necessarium est autem dicere de illis, quoniam oportet justos primos in conditione hac quae renovatur, ad apparitionem Dei resurgentes recipere promissionem haereditatis, quam Deus promisit patribus, et regnare in ea: post deinde fieri judicium. In qua enim conditione laboraverunt, sive afflicti sunt, omnibus modis probati per sufferentiam, justum est in ipsa recipere eos fructus sufferentiae: et qua conditione interfecti sunt propter Dei dilectionem, in ipsa vivificari: et in qua conditione servitutem sustinuerunt, in ipsa regnare eos. Dives enim in omnibus

Not until then does man "have dominion over" nature. Hitherto all his "working" of the earth has been in the sweat of his face.[13] But now the earth bestows its gifts in abundance. This realisation of the first decree for Creation was predicted by Jesus when He said: "Blessed are the meek: for they shall inherit the earth" (Mt. v.5).

The Kingdom of the Son is the beginning of the Consummation, the link between the period of the Church and eternity. The central Irenaean concept of "growth" is natural and necessary to such a transitional stage. Our present existence will move gradually and without any sharp line of distinction to its final perfection. The same powers which are operative in the Church are also operative definitively in the Consummation. The Spirit is given *now* as a first fruits and pledge, but *then* the Spirit will have control of man's body. Resurrection from the dead and becoming "a spiritual body" are identical concepts. Christ is *now* risen, the first-born from the dead, and lives with His own through faith; *then* He will rule the world of men visibly. The resurrection of the just and Christ's coming in power as King will coincide. But even after Christ's Parousia and the resurrection of the just, man will still have to "grow." The resurrection continues in an intensification of man's communion with God. It is only when the earth has disappeared and Christ has "delivered up" the Kingdom that the goal of humanity will have been reached. Christ gives to man and will continue to give as long as there is any need for His gifts, and His creative activity will still continue in His Kingdom. When Irenaeus comes to the point at which he describes how Christ "delivers up the Kingdom," he terminates all discussion of what is to

Deus, et omnia sunt ejus. Oportet ergo et ipsam conditionem reintegratam ad pristinum, sine prohibitione servire justis: et hoc Apostolus fecit manifestum in ea quae est ad Romanos, sic dicens: Nam exspectatio creaturae revelationem filiorum Dei exspectat," *A.h.* v. xxxii. 1 (Stier. ibid.). Irenaeus thereafter quotes Rom. VIII.20 f.

[13] Even in the present age Creation is to serve man in the Church, but it does so in tribulation and in the struggle of faith. When, for instance, martyrdom afflicts the Church, the world is actually serving Christians, for they are receiving eternal life derivatively from "the world," though under the veil of death. See *A.h.* v. xxix. 1 (Stier. ibid.) in its context. In the resurrection of the just, man is encompassed about by the same mighty signs of life as there were in the Garden of Eden before the Fall and the entrance of death into the world.

come, since "no eye has seen, nor ear heard, what God has prepared."[14] There comes a point at which we can no longer speak about the things which belong to the eschatological period. But as long as human life continues, it is a life of growth and development.

For as long as the eschatological event is delayed there will continue to be conflict in some form or another, but when man has reached his destination and grown to the *imago* and *similitudo*, the power of Satan will then have been completely expelled, and God's universal dominion, unimpeded by hostile opposition from any quarter, will be the ultimate reality which "no eye has seen." Only when evil has been destroyed will the struggle abate, but in the Kingdom of the Son this struggle is still continuing. The conclusion of the *regnum* will be the judgement of the unrighteous and the disappearance of death. The Son must reign "till He has put all His enemies under His feet" (1 Cor. xv.25)—only then will He "deliver up the Kingdom."[15] Irenaeus hardly ever gives a specific description of a sin-free state, and there is as little point in attempting to discover in his writings even a broad description of the "original state" as there is in looking for a clear picture of the state after the Last Judgement. What he does describe is the drama which issues in the Judgement. After that, evil is purified and the whole of Creation is in a state of innocence again; and then begins the Kingdom which surpasses description, where God is "all in all."

Since evil is not diminishing or subsiding, but is a power in active conflict against God, and must therefore be put down, the forces of evil reach their point of maximum concentration before the death blow finally annihilates them. Satan is amassing and concentrating his hosts, but it is this very harnessing of his resources which makes possible God's victory. The appearance of Antichrist is thus the beginning of the end, and the increase of evil in all its perversity is, in fact, a sign of hope. Antichrist is a "recapitulation" of evil; the Beast is a "recapitu-

[14] When man has reached his destiny, he is the *imago* and *similitudo* of God. But the only one who really is the *imago* and *similitudo* of God is Christ. When Christ gives, He gives himself. Man reaches his destiny when Christ delivers up the Kingdom, and recapitulation has been brought to its conclusion. The period of the world and the Incarnation has flowed into eternity where "God is all in all."

[15] *A.h.* v. xxxv. 2–xxxvi (Stier. ibid.).

lation" of all iniquity, a concentration of everything demonic, so that all opposition to God can be crushed at a single blow after his short-lived tyranny, and cast into the fire.[16] Christ's return to earth and the appearance of Antichrist will herald the final encounter between God and Satan. The "good" Kingdom on earth, which is under the sway of Christ, is marked by the confinement and imprisonment of the evil power. The end of the Kingdom of the Son will be the Last Judgement when all, even the wicked, have risen. The final expulsion of the power of sin and death will therefore not take place until the *regnum* of the just on earth has reached its appointed end. Growth and conflict will both be brought to an end within the period of the Kingdom of the Son with its last mighty act, and neither is complete until the moment when the Son Himself shall also be subject to the Father. And yet everything has been achieved in the resurrection of Christ. The final, eschatological, outcome of victory over Satan is wholly present in the mighty act of Easter. Everything that takes place between Christ's Resurrection and the Last Day is an extension of Christ's dominion to men. In Christ Himself everything is complete with the Easter event, but He does not include all mankind in His dominion until the Last Day.[17]

Irenaeus's doctrine of the Kingdom of the Son is not an intrusion in his thought, but an organic and natural part of it. It is true, of course, that the chapters v. 32–6 do not appear in all the manuscripts, and there are parts throughout this concluding section where in the main the text is imperfect, but such gaps are almost self-explanatory, since belief in the so-called "thousand years' reign" on earth was rejected at an early

[16] On Antichrist see *A.h.* v. xxv. 1 (Stier. ibid.): "... diabolicam apostasiam in se recapitulans"; v. xxv. 4 (Stier. v. xxv. 5): "... qui in se recapitulatur omnem diabolicum errorem"; and also v. xxviii. 2 (Stier. ibid.) in two passages. On the Beast, see v. xxix. 2 (Stier. ibid.): "Et propter hoc in bestia veniente recapitulatio fit universae iniquitatis et omnis doli, ut in ea confluens et conclusa omnis virtus apostatica, in caminum mittatur ignis"; three further passages in the same part; and finally v. xxx. 1 (Stier. ibid.). Antichrist and the Beast are interchangeable. Irenaeus states quite explicitly that Antichrist has *not* come, but belongs to the future, and that it is fruitless to speculate about the nomenclature of Antichrist. In spite of his doctrine of the Kingdom on earth we cannot count him among writers of apocalyptic. For Irenaeus's use of the term "recapitulatio" in its extended sense, see Scharl, *Orientalia*, 1940, p. 378 f.

[17] Cullmann, *Christ and Time*, p. 141 f.

period, and in the medieval tradition was regarded as a heresy.[18] We must try to understand the objections which the scribes would have felt in regard to passages in Irenaeus which they felt were clearly heretical. The mystery is rather that the passages which dealt with the Kingdom on earth were able to be transmitted in such good condition, as, in fact, they were, through centuries in which, on theological grounds, the actual content of the passages was rejected. If we suppose that another hand inserted into the manuscript of Irenaeus the doctrine of the earthly Kingdom, we are raising more problems than we solve.[19] If we have any suggestions at all to offer in this connexion, they would constitute no more than a fairly satisfactory theory, the theory being, as Harnack conjectured, that certain crudely chiliastic ideas were imposed on a fairly early stratum of thought.[20] But since any reconstruction is quite impossible, such a hypothesis, even though in itself it may be acceptable, has no real significance. The text which we have at present is comprehensible in its main points, and its primary eschatological concepts are in harmony with the theology of Irenaeus as a whole. If Irenaeus has used a special source in his exposition of "*regnum*," he has admirably absorbed its contents. But there are, of course, no misplaced chiliastic tendencies in the *Adversus haereses*.[21]

[18] Irenaeus defended Montanism. In his eschatology he found that his understanding was different from the belief which was shortly to become general, and according to which the thousand years' reign of the Book of Revelation was being realised in the existing Church. On this point see Dufourcq, *Saint Irénée*, pp. 146–9, and 184, n. 3. In the Middle Ages the theology of Irenaeus was of practically no significance; cf. Klebba, *Anthropologie des hl. Irenaeus*, p. 5. Not until the 16th century did Irenaeus become more generally known. But even the Reformers rejected the "chiliastic" interpretation of the Revelation of St John. On the possibility of late textual alterations in the manuscripts see Kraft, *Evangelienzitate des heiligen Irenäus*, pp. 40 ff.

[19] Cremers in *Bijdragen*, 1938, pp. 35–51, maintains that the whole of "millenarianism" is an insertion into *A.h.* It is quite obvious that he rejects any idea that Irenaeus himself could have been responsible for such a serious dogmatic error as "millenarianism." Cf. Scharl, *Orientalia*, 1940, p. 403, n. 1. There is a general criticism of Roman Catholic interpretation of Irenaeus in J. Werner, *Der Paulinismus des Irenaeus*, p. 111, which is not unfair.

[20] Harnack, *History of Dogma*, VOL. II, p. 296, n. 1 (in reference to Overbeck). Cf. Hitchcock, *Irenaeus of Lugdunum*, p. 307 f., and Ehrhard, *Die Kirche der Märtyrer*, p. 225.

[21] When certain scholars have operated with a "presbyter-source" for the "chiliasm" of the fifth book of the *A.h.*, they have tried almost at every point to foist on

But terms like "chiliasm" and "millenarianism" are hardly appropriate expressions for the eschatology of Irenaeus. Both words refer to the fixed period of time mentioned in Rev. xx—the Kingdom after the first resurrection and before the destruction of Satan and the Judgement is to last "a thousand years." Strangely enough, there is not a single mention of the words "thousand years" throughout Irenaeus's description of the Kingdom of the Son. He alludes repeatedly to Rev. xx, but consistently avoids the expression "thousand years," in spite of the fact that the period of time mentioned appears six times in the six verses, xx.2–7, which are doctrinally quite fundamental.[22] There is no doubt at all that this reveals a studious avoidance of the doctrine of the "thousand years' reign." The question is simply whether it was Irenaeus himself who avoided the mention of a definite period of time, or whether it was one of his followers who has made elisions in the text at these points. With all the circumstances in mind, it would be improper to speak of the "thousand years' reign" in Irenaeus.[23] We shall best understand the connexion which Irenaeus makes between Rev.

to this source all that they have disapproved of, and this they cannot therefore allow Irenaeus to have sincerely maintained. See e.g. Hoh, *Die Lehre des hl. Irenäus*, pp. 148–50, 166–8. We find the same tendency, though in a slightly more modified form, in two brief papers which in themselves are very informative, one by W. S. Reilly, "Les 'presbytres' asiates de saint Irénée," in *Revue biblique*, 1919, pp. 217–19, and the other by d'Alès, "Le *ΠΡΕΣΒΥΤΗΣ* de saint Irénée," in *Revue des études grecques*, 1929, pp. 398–410. D'Alès sharply distinguishes between *πρεσβύτης* and *πρεσβύτερος* in *A.h.* Cf. Loofs, *Theophilus von Antiochien*, pp. 302, 310–18. Anyone can see that in his eschatological exposition Irenaeus often cites authorities. But his sources are in agreement with his general view.

[22] Cf. *Novum testamentum sancti Irenaei*, pp. 201, 287.

[23] See, Dufourcq, *Saint Irénée*, p. 147, "mille ans"; Hitchcock, *Irenaeus of Lugdunum*, p. 309, "the thousand years"; Lebreton in *History of the Primitive Church* VOL. III. p. 560, "Thousand Years"; and Cremers in *Bijdragen*, 1938, pp. 37 ff., "het duizendjarig rijk." Böhringer, however, was correct, *Kirche Christi*, VOL. II, p. 598: "... dieses Reich, das aber Ir. nirgends ein 'tausend-jähriges' nennt. . . ." There is the further point that Irenaeus thinks of "regnum" as the sabbath or the seventh day; see on this *A.h.* IV. xxvii. 1 (Stier. IV. xvi. 1) and V. xxxiii. 2 (Stier. ibid.) and V. xxx. 4 (Stier. ibid.). Precisely for this reason it is amazing that he never talks about the "thousand years'" period of the "regnum." On the cosmic week and the division into thousand-year periods, see Moritz Kirchner, "Die Eschatologie des Irenäus," in *Theol. Stud. u. Krit.*, 1863, pp. 330 ff.; and Hans Bietenhard, *Das tausenjährige Reiche*, Bern 1944, pp. 54–7; cf. Werner, *Entstehung des Christlichen Dogmas*, pp. 83–8. Kirchner's comment on p. 330 is as exact as the statement at the top of p. 344 is inaccurate. I myself use the wrong phrase "thousand years" in my essay in *S.T.K.*, 1940, p. 152.

xx and 1 Cor. xv.24–8 if we employ the term "the Kingdom of the Son," a Kingdom on earth before Christ "delivers up" the Kingdom to the Father. If we lay the emphasis on those parts of the line of thought which for Irenaeus were essential, we shall soon see that there is no question of any contrast between *Adversus haereses* and *Epideixis* in the general eschatological view which each has.[24] In the *Epideixis* as well as in the *Adversus haereses* the Church reigns with Christ after the resurrection,[25] Christ's second advent is thought of as bringing changes in the world of nature,[26] and the Son brings man to the Father.[27]

In Irenaeus, consequently, the *regnum* is not described as being of a thousand years' duration, but in fact corresponds to the millenium of the Book of Revelation. There is here a terminological irregularity. The "Kingdom," or the "Kingdom of the Son," is an eschatological term which signifies something purely future, something not yet begun, in spite of the fact that Christ has been born, put to death, is risen, and is now seated in power as the Head of the Church. At the same time Irenaeus uses the term *regnum* in a further sense as being contemporaneous with the dominion of Christ in all its phases from the beginning of His work of recapitulation in His becoming man, through the Cross and resurrection, the Church and the final Kingdom on earth, to His delivering up of the Kingdom. In a sense Jesus inaugurates His dominion as a child, and in a hidden way He has kingly power even in His passion and degradation on the Cross, and in the work of the Church He is continually making men citizens of His eternal Kingdom.[28]

[24] Loofs maintains his theory about the absence of any "chiliasm" in the *Epid.* in *Theophilus von Antiochien*, p. 436 f.; Lebreton, *Histoire de l'église*, VOL. III. p. 560 (see, however, the references in n. 6); and Cremers in *Bijdragen*, 1938, pp. 69–72.

[25] *Epid.* 42, 47. Cf. the last few lines of *Epid.* 57.

[26] *Epid.* 61, beginning. It is no logical objection to belief in the future that freedom in the Church prefigures this *now*, as we shall see later in the present section.

[27] *Epid.* 7. Cf. Wieten, *Irenaeus' geschrift*, p. 15, where the parallel in the *A.h.* is quoted (Stier. v. xxxvi. 2). See also the general criticism in Lietzmann, *Church Universal*, p. 206 f.

[28] Jesus worked as the Christ, i.e. as "anointed" King even when Simeon took Him up in his arms, for Christ had even as early as this already won men and given them the knowledge of salvation. The wise men paid their homage to the child and bowed before Him as before "the eternal King." In the same passage Irenaeus refers to the children who had been slain by Herod as martyrs, whom Christ had sent on before "into His Kingdom": "Propter hoc et pueros eripiebat, qui erant in

From this point of view *regnum* in a more limited and technical sense means a *becoming visible* on *earth* of Christ's dominion —before the world disappears and "new heavens and a new earth" are fashioned. It is of some significance that the Irenaean eschatology gained acceptance in the early Christian world of ideas.[29] In every case it harmonises with Irenaeus's general way of thinking. The work of recapitulation attains the end which has been appointed for it from the beginning in the events of the last times.

Recapitulatio

When Christ returns, it will be to recapitulate and consummate the work which He initiated with His becoming man. To put it in its simplest form, *recapitulatio* or *ἀνακεφαλαίωσις* covers the whole of the period from the birth of Jesus to the eschatological perfection. By far the clearest passage on *recapitulatio* as consummation and the final act is a statement in Book I of the *Adversus haereses* which is preserved both in Greek and Latin: "faith in . . . the ascension of our beloved Lord Jesus Christ into heaven in the flesh, and in His manifestation from heaven in the glory of the Father, to recapitulate all things and to raise up anew all flesh of the whole human race"—this occurs, says Irenaeus in the following section, in order that "at the name of Jesus every knee should bow . . . and . . . every tongue should confess that Jesus Christ is Lord," and that the last, just Judgement of all men may take place.[30] It is one of the merits of

domo David, bene sortiti illo tempore nasci, ut eos praemitteret in suum regnum," *A.h.* III. xvii. 4 (Stier. III. xvi. 4). On the Crucifixion and the Kingdom see *Epid.* 56: "Now in this: *Whose government is upon his shoulders*, the cross is in a figure declared, on which He was nailed back. For that which was and is a reproach to Him, and for His sake to us, even the cross, this same is, says he, His *government*, being a sign of His Kingdom."

[29] Cf. Zahn in *Realencyklopädie*, VOL. IX, p. 140; Bonwetsch, *Theologie des Irenäus*, p. 152; Cullmann, *Königsherrschaft Christi*, pp. 22 f.; and *Christ and Time*, p. 142. On Paulism and chiliasm, see also Werner, *Entstehung des christlichen Dogmas*, p. 140, n. 131. Werner regards chiliasm as being based on Paul, but not on the synoptic Gospels or Jesus Himself.

[30] . . . *καὶ τὴν ἐκ τῶν οὐρανῶν ἐν τῇ δόξῃ τοῦ Πατρὸς παρουσίαν αὐτοῦ ἐπὶ τὸ ἀνακεφαλαιώσασθαι τὰ παντὰ, καὶ ἀναστῆσαι πᾶσαν σάρκα πάσης ἀνθρωπότητος*, *A.h.* I. ii. (Stier. I. x. 1). The Latin reads: ". . . et de coelis in gloria Patris adventum ejus, ad recapitulanda universa, et resuscitandam omnem carnem humani generis"; cf. the whole context.

Scharl's study that he strongly emphasises the connexion, and, indeed, from one point of view, the identity, between recapitulation and consummation.[31] It is very characteristic, too, that Loofs immediately reacts against the passage which we have just quoted with his theories about the division of sources, and notes a contradiction between this final, eschatological recapitulation and other expressions in Irenaeus which speak of recapitulation without any direct reference to the events at the Parousia.[32]

In actual fact the *whole* of Irenaeus's doctrine of recapitulation in all its phases is oriented towards the Parousia. From beginning to end *recapitulatio* involves a continuum which stage by stage is realised in time. When the hostile powers have been defeated and expelled, this work of recapitulation is fulfilled and man restored. There is, however, a definite time-sequence in the conflict—the hostile powers are put down in the order and at the time which God has appointed. Irenaeus refers here to the Pauline statement: "The last enemy to be destroyed is death" (I Cor. xv.26).[33] Sin brought death into the world, and sin will be vanquished before death. We may well say, with regard to the defeat of death in the present, that the final victory over death *in Christ* was achieved through the resurrection on the third day, but we should then have to add that *men* will not fully be clothed in Christ's victory until the resurrection of the dead and the life eternal. When those who belong to Christ are raised, Christ will then have "emptied" death. It is when men receive life and are freed from the clutches of the manslayer, the murderer, the enemy of man, that ἀνακεφαλαίωσις comes to fulfilment.[34] As early as His birth of the Virgin Mary this was the express object of the Lord's coming, and

[31] See Scharl, *Orientalia*, 1940, p. 415 f., and also 396 f. and 407. Cf. Brunner, *The Mediator*, p. 256, n. 1; and Aulén, *Den kristna försoningstanken*, p. 47.

[32] Loofs, *Theophilus von Antiochien*, p. 366, n.1 and the whole context.

[33] *A.h.* III. xxxvi (Stier. III. xxiii. 7) and V. xxxvi (Stier. V. xxxvi. 2).

[34] In *A.h.* III. xxxvi there is a description of the events of the last time, the appearance of Antichrist, etc. In the last time Adam is saved and given life. "Novissima inimica evacuatur mors" (I Cor. xv.26). On Adam's salvation Irenaeus says, "Illius enim salus, evacuatio est mortis. Domino igitur vivificante hominem, id est Adam, evacuata est et mors." We should compare this with III. xix. 6 (Stier. III. xviii. 7), end.

there is an unbroken unity in the whole of Christ's work right up to the events of the last time—everything is *recapitulatio*.[35]

While at the same time there is continuity between Christ's work in the resurrection of the dead and the works which He performed previously in His life on earth, in His Resurrection, and in the Church, there is also something new which takes place in the last time. This eschatological event is also *recapitulatio*, and therein lies its connexion with the past, but it is the *end* of *recapitulatio*, and therein lies its newness and its uniqueness for this phase. In the Church the Spirit has contended against the flesh, but in the Consummation it will have triumphed over the last remnants of resistance. Evil, concentrated in the form of Antichrist, will then have been expelled from Creation.[36] In the Judgement which is to come, however, when evil will be eradicated, matter will not be destroyed, but only sin.[37] Matter will continue, and be taken possession of by the "hands of God," viz. by the Son and the Spirit. Man's body will, therefore, receive eternal life in the resurrection. The final outcome will be a return to the very first condition, and the pure, unblemished resurrection will be the pure, undestroyed Creation. Evil and death belong to a period between these two

[35] Cf. *A.h.* III. xvii. 6–8 (Stier. III. xvi. 6–8), v. xviii. 2 (Stier. v. xviii. 3) and on external Creation in the *regnum*, v. xxxii. 1 (Stier. ibid.): the return of nature to its original purity and abundance in the last age is part of the final phase of recapitulation.

[36] In *Theol. Stud. u. Krit.*, 1863, p. 343, Kirchner points out that Irenaeus does *not* say that Satan "shall be loosed" (Rev. xx.3, 7–9) out of his prison. As there is no mention of the "thousand years" in *A.h.*, there is none either of the prosperity of evil after the millenium. What Irenaeus does assert is that the coming Antichrist is to rule in the heavens for three and a half years *before* the coming of Christ, *A.h.* v. xxx. 4 (Stier. ibid.). The end will be the conclusive defeat of every form of Satanic power.

[37] After the Judgement and the "delivering up of the Kingdom to the Father," the old heaven and the old earth will disappear. Irenaeus adduces here 1 Cor. VII. 31 in which it is said that "the σχῆμα of this world passes away," *A.h.* v. xxxv. 2 (Stier. ibid.). The passage 1. Cor. VII. 31 is introduced again in *A.h.* v. xxxvi (Stier. v. xxxvi. 1) where the Latin text has a slight change: "figura transit mundi hujus." The substantive "figura" is interpreted as "that in which the *transgression* has been committed," i.e. it is *sin* which passes away, not matter. It is expressly stated that the new heaven and the new earth are material though not contaminated by sin: *Οὐ γὰρ ἡ ὑπόστασις οὐδὲ ἡ οὐσία τῆς κτίσεως ἐξαφανίζεται . . . ἀλλὰ τὸ σχῆμα παράγει. . . .* Franz Erdin, *Das Wort Hypostasis*, Frieburg-im-Breisgau 1939, p. 37, deals with this passage, though he does not go deep enough. See the Latin: "Non enim substantia, neque materia conditionis exterminatur."

states, the beginning and the end, without extending into either of them. Man plunged headlong from life into death, but was taken from death to life by Christ. The "child" of Creation has reached his end, and in the conflict has grown to the destiny appointed for him by the Creator.

Against this, however, it may be objected that evil has not been removed, but simply consigned to eternal punishment. Evil as *resistance* has certainly been destroyed, but it still exists as the object of the punishment which is due to it.[38] And furthermore, those who have thus remained in the power of evil right up to the Last Judgement, and who have, therefore, no share in eternal life, have failed to reach humanity's objective, and to come to the state which God has appointed for man. Irenaeus does not see the division of mankind as implying any diminution of God's power, but rather as a revelation of His power.[39] Evil is understood essentially as active disobedience or resistance to God. If this resistance is destroyed, evil is also destroyed. Death is the enemy of God, and when the wicked are ejected from eternal life they fall into the clutches of death, but death's work is limited by the power of the God, who bestows life and who judges men, to destroy that which according to His will *shall* be destroyed, viz. evil. Where death destroys sin and only sin, God is absolute and sovereign Lord, and only *God's* will is done.[40] Irenaeus is quite clearly aware that there are many problems here. He is as little concerned to argue how evil was able to enter God's pure Creation—the "envy" of the Serpent is simply a fact—as to discover why some who have been created by God for eternal life can be damned and lose eternal life. In these matters God has revealed nothing in His Word.[41]

The very fact that part of Creation is transient and not permanent is no sign, says Irenaeus, that death, the enemy of God, is at work. It is natural that that which comes into being in time should disappear in time. There is much that is transient because God has designed that it should be so[42]—the

[38] *A.h.* IV. lxv (Stier. IV. xl. 1).

[39] *Epid.* 8 and 48, *A.h.* V. xxiv. 2–3 (Stier. ibid.).

[40] Cf. *A.h.* IV. lxiv. 3 (Stier. IV. xxxix. 3).

[41] In His sovereignty ("secundum magnitudinem") God is impenetrable. See *A.h.* IV. xxxiv. 4–5 (Stier. IV. xx. 4–5).

[42] See *A.h.* II. iii. 1 (Stier. II. iii. 2).

earthly Jerusalem and the law of bondage are the instruments of God, but they are temporal, transitory, and passing.[43] At times Irenaeus appears to be saying that creation as such is transient, and so it is to a certain extent natural that man as a created being should be moving towards eventual dissolution—there is nothing in him inherently divine, i.e. eternal. But in this regard the concept of destiny and growth complicates the whole issue. It is involved in man's destiny that he is continually to receive from God, and thus grow without interruption and become something more than he is at the present time. In so progressing he is becoming man. Man is created and mortal, but he has been destined to live eternally—to live by receiving from an inexhaustible source. The Spirit makes man "perfect man," but the Spirit is God, and God is Life.[44] It is to this goal, eternal life in the dominion of the Spirit, that man as man is destined. If he suffers death, his destiny is brought to nothing. But the Last Judgement means that the condemned do suffer death, for not all are in Christ. But does this not then mean that *recapitulatio* is never fully realised?

There is the further related question here of death in nature—the death or decay of animals, trees, and organic growth. Irenaeus quite obviously has refrained from introducing the idea of universal death into his discussion of man's death. As soon as he thinks of man's death, he sees death as an enemy, something unnatural and as odious as sin. Death, says Irenaeus, has got dominion over man because of Adam's defeat by the Devil in his temptation—it is disobedience which is primary, and death is a fruit of sin. But when he thinks of death and

[43] The whole exposition in *A.h.* IV. v–vi (Stier. IV. iv. 1–3) emphasises that God also creates what is transient. Transience or transitoriness has been appointed by God. Irenaeus puts it thus: "Quaecunque enim temporale initium habent, necesse est ea et finem habere temporalem. Quoniam igitur a Moyse lex inchoavit, consequenter in Johannem desivit." After this he extends the reference of what he is saying to the "figura" of the whole world: "Et quid de Hierusalem dicimus, quandoquidem et figuram mundi universi oporteat praeterire, adveniente tempore praeteritionis ipsius . . .?" The substantive "figura" recurs in *A.h.* v. xxxvi. (Stier. v. xxxvi. 1), there also denoting what is transient: "Et propter hoc figura haec temporalis facta est." But at the same time "figura" is connected with sin: ". . . hoc est, in quibus transgressio facta est." Cf. the Greek text of this latter passage. "Figura" refers back to 1 Cor. VII. 31 (σχῆμα).

[44] Cf. *A.h.* v. vi. 1 (Stier. ibid.). We shall return to this in the next section in which we shall be discussing immortality, resurrection, and related concepts.

decay in Creation outside of man, Irenaeus sees death and mortality as being at times as natural as life, for what is created comes into existence in time and it ceases to exist in time. The whole of Irenaeus's doctrine of the Kingdom of the Son, however, gives evidence of a completely different view and provides a warning against making too sharp a distinction between life and death. In the resurrection of the just external Creation is also renewed—unprecedented harvests will appear and wild beasts will cease to kill (Is. XI.)[45] In its present state, which is marked by weakness and death, nature is in a measure impaired and cursed by God. But Irenaeus has not speculated on this, and he confines himself to what Scripture has to say on any particular question, and in Scripture he finds that man is the only creature whom God has expressly destined to live and not to die. Man's death is a consequence of his transgression.[46] Whenever death has dominion over man it is an enemy.

And yet, in the Judgement it will be seen that some men are in the Serpent's power and are doomed to an end which completely reverses their destiny. They will not cease to exist—the idea of annihilation is foreign to Irenaeus—but will continue to suffer death and punishment. Despite this, Irenaeus clings to his concept of recapitulation, and repeatedly states that Christ recapitulates *all things* and that he gives life to mankind as a whole. In the same way he says of God the Creator that He has created and is creating *all things*, and that nothing can come into being apart from God, and yet He is not responsible for creating evil. Evil is something incomprehensible both when it enters Creation through the Devil and when it is condemned by God in the Last Judgement. We shall not be able to understand it until all things are made plain to our sight after the Judgement Day. Irenaeus makes no attempt to solve

[45] *A.h.* v. xxxiii. 4 (Stier. ibid.): cf. also the immediately preceding passage. Gen. I. 26–30 is fulfilled in the subservience of animate and inanimate nature to man. "Et oportet conditione revocata, obedire et subjecta esse omnia animalia homini . . . quemadmodum autem in obedientia subjecta erant Adae," v. xxxiii. 4. Cf. *Epid.* 59, 61. The Latin text quoted above is emended by J. A. Robinson in *J.T.S.*, 1931, to "ante inobedientiam" (p. 391). The emendation seems justified.

[46] Cf. Gen. II. 17 and III. 3, and Rom. v. 12. See the important passage in *A.h.* v. xxiii. 1 (Stier. ibid.). There are many similar statements in Irenaeus which might be quoted.

the problem of evil,[47] but he still says a certain amount which makes it possible for him to employ the concept of recapitulation, despite the reality of evil.

In Irenaeus's exposition of the Judgement we find at times the thought that God is active, the only truly active being, producing life out of His own being, while man can only receive from God. And God deals with all men equally according to His own nature. But men differ in their reception of Him. Faith and gratitude "gather up" the goodness which comes from God. Unbelief and ingratitude inevitably absorb judgement and wrath.[48] God's goodness passes unbelief by; unbelief cannot receive goodness, even where goodness exists. God thus acts towards all men equally in His divine nature. Those who are condemned "gather up" the same work of God as the saved, but the way of gathering up and receiving is different. God's dealings are not changed or suspended by any difference in the reception of them—God is what He is, and He acts according to His inner, divine will everywhere and in every thing. The light shines on, even although one blinds oneself to it.[49]

[47] The statement in *A.h.* II. xliii. 1–2 (Stier. II. xxviii. 7) with its reference to I Cor. XIII. 9 is particularly characteristic. When the insoluble questions are left unanswered and "referred to God," it is implied that man must wait until all things are made plain in the future.

[48] "Et Deus quidem perfectus in omnibus, ipse sibi aequalis et similis; totus cum sit lumen, et totus mens, et totus substantia, et fons omnium bonorum: homo vero profectum percipiens et augmentum ad Deum. Quemadmodum enim Deus semper idem est; sic et homo in Deo inventus, semper proficiet ad Deum. Neque enim Deus cessat aliquando in benefaciendo, et locupletando hominem: neque homo cessat beneficium àccipere, et ditari a Deo. Exceptorium enim bonitatis, et organum clarificationis ejus, home gratus ei qui se fecit: et iterum exceptorium justi judicii ejus homo ingratus, et spernens plasmatorem, et non subjectus Verbo ejus," *A.h.* IV. xxi. 2 (Stier. IV. xi. 2).

[49] See *A.h.* IV. lxiv. 3 (Stier. IV. xxxix. 3) where Irenaeus attempts to state what free will can and cannot do. Cf. IV. xi. 3–5 (Stier. IV. vi. 5–7) and IV. lix. 1–lxiv. 2 (Stier. IV. xxxvii. 1–xxxix. 2). Irenaeus always thinks of the double outcome of the Last Judgement, but he has little inclination to depict the punishment of the wicked. He fixes his attention on the victory of life in the Judgement and on the positive side of the last time—the increase of communion with God and sight in place of faith. Since those who are in Christ rise in the first resurrection, and judgement according to works takes place after the second resurrection, judgement as a threat passes to a certain extent from the Church to the world—the Church awaits the last day in unclouded hope and without fear. The background of this whole view is the fact that the Church *now* in the present time is *suffering*, and suffering unjustly, but is patiently bearing its martyrdom.

God's work, however, is bound up with that which happens to man as man, since God has a positive purpose for man, and if man does not receive what God in His goodness gives him, it is not only man who suffers from this failure to receive, but also God, whose purpose for man is thereby frustrated. While it is possible to put the matter thus, it is characteristic of Irenaeus that he never actually says this. He quite certainly does not conceive of God's work as being so unrelated to the life of man—as the line of thought which we have just referred to would appear to indicate—that his picture of God is of a divine being loftily indifferent to the condition of those whom He has created. Irenaeus connects the work of God more intimately with the life of man than is implied merely by saying that God has a purpose for man which may or may not ultimately be fulfilled. To say no more than this would be to isolate the will of God in a decree which existed before the event, and the event itself would take place independently of God. For Irenaeus, however, God the Creator is at work when human life is lived as it ought to be. Human freedom is a part of God's own gracious dealings with man, and His decree for man encompasses man's growth in freedom. To "recapitulate Adam" is to bring man to salvation with true freedom on man's side. If there is no such freedom, man is not saved.[50] This duality, the fact that some believe and others do not, that some receive life while others are subject to death, is an expression of the fact that freedom exists. The very dualism of faith and unbelief is a part of man's recapitulation.

Is it possible for a man to use his freedom in such a way as not to allow himself to be saved? Is he not "recapitulated"? Can we possibly say that God's purpose of recapitulation has been deflected without having effected its object? Irenaeus frequently says that the man who is not in Christ has no freedom—he is a captive. He used the freedom which he possessed

[50] Cf. *A.h.* v. i. 1 (Stier. ibid.): ". . . ea quae sunt sua redimens ab ea, non cum vi, quemadmodum illa initio dominabatur nostri, ea quae non erant sua insatiabiliter rapiens, sed secundum suadelam, quemadmodum decebat Deum suadentem, et non vim inferentem, accipere quae vellet; ut neque quod est justum confringeretur, neque antiqua plasmatio Dei deperiret." Christ "advises," speaks, convinces, and *appeals*, instead of compelling and using force, because man is free and must be saved such. Otherwise ἀνακεφαλαίωσις would not take place. To save men under constraint is not salvation, but rather the destruction of "the old Creation," i.e. of man, of Adam, who at the beginning was created free.

to shut himself up again in his place of captivity, in spite of the fact that the door had been opened by Christ's power. For this man there is no freedom, but the opposite of freedom, and by his choice his very humanity is dislocated. Irenaeus does not begin by thinking of pure humanity as being complete and finished and then go on to argue whether or not this humanity will be saved. Salvation would then be something supernatural, an addition to man's humanity. But salvation is *life*, *human* life, lived under the "hands" of God. To be saved *is* to be man. To resist God is to destroy one's very manhood.[51] But there is no "failure" of God's purpose of recapitulation in such self-destruction, for death is the logical consequence of resistance to God.[52] Salvation embraces all that is man, for salvation is precisely unimpaired human life in its wholeness and uncorrupt form. In Christ this salvation for the whole of mankind is achieved without restriction. The Incarnate One's *recapitulatio* of Adam encompasses the whole of human life to all eternity. Death's destruction of evil is simply another side of the victory of life, and is indeed man's eternal freedom from his two enemies, sin and death, which are now destroying one another. God is "all in all."[53]

Consequently man is not a merely static being to whom salvation is applied as something additional. Man is a child who was ordained by God to grow to full human life, and who is afflicted by Satan, but healed by Christ. The healing work of the incarnate Saviour extends over the period from His birth of the Virgin Mary to the delivering up of the Kingdom to the

[51] See *A.h.* IV. vii (Stier. IV. iv. 3), IV. lxiv. I (Stier. IV. xxxix. I) and V. viii. 2 (Stier. V. viii. 2–3). The possibility of human life depends on fellowship with God. To be man means to be man by receiving life from the Creator. Man without God is a contradiction in terms. The division of humanity which the Last Judgement will involve takes place already in men's response to the *kerygma*. Faith in the Gospel means life, unbelief means death, the destruction of man's life. Cf. Escoula in *N.R.T.*, 1939, p. 563.

[52] We can trace here a sign of an idea of predestination in Irenaeus. Cf. the expression which recurs frequently, that God reveals Himself "to whom He will, when He will, and as He will," e.g. *A.h.* IV. xi. 5 (Stier. IV. vi. 7) and IV. xxxiv. 5 (Stier. IV. xx. 5). Cf. on Pharaoh's hardness of heart IV. xlv (Stier. IV. xxix), where Irenaeus cites New Testament illustrations of God's hardening of men's hearts. The idea of reprobation, however, is based on the foreknowledge of God.

[53] The final result of *recapitulatio* will appear when the Son "delivers up" the Kingdom to the Father, according to I Cor. xv.24–8.

Father after the Last Judgement. The whole of Christ's work in man's salvation is termed *recapitulatio*. By *recapitulatio*, man comes into being as man in accordance with the first decree for Creation. And he does so in growth and conflict. He is not independent of the work of recapitulation, but rather this work of recapitulation is the process in which man is created.[54] Christ enters the world of flesh and contends against the Devil for man. He gives life to the lifeless and captive Creation, which by this act is brought to its original appointed end.[55] In the final Consummation *recapitulatio* will be brought to an end, and man will come into conformity to the image and likeness of God. If, by way of conclusion to the present work, we take up once more the concept of *imago* and *similitudo*, we shall have the opportunity of touching on two problems which up to this point we have not so far discussed. Only now does the possibility present itself to us of dealing with the final questions in Irenaeus, which are of very great importance for our subject.

Imago and Similitudo

Man is created in the image and likeness of God. The Son is the first-born of every creature; He is the image of God and like God. Man is accordingly created in the eternal Son, and destined for Him who in the fullness of time was to become incarnate. In becoming man the Son of God took Adam's flesh. In the birth of Jesus and His victorious human life true man is realised. If those others whose humanity has been strangled in its bondage to the Serpent could only share in Christ's life, they would reach the goal which God intended for them in Creation, and their creation would become complete and perfect. Everything that Christ has done from His becoming man to the final Consummation is a continual giving of Himself to men. When Christ gives and men receive, they in turn progressively become what God intends them to be, as the struggle between flesh and Spirit in the Church continues. Even in the "Kingdom of the

[54] The idea of recapitulation in all its extent brings unity and continuity to the Irenaean theology. We must stress this sharply against Loofs's theories of division. Loofs develops his view of the term "recapitulatio" in relation to the various alleged sources and to Justin in *Theophilus von Antiochien*, pp. 359–64.

[55] Cf. Bonwetsch, *Theologie des Irenäus*, p. 99; also Kirchner in *Theol. Stud. u. Krit.*, 1863, p. 357 f. and Scharl, *Orientalia*, 1940, p. 415 f.

Son" man still grows while fulfilling God's purpose in Creation that he should have dominion over the earth. Man, however, Irenaeus believed, has still some progress to achieve before his destiny is finally attained. Only in the Last Judgement will evil conclusively be cleared out of God's Creation. The conflict between flesh and Spirit will be transformed in the victory of the Spirit through resurrection with Christ.[56] When earth and heaven pass away and the Kingdom is delivered up to the Father, *recapitulatio* will be completed and a new heaven and a new earth will be created. Man will then have attained the end appointed for him, viz. the *imago* and *similitudo* of God. Our main problem in this final section will therefore be: In the final Consummation, will man not be *the same* as Christ?

If man becomes the *imago* of God, then he becomes what Christ in fact is. Does this mean that every distinction between Christ and man disappears? The problem which confronts us here in an altered form is the old one of the relationship between divine and human. The question, Is not Christ's divine nature the same reality as His human nature? emerged earlier as a purely Christological one. In the Incarnate One God and man seemed to be so interrelated as to form a unity. On closer analysis, however, the Incarnation demonstrated the truth that God always creates and man is always created. When God gives and man receives or "grows" (which is the same thing), man is brought to perfection and sin is expelled from him. Christ is man in completely developed and sinless form, because He is God who creates and is victorious. God is one reality and man is another, even in Christ, but when God in the Incarnation gives and creates without limit, and man in the Incarnate One is receptive and created without resisting, God and man are united in the Saviour.[57] When we state it in these terms we see that the problem has shifted from the Incarnation to the eschatological Consummation, and it now no longer relates to Christ alone but rather to man who has been redeemed by Him.

[56] In the resurrection the same "hands" are active as were at work in Creation and in the Church, viz. the Spirit and the Son. On the connexion between the work of the Spirit in faith and the ethical conflict on the one hand, and in the resurrection on the other, see *A.h.* v. ix. 1–4 (Stier. ibid.), and also v. viii. 1 (Stier. ibid.).

[57] See above, Part II, Chapter 1, section 3, "God and Man."

This, however, is simply a new way of expressing the original problem. To put it briefly and concisely, if the Spirit is divine, if Christ gives Himself in faith, and if on the other side the Spirit first makes man *man*, is not man then, as such, divine?[58] Or will he not at any rate become divine in the Consummation?

It may be appropriate initially to make reference to some of Irenaeus's statements in which he clearly says that in the resurrection and eternal life man will become conformed to the *imago* and *similitudo* of God. The man who receives the Spirit in faith has something to wait for and look forward to as long as he lives. The Spirit still cries in him, "Abba, Father!" But when man is wholly compassed about by the Spirit, he becomes like God; he reaches fulfilment in accordance with the decree which the Creator conceived at the very dawn of time.[59] Only then does man attain to the likeness which was the object of Christ's becoming man. He became like us in order that we should become like Him.[60] The transformation to the image of Christ begins in the Christian at baptism and continues afterwards in the life of faith and love in the very midst of death and infirmity, until the moment he awakens from death and attains to perfection.[61] The fulfilment of recapitulation and the realisation of

[58] *A.h.* v. vi. 1 (Stier. ibid.) speaks at one time of the Spirit as something divine, the "hand" of God, and as something which man requires to get in order to be "perfect man." Cf. v. ix. 1 (Stier. v. ix. 2). That man will himself become in the last Consummation what Christ Himself is seems probable, the more so as Christ will then "deliver up" the Kingdom. When God is "all in all" will man not be divine?

[59] "Si igitur nunc pignus habentes clamamus, Abba Pater; quid fiet quando resurgentes faciem ad faciem videbimus eum; quando omnia membra affluenter exultationis hymnum protulerint, glorificantia eum, qui suscitaverit ea ex mortuis, et aeternam vitam donaverit? Si enim pignus complectens hominem in semetipsum, jam facit dicere, Abba Pater, quid faciet universa Spiritus gratia, quae hominibus dabitur a Deo? similes nos ei efficiet, et perficiet voluntate Patris; efficiet enim hominem secundum imaginem et similitudinem Dei," *A.h.* v. viii. 1 (Stier. ibid.).

[60] Scharl, *Orientalia*, 1940, p. 409 f. On the centrality of the idea of Christ in the New Testament concept of *εἰκών*, see Wilhelm Michaelis, *Zur Engelchristologie im Urchristentum*, Basel 1942, p. 53. With regard to the belief in a future realisation of likeness to Christ in the resurrection, cf. E. Schlink in *Der alte und der neue Mensch*, p. 80. Koch stresses this aspect of Irenaeus's view very clearly in *Theol. Stud. u. Krit.*, 1925, p. 203: ". . . erst am Ende aller Tage, als Krönung der *ἀνακεφαλαίωσις*, tritt das Bild und Gleichnis Gottes im Menschen in seiner ganzen Vollendung hervor."

[61] ". . . neque alteram manum Dei praeter hanc, quae ab initio usque ad finem format nos, et coaptat in vitam, et adest plasmati suo, et perficit illud secundum

imago and *similitudo*, as far as man is concerned, both lie in the future.[62]

In his conception of the resurrection Irenaeus lays a strong emphasis on the activity and power of God in regard to man. Man dies—and then God raises him from the dead. The idea of immortality, on the other hand, locates the life-force directly in man as he is in himself—the man who is immortal is not subject to death. When it comes to the question of immortality or resurrection Irenaeus is occasionally ambiguous, as though, in spite of all that he is continually saying about the resurrection of the body, he were anxious to assert the immortality of the soul. There are several explanations for this apparent vacillation, but the most important reason is the specific conception of life which Irenaeus held—in all its aspects life is a receiving of the power of God—and the related concept of "growth" which dominates Irenaeus's whole view of man in fellowship with God, and which makes him unwilling to make a sharp line between the present time and eternity.[63] The theology of Irenaeus is always characterised by a clear continuity. Life in the Church in the present time, human life, that is, is in fact the life of the resurrection; and the new thing in eternity is the absence of man's enemies. On the other hand, however, the concept of growth implies a continual progression from stage to stage, and we might well expect Irenaeus in developing this concept to suggest that in eternal life man leaves his humanity behind and passes over into a divine form of existence. We must

imaginem et similitudinem Dei," *A.h.* v. xvi. I (Stier. ibid.). "Non enim effugit aliquando Adam manus dei, ad quas Pater loquens, dicit: Faciamus hominem ad imaginem et similitudinem nostram. Et propter hoc in fine non ex voluntate carnis, neque ex voluntate viri, sed ex placito Patris manus ejus vivum perfecerunt hominem, uti fiat Adam secundum imaginem et similitudinem Dei," v. i. 3 (Stier. ibid.). Cf. v. xii. 5 (Stier. v. xii. 6) and the whole of v. xv (Stier. ibid.).

[62] See especially *A.h.* IV. lxiii. 2–3 (Stier. IV. xxxviii. 3–4).

[63] Certainly Irenaeus explicitly opposes the doctrine of an immediate transition by way to death to eternal life. The departed await the resurrection. On this point see *A.h.* v. xxxi. 1–2 (Stier. ibid.). But the Spirit, which takes free possession of man in the resurrection life, is no different from the Spirit which seals him in faith in the present, contending against his selfishness, and which makes him man. Coupled with this is the related concept of continuity which the doctrine of the "regnum" on earth implies. There will be some in the Church when the final age begins, and these will pass "in carne" into the Kingdom of the Son. See *A.h.* v. xxxv. 1 (Stier. ibid.).

take each of these problems separately: first, the problem of "immortality," and then that of "deification."[64] Both are variations of the main problem with which we are dealing in the present section: Is man God?

On the question of immortality, Irenaeus says quite explicitly in two passages that the soul is not destroyed and does not perish, but on the contrary continues to exist. It is of particular importance to observe the context in which these statements appear in Irenaeus. In one, Irenaeus is arguing against the theories of metempsychosis or transmigration of souls; and he denies that the soul after death enters another human body.[65] Transmigration from body to body is inconsistent with the idea of Judgement. Man is accountable in the Judgement for the life which he has lived on earth. The soul continues after death and is united with the body in the resurrection. When, as here, the idea of the survival of the soul is associated with resurrection and Judgement, the most specifically Hellenistic features of the idea of immortality are obviously excluded.[66] But to this it has to be added that in the actual context in which he is speaking of the soul, Irenaeus speaks of the soul as having been created in time, and therefore liable to disappear in time, if God, the only eternal one, does not give it life.[67] In himself man is in no respect eternal; he can only receive what is eternal, and he cannot receive it once and for all, but rather must constantly receive it from God who ceaselessly fills up the life which man enjoys in a continuing and extended act of Creation.[68]

[64] Cf. Nygren, *Agape and Eros*, p. 410, n.2. [65] *A.h.* II. lv–lvi (Stier. II. xxxiv. 1–4).

[66] Irenaeus states in several places that the soul is reunited with the body in the resurrection; see e.g. *A.h.* V. xxxi. 2 (Stier. ibid.). In *A.h.* II. xliv (Stier. II. xxix. 1–2) Irenaeus shows how the separation at the Last Judgement shatters the belief in undiscriminating immortality of the soul, and necessitates the dogma of a resurrection of the body, which is the agent of man's actions. In the division which will be made at the Judgement life will be separated from death.

[67] *A.h.* II. lvi. 1 (Stier. II. xxxiv. 2).

[68] "Sicut autem corpus animale ipsum quidem non est anima, participatur autem animam, quoadusque Deus vult: *sic et anima ipsa quidem non est vita*, participatur autem a Deo sibi praestitam vitam . . . Deo itaque vitam et perpetuam perseverantiam donante, capit et animas primum non exsistentes dehinc perseverare, cum eas Deus et esse et subsistere voluerit," II. lvi. 2 (Stier. II. xxxiv. 4). Irenaeus argues in exactly the same way about the life of the *body*, both now and in the resurrection—the body *receives* life from the Creator, the source of life. See the particularly forceful argument in *A.h.* V. iii (Stier. ibid.); cf. V. iv (Stier. V. iv. 2) and V. xv. 1 (Stier. ibid.).

The other context which we have mentioned is that in which Irenaeus refutes the Gnostic theory that the body cannot receive life in the salvation. As usual Irenaeus takes his stand on a Biblical statement, and quite naturally he finds as a basis for his doctrine of the resurrection of the flesh the passage in Rom. VIII. II: "If the Spirit of Him who raised Jesus from the dead dwells in you, He who raised Christ Jesus from the dead will give life to your mortal bodies also through His Spirit which dwells in you." Irenaeus seizes on the adjective "mortal" (*mortalis*) to emphasise the point he wishes to make—it is the mortal who will receive life from God in the resurrection. In this case, then, it is impossible for the Gnostics, Irenaeus maintained, to deny the resurrection of the body.[69] For the purposes of his argument Irenaeus here submited to a thorough analysis the view of the Gnostics that matter in the proper sense is corruptible. The more exclusively he applied the idea of mortality to the body, the more cogently he could argue that Paul's statement refuted the Gnostic case, and the clearer became the proof for the resurrection of the body. When Irenaeus states, therefore, that the soul is immortal, it is in the context of this postulate, and it can at once be seen that the main point of the Hellenistic idea of immortality has no place at all in his view.[70] The affirmative proposition is not for a moment altered—God gives life to man, and it is to the whole man, including his body, that He gives it.[71]

Irenaeus does not think of immortality as a static possession.

[69] Rom. VIII. II is on the whole an unusually exact description of Irenaeus's doctrine of the Spirit and life. Irenaeus expounds the Pauline statement in *A.h.* v. vii (Stier. ibid.).

[70] We should note also that the discussion on the immortality of the soul in v. vii. I (Stier. ibid.) is offered with certain reservations. It is most important, however, to note that Irenaeus *gets right into his opponents' argument* in order to pull it to pieces from within. There is a striking example of the same controversial method in exactly the same question in *A.h.* v. iv (Stier. v. iv. I). So also v. xiii. 3 (Stier. ibid.).

[71] For this reason Irenaeus can at the same time maintain that the soul is mortal. When left to itself and isolated from God it is mortal—the life it has is the life which ceaselessly flows from the Creator. See *A.h.* v. xii. 2–3 (Stier. ibid.). There is a similar quite conscious dualism in Theophilus, *ad Autolycum*, II. xxvii (Otto's edn., Jena 1861, pp. 130 ff.). On immortality in Irenaeus cf. also Nygren, *Agape and Eros*, pp. 410 ff., in which, however, the controversial function of the idea of immortality is not emphasised.

Life is the continuing work of the Creator, and the work of the Creator is an active struggle against Death. The creativity of God and God's contention against the power of Satan are integral parts of the Irenaean concept of life. From one point of view life is a unity. Rain, which falls and makes the dry earth fruitful, and bread, which satisfies man's hunger, serve life and combat death.[72] For modern readers words such as "immortality" and "incorruptibility" might well lead to the idea of something above time, change, and decay. Irenaeus, however, rather thinks of indestructible life as something which is wholly exposed to strife and violence, and, indeed, is ravaged by death, but which still retains its eternal strength in the heart of the kingdom of death itself, and finally shatters every fetter, triumphantly forcing its way from its place of captivity. It is in fact in the trial of the conflict against Satan that true life reveals itself to be "incorruptibility," *ἀφθαρσία*. Life cannot be destroyed, but only momentarily damaged. It is, therefore, in the resurrection from the dead that we shall finally see incorruptible life.[73] Man does not receive immortality from his own nature, but from God the Creator, who is victorious in the resurrection of the body.[74] Such a view of life could hardly be farther from the philosophical doctrine of the natural immortality of the soul.

The question is, however, whether Irenaeus has not instead eventually come to the Hellenistic belief in a "deification" of man. This is consequently our second problem. Does Irenaeus understand man's destiny to be the transformation of man into God? It may be advisable for us to take up here at once the central point at issue, viz. the doctrine of the Spirit, for it is demonstrably true that if man does not consist of body, soul,

[72] Cf. *A.h.* III. xviii. 1 (Stier. III. xvii. 2); IV. xxxi. 3 (Stier. IV. xviii. 4); and V. iii. 3 (Stier. ibid.).

[73] In *Epid.* 72 Irenaeus expounds Ps. XXI. 5 in the following way of Christ: "Now what is this that he says, *He asked life*, since he was about to die? He proclaims his resurrection from the dead, and that being raised from the dead He is immortal. For he received both *life*, that he should rise, and *length of days for ever and ever*, that He should be incorruptible." Cf. *A.h.* V. ii. 3 (Stier. ibid.) and also Gächter in *Z.K.T.*, 1934, p. 523 f.

[74] See *A.h.* III. xxi. 1 (Stier. III. xx. 1); and also V. xxi. 3 (Stier. ibid.), at the end: ". . . ut experimento discat homo, quoniam non a semetipso, sed donatione Dei accipit incorruptelam," Cf. II. xviii. 4 (Stier. II. xiv. 4).

and Spirit, he is imperfect, and if any of these three constituent parts is absent, man's "manliness" is thereby incomplete. At the same time, the Spirit is throughout God's own Spirit, not merely some kind of "gift" of the Spirit, but the Spirit Itself, i.e. God or Christ Himself. And in the resurrection life the dominion of the Spirit extends over the whole man. Before the resurrection, the Spirit dwells in man and is engaged in continual conflict within man, but in the resurrection from the dead, evil is banished and the Spirit reigns supreme. Does this mean, then, that man has been "deified"?

Our impression that such is indeed the case is strengthened by the fact that Irenaeus never says that man's spirit is mortal. His statements about the soul can be ambiguous, and he can say that the soul is corruptible or incorruptible, but in speaking of the Spirit, the one repeated assertion he has to make is that the Spirit cannot die.[75] The Spirit is Life, as God is Life. If the Spirit were a supernatural addition to what is human, so that body and soul by themselves constituted a whole man, the resurrection life could then be understood as an addition or extra gift received by man. Man would then throughout remain man, but in the resurrection he would be given this gift of the Spirit, the gift, that is, of eternal life, which in itself does not belong to man. But when Irenaeus asserts that man as such has been destined for eternal life, that death is an enemy, something contrary to nature, and that the Spirit's dominion over soul and body in the life of the resurrection will make man *man* in the true sense, he is saying quite simply that the Spirit is something characteristic of man, or distinctive in him, that immortality is an attribute of man, and that it is part of man's nature to be

[75] Death is a destroyer who falls upon man as a result of the Fall. Body and soul alike then fell into the clutches of death, and this in a sense was the fulfilment of their own nature, since both originated in time; but it is not the fulfilment of their destiny, since God wills that the whole man, by continually *receiving* life from the Creator, shall *live* and not die. Sin is a severing of the connexion with the Creatro, as a result of which death came into the world. But man, who has been cut off from God, has turned away from the Spirit which he no longer possesses. When the Spirit is given to man, it is given to him in Christ, when sin is destroyed and life takes possession of man again. The Spirit is not itself subject to death. Yet the Spirit is something which belongs to *man*. Man who is in bondage to death, is man without the Spirit. He does not fulfil his true manhood. On death as a consequence of sin, see *A.h.* III. xxi. 2 (Stier III. xx. 2) and *Epid.* 15. On the indestructibility of the Spirit and its victory over both sin and death, see *A.h.* V. xii. 2–3 (Stier. ibid.).

divine, and also little by little to become that which he rightly is, namely, God.[76] The medial position of the Spirit as at one time human and divine would appear to demonstrate quite clearly that man at one time is both human and divine.

There is, however, a by no means unimportant detail which should be mentioned: the word "deification," θεοποίησις, does not in fact appear in Irenaeus.[77] In spite of this, of course, the actual idea is present in his writings. But as far as the main question is concerned, it is at any rate clear that Irenaeus's basic view of man's coming into being as something which takes place in his continuing fellowship with God, and which will be fulfilled in the age to come, makes it impossible that man's human form of existence should be left behind in his "deification."[78] Man does not give up his existence as man and take upon himself a different existence, viz. God's existence, while his human part disappears. There are, perhaps, isolated passages in Irenaeus which might lead to such an interpretation, but these passages too, when seen in the general context, force us to look for a different explanation.[79] Irenaeus saw that in his present condition man is becoming no more than man. But according to God's decree in Creation man as man is to be like God, and when man becomes like God he is in actual fact becoming man.

[76] In Nygren, *Agape and Eros*, pp. 409–12, the limitation of the idea of *agape* in Irenaeus is expressed in the fact that the descent of *agape* has to flow into man's ascent or deification. Nygren sees in this a Hellenistic strain. Apart from this Nygren finds that Irenaeus represents the purest illustration of the *agape*-type in the whole of the early Church.

[77] Cf. Prümm in *Scholastik*, 1938, p. 216, n. 20; and even more clearly, id., *Christentum als Neuheitserlebnis*, p. 253 f. Bousset often uses the term "Vergottung" in his interpretation of Irenaeus; see e.g. *Kyrios Christos*, pp. 416, 424, 426. We see from his own analysis, however, that he deliberately introduces the word "Vergottung" without having any exact equivalent in Irenaeus's own terminology—see *op. cit.*, p. 416, in which "*God-likeness*" and "Vergottung" are equated. On the other hand we come across the term "deification" in the later theology of the early Church, e.g. in Athanasius. Cf. Nygren, *Agape and Eros*, p. 428, n. 3.

[78] The reality under discussion here, man's realised likeness to God, is in all circumstances an eschatological or *future* reality. Irenaeus's doctrine of the future likeness to God has polemical overtones, and he employs it to oppose the Gnostic belief in a present divine nature in man. See Klebba, *Anthropologie des hl. Irenaeus*, p. 186 f. But man's fulfilment too lies in the future. As long as God continues to give and create, man continues to be fashioned. And Irenaeus never depicts a future condition in which God's giving and man's receiving will have come to an end. Man continues to become to the end.

[79] E.g. *A.h.* IV. lxiii. 2–3 (Stier. IV. xxxviii. 3–4).

When Irenaeus represents the idea of a "deification" of man, this "deification" coincides with man's "becoming man." For Irenaeus the question of "deification" becomes in consequence identical with the question of whether he has interpreted man's destiny to imply that in order to reach this destiny man must advance beyond that which is human. Does God have to be in man in order that man may be man? Or are man and God the same?

God and man are not the same. God is the only Creator. The function of creation never passes to man. Man is receptive, and remains such—he is involved in the process of growth. But man's destiny and true being are precisely to grow, i.e. to receive from a source which lies outside man. If this function of growth or receptivity cease, man's humanity also ceases. Man can only be man according to his own nature in communion with God, and if this communion with God is removed, it is not only the "divine" in man's life which is impaired, but his humanity also is lost.[80] Man becomes man, therefore, when the Spirit takes up the struggle against sin, and when Christ dwells in the midst of those who are His Church. Irenaeus maintains that the Spirit or Christ is really in men through faith, baptism, and the Eucharist. God thus dwells in men as the One who defeats the powers in men which are hostile to man. Man becomes what he has been destined for, viz. man, when God in this way begins to enter into full communion with man. This communion with

[80] The Spirit in man means fellowship with God, and therefore life. The fact that the cessation of this fellowship destroys man's humanity as such is expressed by Irenaeus in the assertion that for man separation from God is the same thing as *death*. Cf. *A.h.* v. xii. 2–3 (Stier. ibid.). *Ἕτερον δέ ἐστι τὸ ποιηθὲν τοῦ ποιήσαντος. Ἡ οὖν πνοὴ πρόσκαιρος, τὸ δὲ πνεῦμα ἀένναον· καὶ ἡ μὲν πνοὴ ἀκμάσασα πρὸς βραχὺ, καὶ καιρῷ τινι παραμείνασα, μετὰ τοῦτο πορεύεται, ἄπνουν καταλιποῦσα ἐκεῖνο, περὶ ὃ ἦν τὸ πρότερον· τὸ δὲ περιλαβὸν ἔνδοθεν καὶ ἔξωθεν τὸν ἄνθρωπον, ἅτε ἀεὶ παραμόνιμον, οὐδέποτε καταλείπει αὐτόν . . . Ὡς οὖν ὁ εἰς ψυχὴν ζῶσαν γεγονὼς, ῥίψας ἐπὶ τὸ χεῖρον, ἀπώλεσε τὴν ζωήν· οὕτως πάλιν ὁ αὐτὸς ἐκεῖνος ἐπὶ τὸ βέλτιον ἐπανελθὼν, καὶ προσλαβόμενος τὸ ζωοποιοῦν πνεῦμα, εὑρήσει τὴν ζωήν. Οὐ γὰρ ἄλλο τὸ ἀποθνῆσκον, καὶ ἄλλο τὸ ζωοποιούμενον· ὡς οὐδὲ ἄλλο τὸ ἀπολωλὸς, καὶ ἄλλο τὸ ἀνευρισκόμενον, ἀλλ' ἐκεῖνο τὸ ἀπολωλὸς πρόβατον ἦλθεν ὁ Κύριος ἀναζητῶν. Τί οὖν ἦν τὸ ἀποθνῆσκον; πάντως ἡ τῆς σαρκὸς ὑπόστασις, καὶ ἡ ἀποβαλοῦσα τὴν πνοὴν τῆς ζωῆς, καὶ ἄπνους καὶ νεκρὰ γενομένη. Ταύτην οὖν ὁ Κύριος ἦλθε ζωοποιῶν· ἵνα ὡς ἐν τῷ Ἀδὰμ πάντες ἀποθνήσκομεν, ὅτι ψυχικοὶ, ἐν τῷ Χριστῷ ζήσωμεν, ὅτι πνευματικοί.* Cf. also the Latin. On the Greek text see Holl, *Fragmente vornicänischer Kirchenväter*, p. 75.

God is manifested in a conclusive way in the resurrection of the dead, and the final, unutterable events of the Consummation, when the Spirit, or Christ, finally takes possession of man. The true life of man is fellowship with God.

We shall see the meaning of "deification" in Irenaeus quite plainly if we compare him with later theologians. In both Methodius of Olympus and Athanasius virginity or celibacy is the highest expression of the Christian life. And for both of these Fathers of the Church it is really a Hellenistic deification which is central. The goal of the Incarnation is the virginity of Christian believers.[81] Christ became man in order that men should become gods and relinquish their humanity. There is absolutely no trace of any such ascetic ethic in Irenaeus, and wherever he detects such ascetic tendencies he opposes them. Love of one's neighbour and communion with God constitute a clear-cut summary of Irenaeus's ethical teaching. Christian believers, in whom God dwells through Christ or the Spirit, do not abandon human life, but rather are fitted to become more truly human. God is the Creator who deals in love with His world and His people, and He cannot cease to be what He is when He makes His dwelling through the Spirit in the believer. Even then He remains the Creator who uses those who are in the Church, the members of the Body of Christ, for His continuing work of Creation in the world. This divine work of Creation continues unchanged when the Spirit achieves its total government over man, and man rises from the dead. Since in the Consummation the Spirit reigns over man, it could quite naturally be said that man is then "divine." But man is the one who is raised, body, soul, and Spirit.[82] Hitherto man has been imperfect, for only in unbroken fellowship with God does human life truly exist.

Man has been created in the *imago* and *similitudo* of God, and until man has achieved the *imago* and *similitudo* his humanity is incomplete. Christ is the *imago* and *similitudo* of God, the well-spring of life from which man draws his life. However closely Christ may come to be like man, the distinction between them is never abolished, for Christ creates and man is created. When

[81] See Nygren, *Agape and Eros*, pp. 415–21, 429.

[82] The flesh is created in the image of God and for this reason is destined to rise. Cf. Loofs, *Theophilus von Antiochien*, p. 221.

the Son delivers up the Kingdom and God becomes all in all, man will have been made perfect and sin expelled. In the end man's humanity will be pure, and to that extent he will be the same as Christ, for Christ is the pure man. But Christ is perfect man simply because He is God, the Creator. When Christ brings man to His own likeness, it is Christ who is giving and man who is receiving. The end of Christ's giving and man's receiving will be man's fulfilment according to the *imago* and *similitudo* of God.[83] The Son's delivering up of the Kingdom means that Christ has completed His work as the Incarnate, i.e. as man—He has incorporated mankind into Himself, and given men a righteous and incorruptible life in place of their bondage to sin and death, which was contrary to Creation. Even when this work of recapitulation has been finished, the Son, like the Spirit, remains God, for God is triune from everlasting to everlasting. Man never passes over into God's life.[84] He receives from God, and, indeed, receives the life of God, but in doing so he becomes man.[85] Man's life develops only in communion with God.

It is characteristic of Irenaeus that he thinks of man as God's

[83] In *Theol. Stud. u. Krit.*, 1925, p. 187 f., Koch stresses the difference in meaning between the expression "ad imaginem et similitudinem" and "secundum imaginem et similitudinem." Loofs is rightly critical of this distinction, *Theophilus von Antiochien*, p. 59 f. n. 3. Irenaeus uses the two expressions interchangeably. Cf. Hunger in *Scholastik*, 1942, pp. 168 ff.

[84] Not even in *A.h.* IV. lxiii. 3 (Stier. IV. xxxviii. 4) with its well-known phrase: ". . . primo quidem homines, tunc demum Dii," does Irenaeus refer to anything other than man's receiving of eternal life. He refutes those who refuse to wait for growth, but he has of necessity to explain the phrase from the Psalms, "I have said, ye are gods" (Ps. LXXXII.6), and he does so by projecting man's reception of the divine life into the world of the resurrection. With regard to the present, Irenaeus lays the stress on the immediate sequel of this phrase from the Psalms: "Ye shall die like men" (Ps. LXXXII.7). Man's distinctive characteristic, his receptivity, does not cease; nor does God's—His creativity. In his exposition of man's "deification" Irenaeus very strongly emphasises that man's growth towards his final end lies in submission to God who alone is Creator: *Ὑποταγὴ δὲ Θεοῦ, ἀφθαρσία· καὶ παραμονὴ ἀφθαρσίας, δόξα ἀγέννητος. Διὰ ταύτης τῆς τάξεως, καὶ τῶν τοιούτων ῥυθμῶν, καὶ τῆς τοιαύτης ἀγωγῆς, ὁ γεννητὸς καὶ πεπλασμένος ἄνθρωπος κατ' εἰκόνα καὶ ὁμοίωσιν τοῦ ἀγεννήτου γίνεται Θεοῦ, A.h.* IV. lxiii. 2 (Stier. IV. xxxviii. 3); see the passage following. Man's end is likeness to God; cf. Bonwetsch, *Theologie des Irenäus*, p. 157. On the exposition of Ps. LXXXII.6, cf. *A.h.* IV. iii, pref. (Stier. IV. iv, pref.) and IV. i. 1 (Stier. ibid.).

[85] Even after the Son has delivered up the Kingdom to the Father and God has become all in all, those who live in fellowship with God are "true men," men of flesh and blood. See *A.h.* V. XXXVI. 1 (Stier. ibid.), beginning.

man, God's creation from beginning to end. Human life is only to be found where God is, and where He is freely creating. It is for this reason that sin means death. When fellowship with God is broken in man's disobedience, man's very life is injured. But Christ is righteous, and His life is whole and unimpaired human life. God dwells in Him, and where God is, and freely creates, man's true life comes into being. Through the Incarnation God gives life again to man. In the Church and the Consummation there is re-enacted that which took place in the first pure Creation—man is created. When men rise from the dead and receive eternal life, they are one with Christ, the image of God —they are men.[86] And then the word which God spoke at the beginning is fulfilled: "Let us make man in our image."

Creation and redemption are not completely different, and in the fulfilment of the act of Creation redemption is realised and life is present. Man, in order to be man, must continually transcend himself and have God within himself. Man's life is dependent on communion with God, and if this communion is broken, man is lost. But it does not break, and it cannot break. Christ cannot be destroyed by any power in the world. And Christ means that God is man. By His becoming man the bond between God and man has been made unbreakable, and man has free access to the source from which his life flows. For God alone is the source of human life.[87]

[86] According to Hitchcock, *Irenaeus of Lugdunum*, the restoration of the image and likeness through Christ and the Spirit is a basic feature in Irenaeus which unites *A.h.* and *Epid.* It is characteristic that *A.h.* ends with the following words: "Etenim unus Filius, qui voluntatem Patris perfecit; et unum genus humanum, in quo perficiuntur mysteria Dei, quem concupiscunt angeli videre, et non praevalent investigare sapientiam Dei, per quam plasma ejus conformatum et concorporatum Filio perficitur: ut progenies ejus primogenitus Verbum descendat in facturam, hoc est in plasma, et capiatur ab eo; et factura iterum capiat Verbum, et ascendat ad eum, supergrediens angelos, et fiet secundum imaginem et similitudinem Dei," v. xxxvi (Stier. v. xxxvi. 3). When he says that man "rises above the angels" Irenaeus is not suggesting anything superhuman, but something quite human. Although only a child, man was appointed lord over the angels at the beginning of Creation. See here *Epid.* 11 and 12. Redemption is the fulfilment of the act of Creation, achieved by Christ's becoming man and His victory.

[87] *'Επεὶ ζῆσαι ἄνευ ζωῆς οὐχ οἷόν τε ἦν· ἡ δὲ ὕπαρξις τῆς ζωῆς ἐκ τῆς τοῦ Θεοῦ περιγίνεται μετοχῆς*, *A.h.* IV. xxxiv. 6 (Stier. IV. xx. 5).

BIBLIOGRAPHY
AND LIST OF ABBREVIATIONS

I. SOURCES

Irenaeus

A. Complete Works

Sancti Irenaei episcopi Lugdunensis quae supersunt omnia, ed. A. Stieren. 2 vols. Leipzig 1848–53.

B. *Adversus haereses*

Sancti Irenaei episcopi Lugdunensis libros quinque adversus haereses, ed. W. W. Harvey. 2 vols. Cambridge 1857.

The Third Book of St Irenaeus against Heresies. With short notes and a glossary by H. Deane. Oxford 1880.

Des heiligen Irenäus fünf Bücher gegen die Häresien, trans. E. Klebba. 2 vols. Bibliothek der Kirchenväter VOLS. III–IV. Kempten and Munich 1912.

The Treatise of Irenaeus of Lugdunum against the Heresies. A translation of the principal passages, with notes and arguments by F. R. Montgomery Hitchcock. Early Church Classics. London 1916.

C. *Epideixis*

Des heiligen Irenäus Schrift zum Erweise der apostolischen Verkündigung, trans. K. Ter-Mĕkĕrttschian and E. Ter-Minassiantz, ed. A. Harnack. Texte und Untersuchungen zur Geschichte der altchristlichen Literatur VOL. XXXI, PT I. Leipzig 1907.

Des heiligen Irenäus Schrift zum Erweise der apostolischen Verkündigung, trans. S. Weber. Bibliothek der Kirchenväter VOL. IV. Kempten and Munich 1912.

S. Irenaeus, The Proof of the Apostolic Preaching, with seven fragments, ed. K. Ter-Mĕkĕrttschian and S. G. Wilson. Patrologia orientalis VOL. XII. Paris 1919.

Saint Irénée, Démonstration de la prédication apostolique, trans. J. Barthoulot S.J., ed. J. Tixeront. Patrologia orientalis VOL. XII. Paris 1919.

St Irenaeus, The Apostolic Preaching, trans. J. Armitage Robinson. London 1920.

See also under Literature, WIETEN, L. T.

EUSEBIUS

Kirchengeschichte, ed. E. Schwartz. New edn. Leipzig 1908.

The Ecclesiastical History, trans. Kirsopp Lake. London 1926.

TERTULLIAN

Quinti Septimii Florentis Tertulliani opera, ed. E. Kroymann, PT III, *De carnis resurrectione*. Corpus scriptorum ecclesiasticorum Latinorum VOL. XLVII. Bonn 1906.

THEOPHILUS

Theophili . . . ad Autolycum libri tres, ed. J. C. T. Otto. Corpus apologetarum christianorum saeculi secundi VOL. VIII. Jena 1861.

COLLECTIONS

Die ältesten Apologeten. Texte mit Kurzen Einleitungen, ed. E. J. Goodspeed. Göttingen 1915.

Die apostolischen Väter, ed. Funk. Revised edn. by K. Bihlmeyer. VOL. I. Sammlung ausgewählten Kirchen- und dogmengeschichtlichen Quellenschriften II i. I. Tübingen 1924.

Ausgewählten Märtyrerakten, ed. R. Knopf. 3rd edn. by G. Kruger. Sammlung ausgewählten Kirchen- und dogmengeschichtlichen Quellenschriften n.s. VOL. III. Tübingen 1929.

2. LITERATURE

A. h. = Irenaeus. *Adversus haereses.* See Sources.

ALEITH, EVA. "Paulusverständnis in der alten Kirche," in *Z. NT. W.*, XVIII, 1937.

ALÈS, A. d'. "La date de la version latine de saint Iréneé," in *Recherches de science religieuse*, 1916.

—— "La doctrine de la récapitulation en saint Irénée," in *Recherches de science religieuse*, 1916.

—— "Le mot *oikonomia* dans la langue théologique de saint Irénée," in *Revue des études grecques*, 1919.

—— "Le PREΣBYTHΣ de saint Irénée," in *Revue des études grecques*, 1929.

AULÉN, G. *Den Kristna försoningstanken.* Stockholm 1930.

BARBEL, J. "Christos Angelos," in *Theophaneia*, VOL. III. Bonn 1941.

BARDENHEWER, O. *Geschichte der altkirchlichen Litteratur.* VOL I. Frieburg-im-Breisgan 1902.

BARDY, G. *La Théologie de l'église de saint Clément de Rome à saint Irénée.* Unam sanctam VOL. XIII. Paris 1945.

BARNIKOL, E. *Apostolische und neutestamentliche Dogmengeschichte als Vor-Dogmengeschichte.* Theologische Arbeiten zur Bibel-, Kirchen-, und Geistesgeschichte VOL. VI. 4th edn. Halle 1938.

BATIFFOL, P. *L'Église naissante et le catholicisme.* Les Origines catholiques VOL. I. 6th edn. Paris 1913.

BECKER, S. A. 'Ο ΚΑΝΩΝ ΤΗΣ 'ΑΛΗΘΕΙΑΣ. Copenhagen 1910.

BEUZART, P. *Essai sur la théologie d'Irénée.* Le Puy-en-Velais 1908.

BIETENHARD, H. *Das tausendjährige Reich.* Bern 1944.

BIGELMAIR, A. *Die Beteilung der Christen am öffentlichen Leben in vorconstantinischer Zeit.* Veröffentlichungen aus dem Kirchenhistorischen Seminar München VOL. VIII. Munich 1902.

Bijdragen = *Bijdragen van de philos. en theol. facult. d. nederl. Jerzuieten.*

BILLING, E. *De etiska tankarna i urkristendomen.* 2nd edn. Stockholm 1936.

BÖHRINGER, F. *Kirche Christi* = *Die Kirche Christi und ihre Zeugen.* 2 vols. 2nd edn. Stuttgart 1873.

BONWETSCH, N. "Der Gedanke der Erziehung des Menschengeschlechts bei Irenäus," in *Z.S.T.*, 1923–4.

—— "Der Schriftbeweis für die Kirche aus den Heiden als das wahre Israel bis auf Hippolyt," in *Theologische Studien Th. Zahn dargebracht*, Leipzig 1908.

—— *Die Theologie des Irenäus.* Beiträge zur Förderung der christilichen Theologie VOL. II, PT IX. Gütersloh 1925.

BOSTRÖM, F. *Studier till den grekiska teologins frälsningslära.* Lunds universitets årskrift n.s. I. 28.3. Lund 1932.

BOUSSET, W. *Hauptprobleme der Gnosis.* Forschungen zur Religion und Literatur des Alten und Neuen Testaments VOL. X. Göttingen 1907.

—— *Kyrios Christos.* Forschungen zur Religion und Literatur des Alten und Neuen Testaments n.s. VOL. IV. Göttingen 1913.

—— *Schulbetrieb* = *Jüdisch-christlicher Schulbetrieb in Alexandria und Rom.* Forschungen zur Religion und Literatur des Alten und Neuen Testaments n.s. VOL. VI. Göttingen 1915.

BRING, E. "Till frågan om Pauli syn på lagens förhallende till tron," in *S.T.K.*, 1945.

—— "Till Kritiken av Harnacks syn på den gammalkyrkliga frälsningsuppfattningen," in *S.T.K.*, 1933.

BRUNNER, E. *Der Mensch im Widerspruch.* 3rd edn. Zürich 1941. Eng. trans. *Man in Revolt.* London 1939.

—— *Der Mittler.* 2nd edn. Tübingen 1930. Eng. trans. *The Mediator.* London 1939.

BURKITT, F. C. "Dr Sanday's New Testament of Irenaeus with a note on Valentinian terms in Irenaeus and Tertullian," in *J.T.S.*, 1924.

CAMPENHAUSEN, H. VON. *Die Idee des Martyriums in der alten Kirche.* Göttingen 1936.

—— See Müller, K. and Campenhausen, H. von.

CASPARI, W. "Imago divina," in *Reinhold-Seeberg-Festschrift,* ed. W. Koepp. VOL. I. Leipzig 1929.

CHAPMAN, J. "Did the translator of St Irenaeus use a Latin New Testament?" in *Rev. Bén.*, 1924.

CIRLOT, F. L. *The Early Eucharist.* London 1939.

C.Q.R. = *Church Quarterly Review.*

CREMERS, V. "Het millenarisme van Irenaeus," in *Bijdragen*, 1938.

CRUM, W. E. "Texts attributed to Peter of Alexandria," in *J.T.S.*, 1903.

CULLMAN, O. *Christus und die Zeit.* Zollikon-Zürich 1946. Eng. trans. *Christ and Time.* London 1951.

—— *Die ersten christlichen Glaubensbekenntnisse.* Theologische Studien VOL. XV. Zollikon-Zürich 1943. Eng. trans. *The Earliest Christian Confessions.* London 1949.

—— *Königsherrschaft Christi* = *Königsherrschaft Christi und Kirche im Neuen Testament.* Theologische Studien VOL. X. Zürich 1941.

—— *Urchristentum und Gottesdienst.* Abhandlungen zur Theologie des Alten und Neuen Testaments VOL. III. Basel 1944. Eng. trans. *Early Christian Worship.* London 1953.

DORNER, I. A. *Entwicklungsgeschichte der Lehre von der Person Christi.* VOL. I. 2nd edn. Stuttgart and Berlin 1851. Eng. trans. *History of the Development of the Doctrine of Christ.* Edinburgh 1861.

DUFOURCQ, A. *Saint Irénée.* 3rd edn. Paris 1904.

DURKS, W. "Eine fälschlich dem Irenäus zugeschriebene Predigt des Bischofs Severian von Gabala," in *Z.NT.W.*, 1922.

EHRHARD, A. *Die Kirche der Märtyrer.* Munich 1932.

Epid. = Irenaeus. *Epideixis.* See Sources.

ERDIN, F. *Das Wort Hypostasis.* Freiburger theologische Studien VOL. LII. Freiburg im Breisgau 1939.

ESCOULA, L. "Le verbe sauveur et illuminateur chez saint Irénée," in *N.r.t.*, 1939.

EYNDE, D. VAN DEN. *Normes de l'enseignement* = *Les Normes de l'enseignement chrétien dans la littérature patristique des trois premiers siècles.* Gembloux and Paris 1933.

FROIDEVAUX, L. "Une difficulté du texte de s. Irénée," in *Revue de l'Orient chrétien*, 1931–2.

GÄCHTER, P. "Unsere Einheit mit Christus nach dem hl. Irenäus," in *Z.k.T.*, 1934.

GHELLINCK, J. DE. *Patristique et moyen âge.* VOL. I. *Les Recherches sur l' histoire du symbole des apôtres.* Collection Museum Lessianum, section historique VOL. VI. Gembloux 1946.

GUTBROD, W. *Die paulinische Anthropologie.* Stuttgart and Berlin 1934.

HARNACK, A. "Der Presbyter-Prediger des Irenäus," in *Philotesia, P. Kleinert dargebracht.* Berlin 1907.

—— *Die Pfaff'schen Irenäus-Fragmente.* Texte und Untersuchungen zur Geschichte der altschristlichen Literatur VOL. XX. Leipzig 1900.

—— *Die Terminologie der Wiedergeburt und verwandter Erlebnisse in der ältesten Kirche.* Texte und Untersuchungen zur Geschichte der altchristlichen Literatur VOL. XLII, PT III. Leipzig 1918.

—— *Lehrbuch der Dogmengeschichte*. 4th edn. Tübingen 1909. Eng. trans. of 2nd German edn. *History of Dogma*. 7 vols. London 1899.

—— *Marcion: Das Evangelium vom fremden Gott*. 2nd edn. Texte und Untersuchungen zur Geschichte der altchristlichen Literatur VOL. XLV. Leipzig 1924.

HEILER, F. *Altkirchliche Autonomie und päpstilicher Zentralismus*. Die Katholische Kirche des Ostens und Westens VOL. II, PT. I. Munich 1941.

HERING, J. *Biblischen Grundlagen* = *Die biblischen Grundlagen des christlichen Humanismus*. Abhandlungen zur Theologie des Alten und Neuen Testaments VOL. VII. Zürich 1946.

HERRERA, S. *S. Irénée de Lyon exégète*. Paris 1920.

Historie de l'église depuis les origines jusqu'à nos jours, ed. A. Fliche and V. Martin. VOL. II, J. Lebreton and J. Zeitler, *De la fin du deuxième siècle à la paix constantinienne*, St-Dizier 1935. Eng. trans. *The History of the Primitive Church*. London 1942.

HITCHCOCK, F. R. M. *Irenaeus of Lugdunum*. Cambridge 1914.

—— "Loofs' Asiatic source (IQA) and the Ps-Justin *De resurrectione*," in *Z.NT.W.*, 1937.

—— "Loofs' theory of Theophilus of Antioch as a source of Irenaeus," in *J.T.S.*, 1937.

—— "The Apostolic Preaching of Irenaeus and its light on his doctrine of the Trinity," in *Hermathena*, 1907.

—— "The doctrine of the Holy Communion in Irenaeus," in *C.Q.R.*, 1939–40.

HÖFLING, J. W. F. *Die Lehre der ältesten Kirche von Opfer*. Erlangen 1851.

HOH, J. H. *Lehre des hl. Irenäus* = *Die Lehre des hl. Irenäus über das Neue Testament*. Neutestamentliche Abhandlungen, ed. M. Meinertz, VOL. VII, PTS IV–V. Münster 1919.

HOLL, K. *Fragmente vornicänischer Kirchenväter*. Texte und Untersuchungen zur Geschichte der altchristlichen Literatur VOL. XX, PT II. Leipzig 1899.

HUNGER, W. "Der Gedanke der Weltplaneinheit und Adameinheit in der Theologie des Irenäus," in *Scholastik*, 1942.

JONAS, H. *Gnosis* = *Gnosis und spätantiker Geist*. VOL. I. Forschungen zur Religion und Literatur des Alten und Neuen Testaments n.s. VOL. XXXIII. Göttingen 1934.

JORDAN, H. *Armenische Irenaeusfragmente.* Texte und Untersuchungen zur Geschichte der altchristlichen Literatur VOL. XXXVI, PT III. Leipzig 1913.

—— "Das Alter und die Herkunft der lateinischen Übersetzung des Hauptwerkes des Irenaeus," in *Theologischen Studien Th. Zahn dargebracht.* Leipzig 1908.

J.T.S. = *Journal of Theological Studies.*

KÄSEMANN, E. *Leib und Leib Christi.* Beiträge zur historischen Theologie VOL. IX. Tübingen 1933.

KIRCHNER, M. "Die Eschatologie des Irenäus," in *Theol. Stud. u. Krit.*, 1863.

KLEBBA, E. *Die Anthropologie des hl. Irenaeus.* Kirchengeschichtliche Studien VOL. II, PT III. Münster 1894.

KNOX, W. L. "Irenaeus, *Adversus haereses* 3:3:2," in *J.T.S.*, 1946.

KOCH, H. "Die Sündenvergebung bei Irenäus," in *Z.NT.W.*, 1908.

—— "Irenäus über den Vorzug der römischen Kirche," in *Theol. Stud. u. Krit.*, 1920–1.

—— "Zur Lehre vom Urstand und von der Erlösung bei Irenäus," in *Theol. Stud. u. Krit.*, 1925.

KÖSTERMANN, E. "Neue Beiträge zur Geschichte der lateinischen Handschriften des Irenäus," in *Z.NT.W.*, 1937.

KRAELING, C. H. *Anthropos and Son of Man.* Columbia University Oriental Studies VOL. XXV. New York 1927.

KRAFT, B. *Die Evangelienzitate des heiligen Irenäus.* Biblische Studien VOL. XXI, PT IV. Freiburg im Breisgau 1924.

KUNZE, J. *Die Gotteslehre des Irenaeus.* Leipzig 1891.

LEBRETON, J. See *Histoire de l'église.*

LIECHTENHAN, R. *Göttliche Vorherbestimmung* = *Die göttliche Vorherbestimmung bei Paulus und in der posidonianischen Philosophie.* Forschungen zur Religion und Literatur des Alten und Neuen Testaments n.s. VOL. XVIII. Göttingen 1922.

LIETZMANN, H. *Church Universal* = *Geschichte der alten Kirche.* 2 vols. Berlin and Leipzig 1936. Eng. trans. of VOL. II, *The Founding of the Church Universal.* London 1938. 2nd edn. 1950.

LINDROTH, H. J. "Descendit ad inferna," in *S.T.K.*, 1932.

—— "Irenaeus' kristendomstolkning och kyrkosyn," in *S.T.K.*, 1939.

LIPSIUS, R. A. "Die Zeit des Irenäus von Lyon und die Entstehung der altkatholischen Kirche," in *Historische Zeitschrift*, 1872.

LOEWENICH, W. VON. *Johannes-Verständnis* = *Das Johannes-Verständnis im zweiten Jahrhundert. Z.NT.W.* supplement No. 13, Giessen 1932.

LOHMEYER, E. *Briefe* = *Die Briefe an die Philipper, an die Kolosser, und an Philemon.* Kritischer-exegetischer Kommentar über dem Neuen Testament. 8th edn. VOL. IX. Göttingen 1930.

LOOFS, F. "Das altkirchliche Zeugnis gegen die herrschende Auffassung der Kenosisstelle," in *Theol. Stud. u. Krit.*, 1927–8.

—— "Die Handschriften der lateinischen Übersetzung des Irenaeus und ihre Kapitelteilung," in *Kirchengeschichtliche Studien H. Reuter gewidmet*, Leipzig 1888.

—— *Theophilus von Antiochien* = *Theophilus von Antiochien Adversus Marcionem und die anderen theologischen Quellen bei Irenaeus.* Texte und Untersuchungen zur Geschichte der altchristlichen Literatur VOL. XLVI, PT II. Leipzig 1930.

LÜDTKE, W. "Bemerkungen zu Irenäus," in *Z.NT.W.*, 1914.

LUNDSTRÖM, S. *Studien* = *Studien zur lateinischen Irenäusübersetzung.* Lund 1943.

LUTHARDT, E. *Die Lehre vom freien Willen.* Leipzig 1863.

MARTIN, C. "Saint Irénée et son correspondant, le diacre Démètre de Vienne," in *Revue d'histoire ecclésiastique*, 1942.

MERK, A. "Der Text des Neuen Testaments beim hl. Irenaeus," in *Z.K.T.*, 1925.

MICHAELIS, W. *Zur Engelchristologie im Urchristentum*, Gegenwartsfragen bibliichen Theologie VOL. I. Basel 1942.

MÜLLER, K. "Kleine Beiträge zur alten Kirchengeschichte," in *Z.NT.W.*, 1924.

—— AND CAMPENHAUSEN, H. VON. *Kirchengeschichte.* VOL. I, PT I. 3rd edn. Tübingen 1941.

MUNCK, J. "Billedet af Kaetterne hos Irenaeus," in *Teol. Tidsskr.*, 1936.

NIEBUHR, R. *The Nature and Destiny of Man.* VOL. I. London 1944.

Novum Testamentum sancti Irenaei, ed. W. Sanday and E. H. Turner. Old-Latin Biblical Texts VOL. VII. Oxford 1923.

N.r.t. = *Nouvelle revue théologique.*

NUSSBAUMER, A. *Das Ursymbolum.* Forschungen zur christlichen Literatur und Dogmengeschichte VOL. XIV, PT II. Paderbom 1921.

NYGREN, A. *Corpus Christi (En bok om Kyrkan).* Stockholm 1942.

—— *Den Kristna Kärlekstanken genom tiderna.* 2 vols. Stockholm 1936. Eng. trans. *Agape and Eros.* Revised edn. London 1953.

—— *Pauli brev till Romarna.* Tolkning av Nya Testamenta VOL. VI. Stockholm 1944. Eng. trans. *Commentary on Romans.* Philadelphia 1949.

Orientalia = *Orientalia christiana periodica.*

PERCY, E. *Der Leib Christi.* Lunds universitetets årskrift n.s. I. 38. I. Lund and Leipzig 1942.

—— *Die Probleme der Kolosser- und Epheserbriefe.* Skrifter utg. av Kgl. hum. vet.-samf. i Lund VOL. XXXIX. Lund 1946.

PLUMPE, J. C. *Mater ecclesia.* The Catholic University of America. Studies in Christian Antiquity VOL. V. Washington 1943.

PRESTIGE, G. L. *God in Patristic Thought.* London and Toronto 1936.

PRÜMM, K. *Christentum als Neuheitserlebnis.* Freigburg im Breisgau 1939.

—— "Gottliche Planung und menschliche Entwicklung nach Irenäus Adversus haereses," in *Scholastik,* 1938.

—— "Zur Terminologie und zum Wesen der christlichen Neuheit bei Irenäus," in *Pisciculi F. J. Dölger dargeboten.* Münster 1939.

REILLY, W. S. "Les 'Presbytres' asiates de saint Irénée," in *Revue biblique,* 1919.

—— "L'Inspiration de l'ancien testament chez saint Irénée," in *Revue biblique,* 1917.

Rev. bén. = *Revue bénédictine.*

Rev. des sciences = *Revue des sciences philosophique et théologique.*

REYNDERS, D. B. "La Polémique de saint Irénée," in *Recherches de théologie ancienne et médiévale,* 1935.

—— "Optimisme et théocentrisme chez saint Irénée," in *Recherches de théologie ancienne et médiévale,* 1936.

—— "Paradosis," in *Recherches de théologie ancienne et médiévale,* 1933.

RITSCHL, *A. Die Entstehung der altkatholischen Kirche.* 2nd. edn. Bonn 1857.

RIVIÈRE, J. *Dogme de la rédemption* = *Le Dogme de la rédemption: Études critiques et documents.* Bibliothèque de la revue d'histoire ecclésiastique VOL. V. Louvain 1931.

ROBINSON, J. ARMITAGE. "Notes on the Armenian version of Irenaeus *Adversus haereses*," in *J.T.S.*, 1931.

—— "On a quotation from Justin Martyr in Irenaeus," in *J.T.S.*, 1930.

ROIRON, F. X. "Sur l'interprétation d'un passage de saint Irénée," in *Recherches de science religieuse*, 1917.

SANDERS, J. N. *Fourth Gospel* = *The Fourth Gospel in the Early Church.* Cambridge 1943.

SCHARL, E. "Der Rekapitulationsbegriff des hl. Irenäus," in *Orientalia*, 1940.

SCHERER, W. "Zur Mariologie des hl. Irenäus," in *Z.K.T.*, 1923.

SCHLIER, H. "Vom Menschenbild des Neuen Testaments" in *Der alte und der neue Mensch.* Beiträge zur evangelischen Theologie VOL. VIII. Munich 1942.

SCHLINK, E. "Gottes Ebenbild als Gesetz und Evangelium," in *Der alte und der neue Mensch.* Beiträge zur evangelischen Theologie VOL. VIII. Munich 1942.

SCHMIDT, C. *Gespräche Jesu mit seinen Jüngern. Texte und Untersuchungen zur Geschichte der altchristlichen Literatur* VOL. XLIII. Leipzig 1919.

—— "Irenäus und seine Quelle in Adv. haer. I, 29," in *Philotesia, P. Kleinert dargebracht.* Berlin 1907.

SCHMIDT, W. *Die Kirche bei Irenäus.* Helsinki 1934.

—— "Till förståelsen av Irenaei teologi," in *Teol. tidskr.*, 1934.

SCHUMACHER, H. *Kraft der Urkirche.* Freiburg im Breisgau 1934.

SCHUMANN, F. "Bemerkungen zur Lehre vom Gesetz," in *Z.S.T.*, 1939.

SEEBERG, R. *Lehrbuch der Dogmengeschichte.* VOL. I. 3rd edn. Leipzig and Erlangen 1922.

SILÉN, S. *Den Kristna människouppfattningen intill Schleiermacher.* Stockholm 1938.

SIMONIN, H. D. "A propos d'un texte eucharistique de s. Irénée," in *Rev. des sciences*, 1934.

SLOMKOWSKI, A. *État primitif* = *L'État primitif de l'homme dans la tradition de l'église avant saint Augustin.* Paris 1928.

SPIKOWSKI, L. *La Doctrine de l'église dans saint Irénée.* Strasbourg 1926.

STAERK, W. "Eva-Maria," in *Z.NT.W.*, 1934.

S.T.K. = *Svensk teologisk kvartalskrift.*

STOLL, F. *Lehre des hl. Irenäus* = *Die Lehre des hl. Irenäus von der Erlösung und Heiligung.* Mainz 1905.

STRÖM, Å. V. *Vetekornet.* Stockholm 1944.

Teol. tidskr. = *Teologisk tidskrift.* Helsinki.

Teol. tidsskr. = *Teologisk tidsskrift.* Copenhagen.

Theol. Stud. u. Krit. = *Theologische Studien und Kritiken.*

TIILILÄ, O. *Das Strafleiden Christi.* Annales acad. scient. fenn. B. XLVIII. I. Helsinki 1941.

VERNET, F. "Irénée," in *Dictionnaire de théologie catholique.* VOL. VIII, PT II. Paris 1923.

VOGELS, H. J. "Der Evangelientext des hl. Irenaeus," in *Rev. bén.*, 1924.

WENDT, H. H. *Christliche Lehre* = *Die christliche Lehre von der menschlichen Vollkommenheit.* Göttingen 1882.

WERNER, J. *Der Paulinismus des Irenaeus.* Texte und Untersuchungen zur Geschichte der altchristlichen Literatur VOL. VI, PT II. Leipzig 1889.

WERNER, M. *Die Entstehung des christlichen Dogmas.* Bern and Leipzig 1941.

WIELAND, F. *Der vorirenäische Opferbegriff.* Veröffentlichungen aus dem Kirchenhistorischen Seminar München VOL. III, PT VI. Munich 1909.

WIETEN, L. T. *Irenaeus' geschrift* = *Irenaeus' geschrift "Ten bewijze der apostolische prediking."* Utrecht 1909.

WINDISCH, H. *Der Barnabasbrief.* Handbuch zum Neuen Testament, ed. H. Lietzmann. Tübingen 1920.

WINGREN, G. "Skapelsen, lagen och inkarnationen enligt Irenaeus" in *S.T.K.*, 1940.

ZAHN, T. "Irenäus von Lyon," in *Realencyclopädie für protestantische Theologie und Kirche.* 3rd ed. VOL. IX. Leipzig 1901.

—— *Marcellus von Ancyra.* Gotha 1867.

Z.K.T. = *Zeitschrift für Katholische Theologie.*

Z.NT.W. = *Zeitschrift für die neutestamentliche Wissenschaft.*

ZÖCKLER, O. *Die Lehre vom Urstand des Menschen.* Gütersloh 1879.

Z.S.T. = *Zeitschrift für systematsiche Theologie.*

INDEX OF NAMES

INDEX OF SUBJECTS

INDEX OF PASSAGES FROM SCRIPTURES

Printed in the USA
CPSIA information can be obtained
at www.ICGtesting.com
JSHW020944090724
66076JS00004B/17